The Tenth Muse has been enormously well-received since its initial publication in 1975 and has become a classic study of the American poetic tradition. It has been out of print for several years now and this is the first paperback edition. Albert Gelpi asks the hard questions about how poetry can assume the problems of shaping American identities and he argues that the conditions of American culture have pushed our major poets into a debate between intellect and passion that generates distinctive poetic voices and forms.

Specifically, *The Tenth Muse* focuses on the evolution of American Romanticism out of and against American Puritanism. Through and around detailed discussions of Edward Taylor, Ralph Waldo Emerson, Edgar Allan Poe, Walt Whitman, and Emily Dickinson, this study presents a historical and critical reading of the development of American poetry from Anne Bradstreet to such contemporaries as Adrienne Rich, Robert Duncan, and William Everson. Gelpi's companion volume, *A Coherent Splendor*, also available from Cambridge University Press, elaborates the argument for twentieth-century poetry, focusing on American Modernism as it evolved out of and against American Romanticism and anticipated the Postmodernism of the present time.

The Tenth Muse

THE TENTH MUSE

The Psyche of the American Poet

ALBERT GELPI

Stanford University

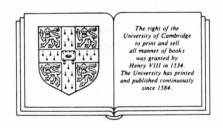

CAMBRIDGE UNIVERSITY PRESS

Cambridge

New York   Port Chester   Melbourne   Sydney

Published by the Press Syndicate of the University of Cambridge
The Pitt Building, Trumpington Street, Cambridge CB2 1RP
40 West 20th Street, New York, NY 10011, USA
10 Stamford Road, Oakleigh, Melbourne 3166, Australia

First published in 1975 by Harvard University Press
First published in 1991 by Cambridge University Press

Printed in the United States of America

Library of Congress Cataloging-in-Publication Data
Gelpi, Albert.
The tenth muse : the psyche of the American poet / Albert Gelpi.
p. cm.
Includes bibliographical references and index.
ISBN 0-521-41339-7 (hardback). – ISBN 0-521-42401-1 (paperback)
1. American poetry – History and criticism. 2. Poets, American –
Psychology. 3. Psychology in literature. 4. Self in literature.
I. Title.
PS303.G4   1991
811.009 – dc20   91-22690
                                                                      CIP

A catalog record for this book is available from the British Library

ISBN 0-521-41339-7 (hardback)
ISBN 0-521-42401-1 (paperback)

This book is for
BARBARA

Contents

Preface
The Muse as Psyche,
The Psyche as Muse

In dens of passion, and pits of woe,
He saw strong Eros struggling through,
To sun the dark and solve the curse,
And beam to the bounds of the universe.

Ralph Waldo Emerson: "Beauty"

Thus I pacified Psyche and kissed her,
And tempted her out of her gloom—
And conquered her scruples and gloom. . . .

Edgar Allan Poe: "Ulalume"

At the moment it comes out   the Muse ('world'

the Psyche (the 'life'

Charles Olson: Letter to Elaine Feinstein

The Psyche of the American Poet is the subtitle of this book for several reasons. I began with a question in literary history: the separation of American poetry from its British parent; the development of qualities of imagination, voice, form, and technique that could be called American. Here and abroad American poetry has continued to receive increasing attention as its importance and originality have come to be

ix

recognized and its influence has extended not just to Britain and Europe but to Latin America, Africa, and Asia as well. Where peoples are engaged in generating national cultures, American literature might well have a special significance since we had to find or project our identity rapidly and self-consciously under the urgent pressures of modern history. For Americans, too, the study of our poetry remains crucial, as we move from a youthful period of exuberant, often ruthless, (we thought) endless expansion into the disturbing self-doubts of the present time, when we must search ourselves if we are to mature, even survive, as a people. Our limits forced upon us, we must figure out how to live within them by exploring the inner continent that we have generally shunned when we could.

From the beginning the way West was a psychological journey as well, but it was conducted by most Americans as much as possible out in the open sunshine of "a commonplace prosperity," as Hawthorne wryly observed in his Preface to *The Marble Faun*. When Jack Burden, in Robert Penn Warren's *All the King's Men*, headed West like Huck Finn to escape his trap and perhaps still find the New Eden over the horizon, he found at last only land's end and had to wedge down, as in fact many of our artists had learned to do before. If now in the middle of our life it is time for a national *nekuia*, our artists will be in many ways our best guides. Our poets have been pioneers of the psyche; many have been map-makers of the underworld. They have been there before most of us, and both the survivors who returned with hopeful clues and symbols and those who did not survive, or barely survived, have lived out aspects of a destiny that is collective as well as personal. Since the cultural situation has forced them to descend, their poetry is—or at any rate represents—their psyches to a degree that has not had to be characteristic of most English and European poets.

The word "mind" suggests a conscious, cerebral activity, engaged with the world or reflecting upon it. Literary and cultural histories account for the "mind" of individual artists or for the "mind" of an epoch or of a nation. Perry Miller, perhaps the most distinguished intellectual historian of America in this century, wrote *The New England Mind, The Life of the Mind in America*, and "The Responsibility of Mind in a Civilization of Machines," and I gave my own book placing Emily Dickinson in various cultural contexts the subtitle *The Mind of the Poet*. Most literary criticism has dealt with poetry as a work of the poet's "mind," analyzable into its constituent linguistic elements and so into its composite meaning. But I have come to see more and more clearly that accounting for the "mind" of the poet or of the poem is only a partial account, an anatomy of what has taken shape at or near the surface of consciousness. "Psyche" is a more inclusive and integrative word. It recognizes that conscious manifestations cannot be separated from the mysterious promptings and impulses of the unconscious that either engender those manifestations or struggle against them; it recognizes, further, that external conditions of social and cultural history affect and provoke not just those conscious phenomena, but the volatile, turbid unconscious as well. All artists are more rooted in and susceptible to that shadowy area than most of us. Many artists explicitly take the unconscious as the matrix of their art, and even those who rely more strongly on conscious formulation do so with a vivid sense of the power of the unconscious and consequently live more from the "psyche" than do people committed to the operation of the rational "mind" on data from the external world: scientists, social scientists, businessmen, behavioristic psychologists, even most philosophers, scholars, and critics.

In this study of American poetry, therefore, I wanted to see the poet's mind as part of his psyche. Most psychological criticism has been rather narrowly and rigidly Freudian and, taking the work of art as clinical evidence, has dissected it in order to draw out of it the conflicts that constitute the artist's neurotic problem in adjusting to external reality. The frequent result has been not an amplification or enrichment but a reduction of a complex work to symptoms and clinical labels. If I was going to find a way of bringing to bear psychological questions and insights that would extend the poem, open it to new depths, I knew that I would have to avoid single doctrinaire systems or schools of psychology. Just as an eclectic and synthesizing combination of critical approaches to a poem—historical, philosophical, and explicatory, let us say—permits a fuller reading of the text, so an eclectic and synthesizing responsiveness to various psychological theories and approaches was necessary for the widest and deepest comprehension of the poem at that level, most particularly a responsiveness to approaches that trusted, affirmed, and worked from the unconscious. So in writing the chapters of this book, I have drawn on a variety of psychologists and psychiatrists: Freud himself (particularly what Robert Duncan designated "Freud's mythic imagination"); even more extensively, the archetypal psychology of C. G. Jung and Jungians like Erich Neumann and Marie Louise von Franz and James Hillman; neo-Freudians like Erik Erikson and Norman O. Brown; and others who belong in neither "camp," such as R. D. Laing and Robert Ornstein. I used whoever could help me read more clearly the operations of the poet's psyche—at once private and representative, personal and collective—as it expressed itself in the structures of language. For only then can there be a more genuine integration of the poem, just as the writing of the poem was for the poet an effort at integrating the unconscious and conscious aspects of his psyche. My purpose has been similarly integrative: to combine a literary-historical and textual reading of the poems with a psychological sensitivity.

If all art proceeds from the unconscious, more openly or less, more positively or less, then all art proceeds from and expresses what Freud called the erotic energy of the libido and what Jung described as the instincts imaged in our dreams and myths and art. The myth of Psyche—a late creation that seems very "modern" in its implications—links Psyche to Eros; the long story that is their myth and literary monument tells of the perplexing difficulties that beset their long-sought, long-delayed, necessary union. Freud contended that all aesthetic creation was the sublimation of—often the perverse deflection of—the libido. But the more penetrating insight would seem to be that language and imaginative expression are the substantive, substantiating means whereby poets—and through them, all of us—strive toward psychological wholeness and completion. This is all the more true, perhaps, in the case of American poets, challenged by their culture and so driven more deeply than others into the erotic and instinctual resources of the individual psyche. The poetry of each of the poets studied here dramatizes a particular interaction between eros and psyche. Whitman and Dickinson claim the most extended attention not because they represent, simply and separately, Eros and Psyche, but because, as a man and a woman, they represent more compellingly than the other poets the loving, lifelong contention of eros and psyche to work out the terms of their reconciliation.

I found myself, therefore, considering a phenomenon in literary history by attempting to reach as well the poet's psyche, especially as it came to the creative act of expression. My aim was not to mount a rigorously or exclusively psychoanalytic investigation but to discern the elusive connections between the cultural situation and the psychological situation of the poets as those connections contributed to poetic theory and practice during the formative period of American literature. As we have come to perceive more deeply the interdependence of the social and subjective terms on which we live, we have realized not just the political aspects of psychology but also the psychological dimension of history, including literary history.

The first chapter presents the cultural situation in sweeping terms; the subsequent chapters study the five major American poets before the twentieth century, four of them from the nineteenth century, when the existence of an American poetry was being thrashed out, proclaimed, and tested. As would be expected, the issues are most deeply engaged by Whitman and Dickinson; this pair, curiously related in their contrasts, reflected much of the literary situation of their times, subsumed much of the imaginative currents of previous decades, and cast all this into sustained literary achievements. Moreover, their work exemplifies a masculine and feminine psyche enacting the premises and limits of the myth of the self-reliant individual, which, despite the attempts then and more recently to balance it through countermyths of social responsibility and fraternal communities, remains today the dominant myth of the American experience.

The major poets from the formative period of American poetry demonstrate the inseparability of, indeed the interaction between the cultural situation and the psychological situation, between social factors and private responses, between "mind" and "psyche," between psyche and eros. The poets who came to maturity between 1910 and 1920 or so, with World War I as a grim enactment of a turning point in civilization and the transition into the twentieth century, constitute the American Poetic Renaissance. The most important members of that generation are Robert Frost, Ezra Pound, William Carlos Williams, H. D., T. S. Eliot, Wallace Stevens, John Crowe Ransom, Allen Tate, and Hart Crane. So original and individual were their accomplishments that they made American poetry pre-eminent not only in English-speaking countries but in the world at large. Building on or reacting against what the poets in this volume represented, they elaborated and complicated and internationalized American poetry. A projected companion volume to *The Tenth Muse* will study the major figures of the American Poetic Renaissance. Their efforts and achievements comprise another phase of the American tradition, both the extension and the counterthrust to the initial sorting out of possibilities in the poets studied in these chapters.

The scholarship and criticism of the last several decades—most of it studies of individual poets—have created the contextual basis necessary for an attempt like this one to begin to trace out the tradition of a poetry that began with a worry about having no tradition. The notes to the chapters indicate only the most obvious of indebtednesses. I want to cite especially here two books that develop powerful arguments about the American poetic tradition with a different perspective from mine: Hyatt H. Waggoner's *American Poets from the Puritans to the Present* (1968) and Roy Harvey Pearce's *The Continuity of American Poetry* (1961). I want, too, to remember the following people particularly: the late Perry Miller, not only because he led me into a consideration of the subject years ago through his lectures, seminars, and writings, but because he will always stand in my intellectual life as a Promethean Demiurge; friends and colleagues, because in various ways they offered support, encouragement, inspiration, and constructive criticism: Joel Porte and Robert Kiely at Harvard, David Levin at Virginia, Claude Simpson, Jr., at the Huntington Library, Hyatt Waggoner at Brown, Albert Guerard, Herbert Lindenberger, Donald Davie, and Thomas Moser here at Stanford; Adrienne Rich and William Everson, because the fact that my critical remarks about the poet's psyche made sense to such different poets with special affinities for Whitman and Dickinson confirmed for me that I was on the right track; Josephine Guttadauro, for typing the manuscript; David Langston, for preparing the permissions file; and Barbara Charlesworth Gelpi, because in all aspects of my life, including the writing and revision of this book, she has made possible the creative interchange of eros and psyche.

Stanford University
October 1, 1974

Preface to This Edition
A Backward, and
Prospective, Glance

"Gods always face two ways," says H. D. in *Trilogy*, by which she also meant that humans always face two ways. The welcome offer of Cambridge University Press to reissue *The Tenth Muse* presents the moment for me to look backward and forward. Walt Whitman called his last preface "A Backward Glance O'er Travel'd Roads," and the present occasion invites a stock-taking of my critical purposes in relation to the present state of literary study. I want to reflect on this book in relation to its sequel, *A Coherent Splendor* (1987), and to relate that project, which has been the radiating center of my professional life until now, to the changes that have conflicted literary study in the 16 years since the initial publication of *The Tenth Muse*; and out of that muddle I want to muse on the prospect for literary study in this decade and into the next century.

My graduate study in the 1950s and early 1960s trained me in what is shrugged off by contemporary critical theory as the "old" historicism and the now-"old" New Criticism. I was very fortunate to have had Perry Miller as my mentor during my doctoral studies at Harvard University; Joel Porte and I were, I believe, his last dissertation students. I had begun serious study of American poetry under Richard Fogle at Tulane University; and, listening at Harvard to Reuben Brower's subtle, supple explications of the poems of Dryden and Pope, I learned

xv

that the New Criticism represented not a political agenda but a technique for accurate reading and that textual explication need not forego the insights of intellectual and social history and even biography.

My doctoral dissertation, published as *Emily Dickinson: The Mind of the Poet*, grew out of the received humanistic association of art and morality, and combined an interest in history and in the psychology of poetic creation to delineate the poet's inner life in language. Working out of my readings in American Puritanism and Romanticism, I set out to show how the play and counterplay of Emily Dickinson's psyche mediated her New England heritage and nineteenth-century culture into the idiosyncratic shape and rhythm and imagery of those apparently inexhaustible poems and letters. Without fully realizing it, I had fastened on the issues that have continued to tease and challenge me; and I found myself fascinated by the reciprocal interaction between "tradition and the individual talent"—though Eliot's "classicist" norms would have found my aspirations too "romantic" in trying to discern how history and psychology inform the epistemology of creative expression. Or, to put this last point the other way around, how poetry mediates history and psychology. So I set about understanding the complex ways through which poets make their meanings—the conscious and unconscious processes impelling acts of imaginative creation in particular poems and in the shaping of a life in poetry; and I also sought to understand that alchemy working not just in individual poets like Dickinson but in the pattern evolving over the years and decades within the culture shaping and shaped by those individual careers in poetry.

Together *The Tenth Muse* and *A Coherent Splendor* comprise my account of the American poetic tradition through the poetry and poetics of the major figures constituting the tradition. *The Tenth Muse* follows out the emergence of American Romantic poetry from its Puritan foundations. The religious, moral, and aesthetic heritage of Puritanism, for which Edward Taylor is the strongest poetic voice, persisted through the spate of Neoclassical imitations during the Revolutionary period to fuse with the new imaginative energies coming over from England and Germany. That fusion informed the imagination of all the major American Romantic poets—Emerson, Poe, Dickinson—except Whitman. Extending the historical argument into the first half of the twentieth century, the period I dubbed the American Poetic Renaissance, *A Coherent Splendor* traces the continuities and discontinuities between Modernism and the Romanticism that it in some respects rebelled against and in other respects reconstituted. The central chapters of *A Coherent Splendor* examine the careers of most of the major American Modernist poets—Wallace Stevens, T. S. Eliot, Ezra Pound, H. D., William Carlos Williams, Allen Tate, Hart Crane—flanked by chapters on a pair of pre-Modernists, Robert Frost and John Crowe Ransom, and a pair of anti-Modernists, Robinson Jeffers and Yvor Winters.

A long essay entitled "The Genealogy of Postmodernism," published in the summer of 1990 in *The Southern Review*, represents my first sortie into the largely uncharted territory of the contemporary poetic scene. I argue that Postmodernism, at least in American poetry, has defined itself by finally extirpating the Romantic aspect of Modernism, and that American poetry since World War II can therefore be read as a dialectic between the Postmodernist inclination and a counterinclination that I see as Neoromantic. The essay offers a sketch for a possible third volume on the American poetic tradition.

So I have set out to make a sweeping historical argument through close attention to poetic texts. There is nothing else quite like it in the scholarship of the field. I did not attempt the compendiousness of Donald Stauffer's *Short History of American Poetry*, but instead concentrate on those major poets whose poetry and poetics most saliently exemplify the tradition as I saw it defining itself. At the same time, the scale of presentation was larger and more detailed than that of Stauffer's book or of such other studies of the American poetic tradition as Roy Harvey Pearce's *The Continuity of American Poetry*, Hyatt Waggoner's *American Poets*, and Edwin Fussell's *Lucifer in Harness*. Because I wanted the historical argument to emerge gradually and inductively from the give-and-take of individual, lifelong commitments to poetry, the chapters on those individual poets I chose to discuss are monographic in length and scope.

Returning to *The Tenth Muse*, I had to ask myself whether I might do it differently now, especially in view of the ferment in the literary academy that the accession of various theoretical schools—feminism, marxism, deconstruction, semiotics, new historicism, culture studies—has precipitated. My conclusion was, not surprisingly perhaps, that while no doubt there would be local differences in interpretation and perspective and emphasis, due in good part to exposure to recent "theory," this book, and *A Coherent Splendor* as well, would not be substantively different in conception and structure or in argumentative tenor and intention. I want to offer, especially to those who have accepted "theory" as the new hegemonic orthodoxy in institutionalized literary study, not an apology but an explanation. Or rather the kind of apology that Cardinal Newman meant in naming his autobiography *Apologia Pro Vita Sua*.

I recognize the salutary function of certain theoretical perspectives in stressing race, class, and gender in an academic and literary arena still dominated by white males, and in analyzing the structures through which literature and literary study have come to be canonized and institutionalized. Through the witness and writings of Barbara Charlesworth Gelpi and Adrienne Rich, I came to understand and draw on the feminist critique of literature and society from the early days of the movement.

At the same time, deep-seated convictions keep me from committing myself to the deconstructionist and new historicist venture. My purposes and ends remain different and to some extent antithetical to those of most Poststructuralist inquiries. I do not believe that individuals are merely functions of the political and economic—and so literary—systems within which they operate; that literature and art merely reinscribe the institutionalized social order; that consciousness is merely a function of language, and language merely a self-reflexive, arbitrary semiotic code; that a word is merely a signifier without a genuine signified; and that religion, morality, and politics merely legislate the dominant ideology. The word "merely" in the previous clauses is the key to the demurral I would lodge. Some theorists, I know, want to allow for individual choice and social change, but Poststructuralism is, for the most part, dogged by a numbing, finally nihilistic and self-defeating, determinism.

Emerson summed up all the uncontrollable, destructive, destabilizing factors limiting human existence as Fate, but opposed to Fate the potentially superior power of the human Will. Poststructuralists view Emerson with suspicion and even contempt for a *faux-naif*, idealistic individualism that masked the imperialism of the white male capitalist. Even granting Emerson's vulnerability up to a point, I draw a confirming strength from his conviction. I reject the Poststructuralist inclination to authorize a network of systems so overdetermined yet indeterminate, so fixed yet relativistic, so closed yet open as finally to denigrate and sometimes even to deny the psychological integrity, the moral and political responsibility, the religious vision of the individual and so of society.

The deconstruction of the individual into an inscribed code means, in Yeats' words, that "the centre cannot hold;/Mere anarchy is loosed upon the world." Indeed, the point is that there *is* no center to hold. As Lacan and Derrida have gone on to demonstrate, with that slippage everything starts sliding and skidding: the efficacy of language in engaging and interpreting a physical or social or metaphysical reality; the capacity to make discriminations and judgments about identity and commitment, meaning and value; the authority of art and philosophy and religion in construing and constructing private and public life.

So, among other consequences, the effect of the ascendancy and institutionalization of Poststructuralism has been the erosion of literary study as an intellectual discipline. The hue and cry in the academy since the 1970s has hectored literature and the humanities in general to abandon their aestheticist elitism, sterile formalism, and disciplinary parochialism for the widening vistas of interdisciplinary study. It goes without saying that literary critics should be as broadly cultivated as possible, but the call for humanists to join social scientists—principally sociologists, anthropologists, psychologists—in interdisciplinary study has a hidden agenda: not the enrichment or extension of literary and humanistic study but its subversion into the methodology and goals of the social sciences. The list of journal articles and books published by university presses in recent years chronicles the steady surrender of literary study to a certain kind of ideologically driven social science that has arrogated to itself the term "culture studies."

For, strictly speaking, there can be no such thing as interdisciplinary study. Literary critics, historians, philosophers, linguists, psychologists, and anthropologists bring their interests, however broad and interdisciplinary, to focus and use within the purposes, materials, and methods of a particular discipline. Disciplines can overlap and intersect and illuminate one another, but scholars who ignore defining distinctions and adopt the methods and aims of other disciplines do so at the risk and sacrifice of their own. They do not cross over into a neutral no-man's land—such a place would be desolate anyway—but cede themselves into somebody else's intellectual and methodological territory.

The distinctive and defining responsibility of literary study is to study literary materials on their own terms—in formalist terms as verbal structure and technique—since the unique constellation of words constitutes the unique fusion of thought and feeling, of psychology, politics, and morality that is the irreducible text. It exists in vital interrelation to the society and culture within which it functions, but it exists on its own terms. Characteristically, interdisciplinary study focuses not on the complexities of the text but instead on the political, anthropological, psychological, and linguistic theory for which the text is evinced, often reductively, as empirical evidence. By contrast, the literary critic's experience, personality, religion, morality, politics, knowledge of history and psychology, study of language and literature, sense of formal convention and experimentation all come to bear on the text: interpreting how this selection of words constitutes and enacts an experience of a particular political, moral, religious, psychological, emotional texture and character; and then judging both its aesthetic success and its moral, social, or religious value to the reader and the world it addresses.

At the base of such an apologia for the literary discipline is, quite unapologetically, the conviction that literature performs a function in the moral, psychological, religious, and political life of the individual and thereby of the society. Not at all a simple or unproblematic function—quite the contrary; but a basic and essential function. Otherwise I could not conscientiously be a literary scholar and critic. If language, no matter how slippery the relation between the signifier and the signified, is not a genuine act of or effort at signification, if the language act does not mediate an engagement between subject and object that illuminates both subject and object—no matter how ambiguous the assumptions of that mediation, how muddled its means, how unresolved its conclusions—then literary study is indeed in a parlous way.

I am aware that such ideas—ideals, really—are dismissed by Poststructuralists as "essentialist"; I have no quarrel with that description. I am aware, too, that some would dismiss religion, humanism, even formalist criticism as expressions of an individualist ideology manifestly deconstructed by a history of racist, sexist, classist oppression. But one must make a distinction, again an essentialist distinction, between principles and the inevitably tainted historical record. Ideas, ideals, values will, in their historical expression, be imperfectly realized, often corruptly used and abused. But if one believes in those values—Christian, Jewish, Buddhist, secular humanist, feminist, marxist, ecological, or whatever, or any synthesis thereof—then historical failure is all the more reason to keep trying to refine and realize them. I reject the notion that ideas and ideals are *merely* historically bound. Their expression and realization are, again and again, up to us; in discerning what our ideas and values are, and what they might be, lies the challenge of freedom and responsibility, including the freedom and responsibility of literature and literary criticism.

So I let *The Tenth Muse* and *A Coherent Splendor* stand witness—in this Postromantic, Postmodernist, Poststructuralist fin de siècle—to the efficacy of the literary discipline and to the power of humanistic, moral, and religious values to discern meaning, move readers, and change history. My colleague Marjorie Perloff, who studies the avant-garde, recently remarked to me that a position like mine is so rear-guard that it might represent the vanguard of what lies ahead in literary study. She meant the joke seriously, and, facing both ways on the cusp of the two centuries, I hope she is right.

Stanford University
May 18, 1991

Acknowledgments

I wish to acknowledge permission for use of the following poetry: Lines from Emily Dickinson reprinted by permission of the publishers and the Trustees of Amherst College from *The Poems of Emily Dickinson*, edited by Thomas H. Johnson, Cambridge, Massachusetts: The Belknap Press of Harvard University Press, Copyright, 1951, 1955 by the President and Fellows of Harvard College. In addition, lines from poems 1545 and 1072 from *The Life and Letters of Emily Dickinson* by Martha Dickinson Bianchi reprinted by permission of Houghton Mifflin Company. And lines from poems 61, 306, 1247, 1461, 1705, 1677 (Copyright 1914, 1942 by Martha Dickinson Bianchi), from poems 248, 370, 448, 461, 473, 569, 597, 601, 642, 679, 750, 1247 (Copyright 1929, © 1957 by Mary L. Hampson), from poems 378, 420, 648, 798, 802, 1090 (Copyright 1935 by Martha Dickinson Bianchi, © 1963 by Mary L. Hampson) reprinted by permission of Little, Brown & Company.

I express my thanks also for permission to reprint the following: Lines from Robert Frost from *The Poetry of Robert Frost*, ed. Edward Connery Lathem. Copyright © 1969 by Holt, Rinehart & Winston, Inc. Copyright © 1970 by Lesley Frost Ballantine. Reprinted by permission of Holt, Rinehart & Winston, Publishers. British rights by permission of Jonathan Cape, Ltd. Lines from Canto 81 from *The Cantos* by Ezra Pound. Reprinted by permission of New Directions Publishing Corp. Copyright 1948 by Ezra Pound. British rights by permission of Faber & Faber Ltd., London. Lines from "I Am in Danger–Sir–" from *Necessities of Life* by Adrienne Rich. Reprinted by permission of W. W. Norton & Company, Inc. Copyright 1966 by W. W. Norton & Company, Inc. British rights by permission of Chatto & Windus Ltd.

Permission was also received to quote: Lines of Edward Taylor from *The Poems of Edward Taylor*, edited by Donald E. Stanford. Copyright © 1960 by Yale University Press, Inc. Reprinted by permission of Yale University Press. "Meditation One," and selections from "The Reflextion," "Meditation Eight," Meditation Twenty-Nine," "Meditation Thirty-Eight," and "Meditation Forty-Two," in *The Poetical Works of Edward Taylor*, ed. Thomas H. Johnson (Princeton Paperback, 1966). Copyright Rockland, 1939; Princeton University Press, 1943, pp. 123, 125, 129/130, 140, 146/147, and 148. Reprinted by permission of Princeton University Press. Lines from *Sacramental Meditations*, 1st Series, 40th Meditation, and from "Upon a Wasp Child with Cold" reprinted by permission of *New England Quarterly* from T. H.

Acknowledgments

Johnson, "Some Edward Taylor Gleanings," *New England Quarterly*, 16 (1943), 280–296. Lines from "In Gratitude to Beethoven" and "The Man in the Silver Ferrari" from *Inside the Blood Factory* by Diane Wakoski. Reprinted by permission of Doubleday & Company, Inc. Copyright 1962, 1968 by Diane Wakoski. Lines from "The Choice" from *Collected Poems* of William Butler Yeats. Copyright 1933 by Macmillan Publishing Company, Inc., renewed 1961 by Bertha Georgie Yeats. Reprinted by permission of Macmillan Publishing Company, Inc. British rights by permission of M. B. Yeats, Miss Anne Yeats, Macmillan of London & Basingstoke and Macmillan Company of Canada.

He who endeavors to fix the personality of America in one
eternal, unchangeable pattern not only understands nothing of
how a personality is created, but comprehends little of how this
nation has come along thus far . . . . he fools himself if he
supposes that the explanation for America is to be found in the
conditions of America's existence rather than in the existence
itself. A man *is* his decisions, and the great uniqueness of this
nation is simply that here the record of conscious decision is more
precise, more open and explicit than in most countries. This gives
us no warrant to claim that we are higher in any conceivable
scale of values; it merely permits us to realize that to which the
English observer calls attention, that being an American is not
something inherited but something to be achieved.

Perry Miller

"The Shaping of the American
Character," *Nature's Nation*

Leaving aside all questions of style, there is a difference between
Tennyson's *Ode on the Death of the Duke of Wellington* and
Whitman's elegy for President Lincoln *When lilacs last in the
dooryard bloom'd* which is significant. Tennyson . . . mourns for a
great public official figure, but it would be very hard to guess
from the words of Whitman's poem that the man he is talking of
was the head of a State; one would naturally think that he was
some close personal friend, a private individual.

To take one more example—two poets, contemporaries, both
women, both religious, both introverts preoccupied with
renunciation—Christina Rossetti and Emily Dickinson; could
anyone imagine either of them in the country of the other? When
I try to fancy such translations, the only Americans I can
possibly imagine as British are minor poets with a turn for light
verse like Lowell and Holmes; and the only British poets who
could conceivably have been American are eccentrics like Blake
and Hopkins.

. . . every European poet, I believe, still instinctively thinks of
himself as a 'clerk,' a member of a professional brotherhood,
with a certain social status irrespective of the number of his
readers . . . and taking his place in an unbroken historical
succession. In the States poets have never had or imagined they
had such a status, and it is up to each individual poet to justify his
existence by offering a unique product.

W. H. Auden

"Introduction," *The Faber
Book of Modern American Verse*

You can only live for yourself; your action is good only while it is alive—whilst it is in you. The awkward imitation of it by your child or your disciple is not a repetition of it, is not the same thing, but another thing. The new individual must work out the whole problem of science, letters and theology for himself; can owe his fathers nothing. There is no history; only biography.

Ralph Waldo Emerson
Journals, May 28, 1839

No poet, when he writes his own *art poétique*, should hope to do much more than explain, rationalize, defend or prepare the way for his own practice: that is, for writing his own kind of poetry. He may think that he is establishing laws for all poetry; but what he has to say that is worth saying has its immediate relation to the way in which he himself writes or wants to write: though it may well be equally valid to his immediate juniors, and extremely helpful to them. We are only safe in finding, in his writing about poetry, principles valid for any poetry, so long as we check what he says by the kind of poetry he writes.

T. S. Eliot
"From Poe to Valéry,"
To Criticize the Critic

Nothing could be more inappropriate to American literature than its English source since the Americans are not British in sensibility.

Wallace Stevens
"Adagia," *Opus Posthumous*

I

The American as Artist,
The Artist as American

In 1820 Sydney Smith, cofounder of *The Edinburgh Review* and a critic renowned for the deadly accuracy of his wit, aimed all his hauteur at the pretensions of the new American nation in a single barrage entitled "America" that was meant to settle the matter once and for all:

> In the four quarters of the globe, who reads an American book? or goes to an American play? or looks at an American picture or statue? What does the world yet owe to American physicians or surgeons? What new substances have their chemists discovered? or what old ones have they analyzed? What new constellations have been discovered by the telescopes of Americans? What have they done in mathematics? Who drinks out of American glasses? or eats from American plates? or wears American coats or gowns? or sleeps in American blankets?[1]

If Smith's questions have boomeranged during the last hundred and fifty years, at the time he need not have worried about sounding silly. Smith's excuse for calling attention to the deficiencies of his inferiors was the outrageous provocation of the Americans' own loud boasts about their accomplishments. If they beat their own drum and breasts so noisily, why should he not puncture the drum and silence the upstarts? His superciliousness and their breast-beating were complementary indications of the Americans' defensiveness. In a previous article Smith had disposed of American literature in a succinct summary which condemned as much by the brevity of the list as by the paltriness of what was listed:

> Literature the Americans have none—no native literature, we mean. It is all imported. They had a Franklin, indeed; and may afford to live for half a century on his fame. There is, or was a Mr. Dwight, who wrote some poems; and his baptismal name was Timothy. There is also a small account of Virginia by Jefferson, and an epic by Joel Barlow; and some pieces of pleasantry by Mr. Irving. But why should the Americans write books, when a six weeks' passage brings them, in their own tongue, our sense, science and genius, in bales and hogsheads? Prairies, steam-boats, grist-mills, are their natural objects for centuries to come.[2]

In 1820, however, Washington Irving published *The Sketch Book* and launched a career which would make him the lionized lamb of salons on both sides of the Atlantic. By 1820 William

1

Cullen Bryant had written many of his best poems and would bring out a collected edition the next year. That same year, 1821, James Fenimore Cooper published the first of the romances which were to make him an acknowledged master of fiction in England and Europe as well as at home. And yet, though Sydney Smith's supercilious questions began to receive prompt reply, the taunt behind the questions—and all that it implied about the possibilities of art and civilization in America—continued to sting the American consciousness. "Who reads an American book?" Would the conditions of life on the North American continent permit Americans to write books worthy to be read, compose music worthy to be remembered, create paintings and statues worthy to be treasured? If America had no cultural past, would it, in fact could it have a cultural future?

As the most widely acclaimed poet of his day, William Cullen Bryant was invited in 1825 to lecture on poetry at the Athenaeum Society in New York. His four lectures reveal a great deal about the worried situation of the American poet in the early nineteenth century. The third lecture, "On Poetry in Its Relation to Our Age and Country," addressed itself specifically to the problem which disturbed every cultivated American. Bryant took full measure of the hardheaded doubts of men, even some Americans, who thought like Smith. Bryant was not speaking for himself but he was speaking for many when he drew up the case against the future of the arts in America:

> Our citizens are held to possess, in a remarkable degree, the heedful, calculating, prosaic spirit of the age, while our country is decried as peculiarly barren of the materials of poetry. The scenery of our land these reasoners admit to be beautiful, but they urge that it is the beauty of a face without expression; that it wants the associations of tradition which are the soul and interest of scenery; that it wants the national superstitions which linger yet in every district in Europe, and the legends of distant and dark ages and of wild and unsettled times of which the old world reminds you at every step. Nor can our country, they say, ever be more fruitful of these materials than at present. For this is not an age to give birth to new superstitions, but to explode and root out old. . . . Is it likely, then, that a multitude of interesting traditions will spring up in our land to ally themselves with every mountain, every hill, every forest, every river, and every tributary

brook. . . . The genius of our nation is quiet and commercial. Our people are too much in love with peace and gain, the state of society is too settled, and the laws too well enforced and respected, to allow of wild and strange adventures. There is no romance either in our character, our history, or our condition of society; and, therefore, it is neither likely to encourage poetry, nor capable of supplying it with those materials—materials drawn from domestic traditions and manners—which render it popular.[3]

The problem is perhaps not susceptible of a final answer, but it was and still is basic. Can art flourish in a land admittedly filled with natural marvels, but raw and wild, devoid of history and customs and tradition, diverse in its moral values and social criteria? We were "Nature's nation," a cliché that was fresher then and expressed a pious hope. The very fact that we were less civilized than Europe, closer to the teachings of Nature provided the peculiar moral imperative of our rugged individualism and would secure, if we were worthy, our exemption from the tragic course of history's rise and fall. Our manifest destiny made us antihistorical and anticultural, or so one side of the national consciousness intuitively felt.

Bryant wanted to soothe these cultural anxieties with a positive assurance, but the very hesitancy of his affirmative formulation—the interrogative and conditional drift of the syntax—suggests his own anxiety:

Where the fountains of knowledge are by the roadside, and where the volumes from which poetic enthusiasms are caught and fed are in everybody's hands, it would be singularly strange if, amid the multitude of pursuits which occupy our citizens, nobody should think of taking verse as a path to fame. Yet, if it shall be chosen and pursued with the characteristic ardor of our countrymen, what can prevent its being brought to the same degree of perfection here as in other countries? . . . I infer, then, that all the materials of poetry exist in our own country, with all the ordinary encouragements and opportunities for making a successful use of them. . . . If under these circumstances our poetry should finally fail of rivalling that of Europe, it will be because Genius sits idle in the midst of its treasures.[4]

Questions and ifs, leading to a speciously rational conclusion: "I infer, then . . . ." However, Bryant's response reveals itself as no

3

rational deduction but a visionary hope. He assumed strategically that the terms of American life, bountiful with natural resources but bare of human heritage, do recognize and nourish and sustain the activity of the poet and artist. If his assumption were false, the opportunities of the New World would represent nothing but a bloated materialism, and our hard-won gains would be reduced to plunder. Surely some of our energy would go into making a great as well as a productive society. Still, dreams and ideals—no matter how frequently asserted nor how ardently invoked—can never assuage doubts for long. Consequently from the beginning of our written record until now, some form of Sydney Smith's questions has haunted our boldest artistic endeavors and often raised even before some of our most ambitious artists the dread specter of failure, half-expected and half-believed.

In the flush days of the late eighteenth century the poems of John Trumbull and Timothy Dwight projected democratic vistas stretching almost illimitably west from the thinly settled eastern shore. But even these poetic depictions gave empire precedence over art, as the poet's farsighted eyes explored America:

> To glory, wealth and fame ascend,
> Her commerce wake, her realms extend;
> Where now the panther guards his den,
> Her desert forests swarm with men;
> Gay cities, tow'rs and columns rise,
> And dazzling temples meet the skies;
> Her pines, descending to the main,
> In triumph spread the wat'ry plain,
> Ride inland seas with fav'ring gails,
> And crowd her ports with whitening sails:
> Till to the skirts of western day,
> The peopled regions own her sway.[5]

The climactic vision of Joel Barlow's epic *Columbiad* disclosed "the progress of arts in America" but the steps of the progress laid out a sequence of development which placed art and poetry last: "Fur trade. Fisheries. Productions. Commerce. Education. Philosophical discoveries. Painting. Poetry."[6]

Then and now, many, including so flinty a critic of American culture as Ezra Pound, argued that the arts could grow only in a stable and healthy economy. Or did that order of things betray, however unwittingly, a hierarchy of values that damned us from the start as a venture in mindless and soulless capitalism? Our first worry was that our privileged status as "Nature's nation" precluded cultural achievement; as we set about exploiting nature's bounty, another question, not unrelated to the first, confronted Americans: can culture root itself in a society whose norms are economic, the profit motive fixing us on commercial expansion under a republican form of government? Were we, in fact, Mammon's nation?

So rapidly was the continent spanned, so rapidly was it being peopled and urbanized and mechanized that many began to wonder if we had not abandoned the ideals that had kindled earlier generations and lost touch with our peculiar source of inspiration: the economy of nature itself. What happened to John Winthrop's vision of a city set on a hill for all to see? Or to Thomas Jefferson's idea of the balanced perfection of an agrarian society? Or to Fenimore Cooper's sense of natural social classes and a natural aristocracy as the genius of American democracy? In a country of such extremes—unbridled commerce and untamed nature—what could be the sources of civilization? Or—to turn the question around—what would be the artist's and the poet's role in reconciling the American people and the American land in an American civilization?

Philip Freneau aspired to be the first great American poet, and his career typifies in bold outlines the problem of the artist in America. Even before the Declaration of Independence he hailed "The Rising Glory of America," as if the curve of our history were ever ascendant, freed of the wheel of fortune and the cyclic course of empire. "Bless'd by the genius of the rural reign," "uncultured nature" would "tame the soil, and plant the arts."[7] In anticipation of the westward progress which T. S. Eliot would look back on in The Dry Salvages, Freneau saw the Mississippi, the "Great Sire of Floods," submitting to the service of the settlers:

Nor longer shall your princely flood
From distant lakes be swelled in vain,
Nor longer through a darksome wood
Advance, unnoticed, to the main,
Far other ends, the heavens decree—
And commerce plans new freights for thee.[8]

5

In this "Millennium" our "Canaan" was "a new Jerusalem"; here "Paradise anew/ Shall flourish, by no second Adam lost." Moreover, Paradise regained not as a garden but as a city, belles lettres would spring up unforced, alongside trade, and we need never stoop to the study of dead languages or to "literary importation" from abroad.[9]

Did Freneau believe this ideal America, or did he, more than he was able to realize, merely believe in this ideal of America? In any case the ideal was soon challenged in Freneau's own experience. When he listed his literary models, he could cite only Englishmen: Shakespeare and Spenser and especially the neo-classicists, Dryden, "heav'nly Pope," and "godlike Addison."[10] Moreover, so painfully was his society not the new Jerusalem that soon after the Revolution he began to project the American dream toward the frontier—the forest and prairies and mountains—as Natty Bumppo and Huck Finn were later to find themselves forced west before the advance of "civilization." Even Whitman would have to admit, after another war (and a fratricidal war at that) in the name of the national ideal, that the promise lay beyond the convulsive present along the road open west to the future. Freneau could blame corruption on the lingering taint of "civilized" Europe, but then the snake had entered the garden with the first settler. The new republic could seem to present a panorama of "the worst of men in worst of times."[11] The poet was the least of citizens; the merchant-baron throttled him and then went on to snivel that "these States, as yet, can boast no bard":

> With such a bold, conceited air
> When such assume the critic's chair,
> Low in the dust is genius laid,
> The muses with the man in trade.[12]

The poet had, then, two courses open to him: he could either turn east back to the society of the Old World:

> Thrice happy Dryden, who could meet
> Some rival bard in every street!
> When all were bent on writing well
> It was some credit to excel:–[13]

6

ot turn west to the far frontiers of the private dream:

> O waft me far, ye muses of the west—
> Give me your green bowers and soft seats of rest—
> Thrice happy in those dear retreats to find
> A safe retirement from all human kind.
> Though dire misfortunes every step attend,
> The muse, still social, still remains a friend—[14]

Freneau's solitude proved more misfortune than safe retirement, and the muse kept no steady vigil against his mounting wretchedness. His old age, like Melville's and Twain's, was anticlimactic. Denounced as a political radical, neglected as a poet, poor, increasingly given to the "tavern and the flowing bowl," Freneau died from exposure after losing his way back home in a snowstorm. Carved on his tombstone is an epitaph so simple it seems portentous and symbolic: "Poet's Grave."

2

Nathaniel Hawthorne, looking back on his own literary career, put the problem with his usual honesty and rueful ambivalence: "No author, without a trial, can conceive of the difficulty of writing a romance about a country where there is no shadow, no antiquity, no mystery, no picturesque and gloomy wrong, nor anything but a commonplace prosperity, in broad and simple daylight, as is happily the case with my dear native land."[15] Nevertheless, for all Hawthorne's modesty the supreme fact about his career is his achievement: shadowy, mysterious romances about America which made him an inspiration and example to others striving to cope with their situation as artists in the New World.

Herman Melville, primed by the literary nationalism of the "Young America" group in New York, found in Hawthorne's stories such strong validation of his own efforts that he could publicly scorn Irving's "imitation of a foreign model" and rank his new-found hero with Shakespeare. Since Hawthorne had demonstrated what could be accomplished with our own spirit and materials, "let us away with this leaven of literary flunkeyism toward England. If either must play the flunkey in this thing, let

England do it, not us." In fact, the time had come to see the English tradition as in many respects "alien to us." At this point Melville felt brash enough to aim Sydney Smith's loaded question back across the Atlantic: "the day will come when you shall say, Who reads a book by an Englishman that is a modern?" But even with his head swimming, the realist in Melville had also to concede the futurity of America's laurels and the poverty of the immediate literary scene, which *Pierre* would gloomily satirize a year or so later. Indeed, so few "as yet have evinced that decided originality which merits great praise" that America should "first praise mediocrity even, in her children, before she praises . . . the best excellence" in foreigners. For "the truth is, that in one point of view this matter of a national literature has come to such a pass with us, that in some sense we must turn bullies, else the day is lost, or superiority so far beyond us, that we can hardly say it will ever be ours."[16] The juxtaposition of the American artist as bully and weakling in this single short essay may have betrayed more uncertainty than Melville intended. In any case, while Walt Whitman emerged during the 1850s as the bard of modern America, Melville receded from the active contention of authorship.

Hawthorne cut a quainter and clumsier figure in the eyes of Henry James almost thirty years after Melville's comments, but Hawthorne's writings, for all their limitations, called forth James's most extended critical piece, and the first full-length critical work on an American author. Writing for an English audience, James had to accommodate Hawthorne before he could find his own posture as an American-British novelist. He appreciated Hawthorne's "great courage" in daring to write at all. If "the profession in the United States is still very young, and of diminutive stature . . . in the year 1830 its head could hardly have been above ground." In fact, James, unlike Melville, wondered solicitously whether we did not render Hawthorne "a poor service in contrasting his proportions with those of a great civilization." On the other hand, since our best writers had been more or less "of trans-Atlantic growth," the heartening sign to James was the fact that the more recent American writers seemed "now almost inevitably more cultivated," "more cosmopolitan," "more Europeanized in advance."

However, even Henry James could not but be somewhat of two minds on this point. The crux of the problem was whether the American artist found himself by looking at home or abroad, by seeking the fuller context of the established tradition or rooting himself in his intrinsic possibilities for whatever they yielded. James would make his own determination; but the paradox which "poor Hawthorne" presented to him in 1879 was the odd fact that although he was a "provincial" and "solitary worker" he was also a profound and original genius, and, further, that his eccentric genius proceeded in many ways out of and not despite his circumstances. The British themselves recognized this fact in asking James to write the book for the English Men of Letters series; Hawthorne was the only American author honored by inclusion in the series.[17]

For the next generation Pound, in his strong-voiced expatriation, denounced the literary nationalism of his friend William Carlos Williams. How could Williams live in New Jersey and write such fine verse? Because, Pound had to conclude, Williams' mixed ancestry held him off as an "observant foreigner" who had to absorb America "as something put there for him to look at."[18] So by Pound's curious twist of thought Williams could be a poet in America because he was not really American, while he, Pound, had to remain a poet in exile because as a thorough American he was too deeply involved in the outrageous actuality of home to live there. Williams retorted flatly that Pound was "aching to make me something that I ain't"[19] and remained opposed to the seductions of the Old World. Almost twenty-five years later he wrote to young Robert Lowell abroad, attacking T. S. Eliot for declining "to remain here and put his weight behind" the making of an American poetic speech and warning Lowell against losing himself to the "European Circe":

> ... it is another Odyssey from which, not like some earlier American writers, I hope to see you return to your Penelope (American) much enriched in your mind and ready to join your fellows here in pushing forward the craft. You can bring great riches to us or you can ignore us; it's your choice. . . . come back; do not allow yourself to be coaxed away from us. I say this not for myself, after all, but for you.[20]

The course of American poetry can be measured by the poets' persistent crises of identity which involved in some way a crisis of place and role. The accommodations of other or older American poets, even when successful for them, were generally powerless to allay the restlessness of the next generation. Each poet had to confront his own situation and attempt to identify himself within it. Since the nineteenth century, poets everywhere have felt more and more displaced from their increasingly urbanized and technocratic societies, but the situation here is an extreme testing of the ability of the human spirit to adjust to the modern reality. Consequently, seldom—perhaps never before—have a nation's poets been as consistently concerned with and self-conscious about their purpose and role as American poets have been—indeed have had to be—from the start. As a result they have asked, perhaps more urgently than other poets in other times and places, the fundamental questions about their calling and their craft: what is poetry? what are its deepest sources and richest materials? what are its ends? how is the poem made? what is the relation of the poet to the poem, of the poem to the public? is the poet foreign to his native environment, or can he draw from it and help shape it?

Thrown back on himself more than his counterpart in England or on the continent, the American is forced to name his identity on his own ground and root his speech in that self-defined ground. Without the security of an accepted role or range of roles in society, without the assurance of a literary class or a literary audience, however small, without the expectations and norms given and acknowledged—all these prerogatives of the poet in a more traditional society—he has had to justify and comprehend the poetic act before he can speak to others. Emerson had optimistically placed the poet in the new society as the "representative man," but many poets and artists found themselves among Melville's "isolatos," their self-reliant individualism turned darkly and sourly inward. In both ways the artists have been profoundly representative; in Whitman's words "by its popular poets the calibres of an age, the weak spots of its embankments, its subcurrents, (often more significant than the biggest surface ones,) are unerringly indicated."[21]

Nevertheless, whatever theoretical position one adopts toward the possibilities for poetry in America or the place of the poet in America, the promise of American poetry has in a short time come a long way toward fulfilling itself. Moreover, it is precisely the contradictions of the cultural situation which give American poetry its fascination and character: the high hopes and the fear of failure, the arrogance and the defensiveness, the bold front and vulnerable flank, the loud mouth and soft heart, the energy at once searching and unsophisticated, the thrust toward originality against the domination of the past, the sense of limitations and the refusal to rest in them, the lonely isolation and the consequent assertion of individuality, the soaring idealism and the sober realism, the insistence on absolutes and the impatience with imperfections. One way and another, America—Nature's nation and commercial empire—has produced a remarkable number of poets and an increasing number of excellent poets over the three hundred years during which farms and cities have threatened to supplant the wilderness—poets for whom the enigma of their identity has been an insistent and subsuming theme.

II
EDWARD TAYLOR:
Types and Tropes

Although Edward Taylor left no treatises on poetic theory or practice and even forbade the posthumous publication of his poems, he is the first major poet in America. His boldness and originality can be appreciated more dramatically if his poetry is made to resonate against the sounding board of conventional Puritan literary theory, a position clearly thought out and tersely propounded in parenthetical remarks, prefatory notices, and occasional essays. The literary principles of the Puritans could be axiomatic, at least for the first generations, because the written word was intended to be all of a piece with the theological vision strong enough to propel a handful of people across the seas to a wilderness to found the City of God. Anne Bradstreet was voicing the courage and the fear of them all when she remembered coming "into this country, where I found a new world and new manners, at which my heart rose."[1] To the minds and tastes of Anglicans like John Donne and George Herbert or of Catholics like Richard Crashaw, the aesthetic attitudes of these colonials would have seemed narrowly and rigidly prescriptive, but these attitudes grew out of their special conception of human nature and man's place in the scheme of things just as much as did Donne's and Crashaw's. Read against the background of the Puritan notion of poetry and language, Edward Taylor's poems stand out in vivid relief, foreshadowing an indigenous American poetic tradition.

William Bradford prefaced his history with the reminder that the story would be rendered "in a plain style, with singular regard unto the simple truth in all things."[2] In the meeting-house, attention to art and artistry—pictures and statues, or music and vestments and ritual—distracted from the essential concern: the focus of God's creatures should be in all things on God's truth. Scholars and historians have long since demolished the caricature of the Puritan as a boorish philistine hostile to refinement or taste. One need only look at an old New England church for evidence of the Puritans' sense of grace and beauty expressed in simple forms. And they imposed similar limits on literary composition: the style of the artist, his approach to his materials and his medium, must be scrupulously suited (and it was a matter of conscience) to the usefulness of the creation under God in the society, not to the artist's indulgence in the imaginative flights of his titillated senses.

The presuppositions about the written word became a matter of pressing concern and so of precise specification, because if the Puritans produced understandably little music or painting or sculpture, they immediately and copiously began to write book after book. Before anything but a few patches of forest had been cleared for habitation, a printing press was set up in the New World. Since they were a remarkably literate and intellectual group, their leaders, most of whom had received a classical education and training in rhetoric at Cambridge, felt the compulsion, indeed the religious obligation, to write and publish. Their words conveyed God's Word—spoken from the pulpit, sung from the hymnal, preserved between the covers of a book. The purpose and end of writing had, therefore, to be explicit: that writing is best which makes the clearest and most effective translation of God's Word into human speech for the community. No wonder that much of their verse was in fact translation from Scripture. The author's ideas and responses, his talents and invention, were quite irrelevant to the unravelling of complicated matters to the ordinary understanding of ordinary men and women. Though a poet, Anne Bradstreet wanted to make it clear to her children that "I have not studied in this you read [a manuscript book of prose meditations and poems] to show my skill, but to declare the truth, not to set forth myself, but the glory of God."[3]

Needless to say, such assumptions would encourage expository and didactic prose over belles lettres. Even in intellectual prose, however, the writer had to move the reader to the truth of his words, and in order to compel the reader's will he had to move his emotions through affective images and concrete examples. But this emotive appeal of language particularly had to be controlled with a purposeful hand; no ornamental excrescences, no merely human fable, no merely personal touch, no merely individual response should tease the writer's and reader's direct and outward gaze. At the root of this notion of language lay the conviction that the truth or meaning of the written word existed independent of the written word, beyond the skill and personality of the writer, whose task was to investigate objective reality, ferret out the inherent truth and convey it to others less perspicacious than he.

Consequently Bradford's "plain style" utters "the simple truth in all things." Almost a century later, in 1725, John Bulkeley drew a commonly accepted distinction between the "Accomplished Poet" and the "Great Man":

> whereas what is properly call'd *Wit*, (which is no other than a ready Assemblage of Ideas, or a putting those together with quickness & variety wherein there can be found any *Congruity* or *Resemblance;* or to speak more plain, an aptness at Metaphor and Allusion) is what, as I take it, makes the *Accomplish'd Poet;* exactness of Judgment, or Clearness of reason (which we commonly and truly say makes *the Great Man*) on the other hand lies in an Ability of Mind nicely to distinguish its Ideas the one from the other, where there is but the least difference thereby avoiding being misled by Similitude, and by Affinity to take one thing from another.

In other words, the poet concocted the connections and relationships of figurative language, whereas true greatness of mind and spirit lay in discriminations which saved one from being "misled by Similitude." Since the poet synthesized by erratic intuition and the great man analyzed by rational discourse, subject to proof and disproof, and since "the process of the Mind in these two things [is] so *contrary* the one to the other," it was difficult to find a literary man who had not been betrayed by his own wit.[4] The human lot is to dissect, not to create; the creative inspiration came, when it came, from God. Mere "Metaphor and Allusion" are verbal tricks.

For all this overriding insistence on the dry control of what Wordsworth would suspect as "meddling intellect," there was a gradual relaxation of attitudes in the century between the arrival of the *Arbella* and the Revolution. Speaking for his fellow translators whose *Bay Psalm Book* (1640) was the first volume printed in America, Richard Mather voiced the early literalism as their avowed purpose: "to make a plaine and familiar translation of the psalmes and words of David into english metre." The refusal even to paraphrase lest the sense be lost "attended Conscience rather then Elegance, fidelity rather then poetry," as if poetry would violate conscience.[5] To the sophisticates at home in England, the Puritans would say with Thomas Hooker:

> That the discourse comes forth in such a homely dresse and course habit, the Reader must be desired to consider, It comes *out*

of the wilderness, where curiosity is not studied. Planters if they can provide cloth to go warm, they leave the cutts and lace to those that study to go fine. . . . They who covet more sauce then meat, they must provide cooks to their minde.

For a mind like Hooker's, intent on a rational balance he thought more possible in the wilds than in British society, "substance and solidity," "plainesse and perspicuity, both for matter and manner of expression" rule out "nicenesse," quaintnesse," "loosenesse of language," and "daintinesse of speech."[6] When Cotton Mather defended the blank verse of his own translation of the psalms over his grandfather's rhymed meters, it was on precisely the same grounds: a more effective elimination of *"Humane Debasements"* from the *"Divine Matter."* But now in 1718 Mather was wondering whether we had "tied ourselves" to language more literal "than there is a real occasion for" in rendering the poetry of the psalms: "if any *Beauties* be wanting, 'tis owing to the lowness [no longer plainness] of the *Language,* whereinto a strict and close *Translation,* is what we are here tied unto."[7] The repetition of the word "tied" suggests a fretful constraint. His annoyance with the restrictions of an outmoded literary formula is more explicit in the chapter "Of Poetry and Style" from his tremendously influential manual for ministers. He issued the stock warnings against "the Circaean cup" of "muses that are no better than harlots" and against the libraries compiled by "the powers of darkness," "whereof the poets have been the most numerous as well as the most venomous authors." But what is by hindsight more notable about Cotton Mather's literary guidelines is that he opposed his more literal-minded confrères with the hope that no one could be "wholly unpoetical." Seventy-five years after Hooker had declared his contempt for "cutts and lace" Mather praised a style so highly embellished that it was "not only a cloth of gold, but also stuck with as many jewels as the gown of a Russian ambassador." After all, style expressed the individuality inseparable from the tone and turn of temperament; since "every man will have his own stile, which will distinguish him as much as his gait," various styles "may please in their several ways."[8]

By the middle of the eighteenth century the religious and cultural circumstances of New England had changed so much that Mather Byles could write a literary essay in a secular magazine in order to "cultivate *polite* Writing, and form and embellish the Style of our ingenious Countrymen." Byles was an orthodox enough Calvinist in the manner of his day, but his religious inclinations did not interfere any longer with gentlemanly breeding and taste in what he hoped would become a polite society in the accepted eighteenth-century manner. Against the "false Glare" of "a good *Genius* run wild," Byles counseled "Cultivation from Study, and the Rules of Art": "Purity," "Elegance," "Symmetry of Arrangement and Disposition."[9] Wild geniuses were still offensive, as they had been to Bradford and Hooker—but now on literary and social grounds. Style was a matter of aesthetic concern in a community aspiring to culture, and both Massachusetts and Virginia strove to offer versions of the chaste neoclassical ideal. In the progression from Richard Mather through Cotton Mather to Mather Byles, between the founding of the colony and the establishment of the nation, a sense of language as exposition had opened up to include a sense of language as belles lettres.

Despite the severity of the literary criteria which lingered almost till the Revolution, the quantity of Puritan poetry is amazing not because it amounts to a legacy of good or even mediocre poems, but simply because so small a band fighting to maintain its hold on a savage continent managed to write as much verse as it did. The humanistically educated Puritan would be expected, even encouraged, to allow "a little recreation of poetry in the midst of your painful studies," as long as it remained "sauce, rather than food for you."[10] The strictures were, after all, more pious suspicions than categorical condemnations of fancy. Pegasus could flap and fly—but tethered, lest he break into fancy swoops and swirls or attempt to wing his way past the circumference set by the rational intelligence. The poet could loose his words and illustrative figures of speech as long as they were improving to himself and edifying to others. As a result, many Puritans did, as a matter of course, write religious and occasional verse: meditations, eulogies, elegies, family commemorations, and versified jeremiads such as John Wilson's *Song of Deliverance* and Michael Wigglesworth's *Day of Doom.* Not surprisingly, almost all of it is stiffly conventional in theme and expression: the Muse in Puritan mufti and starched collar, Pegasus pegged to the stake and hobbling his mostly iambic gait wearisomely round and round. Perhaps Cotton

Mather was right in worrying whether the plain style was unpoetical; certainly, at any rate, it was more suited to discursive
prose, and the Puritans wrote more vigorous prose than verse.

The contrast makes the poetry of Anne Bradstreet and Edward Taylor seem all the more remarkable, for they demonstrated
that genuine poetry was possible, though perhaps only by stretching the limits of the plain style. Here and there in Anne Bradstreet's long historical-allegorical chronicles, more often in her
elegies, and quite often in her short lyrics, she managed to achieve
that individuation of experience which invests verse with the
cadence and timbre and diction of a poetic voice. Hers is the first
book of American poetry, published by friends in London in 1650.
The consciously auspicious title—*The Tenth Muse Lately Sprung
Up in America . . . By a Gentlewoman in Those Parts*—proclaims
a native birth of poetry: no mere translation or migration of the
European sisters, but a distinct, creative female-spirit for the new
land to round out and complete the number of Muses. It would be
easy enough to point out how derivative Bradstreet's style and
devices were, how many of the conventions of Sidney and Donne
and the Renaissance poets she had carried with her to these parts;
but literary antecedents do not fully account for nor describe her
best poems. Here the exuberance of Renaissance convention took
a distinctive turn: muted by the cautions of the plain style and
transmuted into the tones of a Puritan woman of strong mind and
heart struggling with the harsh vicissitudes of life in the Massachusetts wilds. Her verse discloses a world in almost every way
more restricted than that of the great Renaissance poets: a domestic Calvinist world on the fringe of the forest and the edge of
civilization. But her sensibility made it a complete world, and the
plain style takes on a personal voice. She wrote from the freedom
of dwelling deeply within that small and separate world, for all
the rigor preached in the pulpit, for all the disease and hardship
which afflicted her family, for all the forest-terrors outside her
window. Somehow, quite improbably, there came to the New
World on the *Arbella* with Governor Winthrop a woman-poet
who found her own terms for the love of God, husband, children,
and much of life in this vale of tears. Mythologically the Muses
are feminine because woman as progenetrix symbolizes the fertile
and emotive energies of the imagination, at least to the almost

exclusively male line of poets. In "The Author to Her Book" Bradstreet describes her poems as uncouth, ragged offspring, but the ostensible maternal solicitude is laced with the shrewd ironic recognition (which Margaret Fuller and Emily Dickinson and Marianne Moore would in time come to share) that her poems would be read and judged by male critics. Nevertheless, it is a happy augury that a woman of her passion and spirit stands at the sourcing of our poetry: the American Muse, the *genius loci* at the wellspring.

It was in the verse of Edward Taylor, however, that the Puritan spirit received its majestic (and uncharacteristic) poetic statement. Taylor was of the generation following Bradstreet, born thirty years after her and already in his twenties with his education under way when he arrived in the Massachusetts Bay Colony with his family in 1668. After graduating from Harvard College a few years later, Taylor became minister of Westfield, a hamlet so remote that it was endangered by the Indian massacres of King Philip's War. From the first he was recognized as a man of singular intellect and piety, and from this outpost word spread of his strict adherence to orthodoxy in the administration of his stewardship. His 200-book library, one of the largest in America, consisted almost completely of works of philosophy and science and divinity; there was strikingly little of that "venomous" poetry bred by "the powers of darkness." In fact, Taylor's long public career until his death in 1729 was a losing battle against the insidious weakening of doctrine and practice which he saw rending, small point by larger, the seamless integrity of the Puritan Covenant.

Since Taylor was known as the stern voice raised in the Commonwealth against any abrogation of the covenantal ties, the poetry seems all the odder: written in secret and so private that he would forbid publication even after his death. He would have known the established literary guidelines as he would have known the orthodox position on infant baptism and the Real Presence. Yet he wrote, preserved, and passed on the 400 manuscript pages of poetry marked by personal idiosyncrasy, rhetorical intricacy, elaborate conceits, alliterative and onomatopoetic effects, a thick profusion of images, and an intellectual and emotional intensity that would have jolted the wits of the ordinary reader, had Taylor seen his way to exposing himself thus by publication. The discovery of the manuscripts forty years ago demanded a critical reassessment of the Puritan character and of Puritan poetry. In its evolution Puritanism was for some time resilient enough to contain and nourish its supreme and questioning intellects—Roger Williams and Jonathan Edwards, for example—but not without permanent consequences. By the force of their word and presence these geniuses explored new possibilities in the name of their very Puritanism, thereby expanding its previous formulation and undermining to some extent the substance of Puritanism and its notion of itself. Taylor's poems issued no public challenge to the old order which the poet otherwise staunchly upheld, which indeed he affirmed in his unusual poems; in fact, they present the Puritan consciousness confronting itself in the privacy of its isolation (in the words of Edwards' own resolution) "with all the power, might, vigour, and vehemence, yea violence, I am capable of."[11]

Taylor's sequestration on the outskirts of the colony undoubtedly contributed to the theological conservatism which set him off more and more from the larger community, but in this case intellectual conservatism led to what the community could only consider radical experiments in language. The same conviction that led him to live out in his orthodox fastness the experience of faith issued in poems whose unorthodox language violated not only the restrictions of Bradford and Hooker but also the neoclassic norms of Mather Byles and thereby created the first distinctive poetic style in America.

By the time Taylor arrived from England, his education and poetic tastes had been thoroughly formed. He had read the Renaissance poets, more particularly the metaphysical poets, and most especially George Herbert (judging from the many lines echoed and adapted from Herbert). Among the Puritans in general even the devotional poets of the seventeenth century were little read and imitated because Puritans viewed with alarm Catholicism and its vestiges in Anglicanism as base pandering to the senses and passions of men:[12] "the senses are seduced by Objects, these help to abuse Imagination, which excites disorders in the inferior parts of the soul, and raiseth Passions."[13] Only the otherworldliness of Herbert spared him from the distrust which fell on Donne and

22

Crashaw, with their strongly erotic appeal through imagery and rhythm to the physical senses and the passions.

In a Foreword to Donald Stanford's edition of Taylor's *Poems*,[14] Louis Martz pointed out the many parallels between Taylor and Herbert and also made the equally important observation that substantial differences in sensibility, diction, and technique set Taylor off from the English predecessors to whom he is indebted—from Herbert on the one hand and from Donne and Crashaw on the other. Taylor's poems consist principally of two long sequences: one (part lyrics, part allegorical morality play) depicting the drama of salvation under the title *God's Determinations Touching His Elect* and two Series of *Preparatory Meditations*. In the poems which make up *God's Determinations* Taylor tried to imitate Herbert's versatility with meters and stanzas but fell far short of Herbert as a virtuoso performer; he simply lacked Herbert's subtlety and adaptability at versification. At the other extreme, the 221 *Preparatory Meditations*, which comprise the bulk of Taylor's work, are all written in the same stave of six (the quatrain and couplet of Herbert's longest poem, "The Church Porch"). Over the decades, during which he wrote "a Meditation" in the same stanza form every six weeks or so, there is notably little limbering or variation; the units remain on the whole sturdy and separate building blocks stacked into a poem.

The real liveliness and originality of Taylor's poetry reside not in prosody but in the qualities of the language, diction, and imagery. Taylor's ear and tongue have a rougher, coarser edge than Herbert's, and the language moves into blunter, more tough-grained effects. At the same time Taylor's language does not recall the more strenuous metaphysical poets. The phrasing and texture suggest neither the baroque energy of Crashaw's best passages nor the nervous athleticism of Jack Donne nor the sinewy strength of Dean Donne but, instead, the bulging muscularity of Edward Taylor of Westfield. At its worst his language can tie itself into knots, the syntax muscle-bound, the word order awry; but no passage of Taylor—good or bad—would be mistaken for lines by any of the English metaphysicals.

The range of Taylor's diction is greater by far than Herbert's, greater even than Donne's: from learned and pedantic terms to expressions from his Leicestershire dialect to words coined for the occasion to colloquial expressions, many of which are obsolete and require a glossary at the back of Professor Stanford's edition. Moreover, many of the unfamiliar and colloquial words have the heavily monosyllabic and consonantal thickness of the Germanic roots of the language, so that the words have the lumpish shape and weight of objects on the tongue: squitchen, sprindge, hurden, haump, panchins, hift, chuffe, frim, blin, tills, quorns, poother, thrumping, pipkin, cades, crickling, flur, gastard, glout, keck, rigalled, skeg, snick-snarls, and so on. After Herbert's calm limpidity Taylor's diction sounds out with a rude eccentricity and almost primitive power.

Although Herbert frequently applied domestic metaphors to sacred subjects, Taylor pressed his homely images more forcefully and at greater length than either Donne or Herbert. The more sophisticated Englishmen would have found some of his images distasteful and uncouth, as when he dwells on excremental details or on a conceit of circumcision or of the seed's activity in the womb. At times he pushed a single metaphor too hard; at other times he compounded his metaphors into confusion. But even this irrepressibility suggests not so much the indulgent excesses of the minor metaphysical poets as the earnestness of the Puritan-amateur poet. His own sole judge and critic, he was determined at least to exhaust his materials and push his powers to their limits; he would pursue an idea relentlessly rather than risk abandoning it with possibilities unplumbed.

A juxtaposition of analogous passages from Herbert and Taylor should make the contrast plain. Both Herbert's "Redemption" and Taylor's 38th Meditation of the First Series develop a single and similar conceit. Here is Herbert's sonnet:

> Having been Tenant long to a rich Lord,
>   Not thriving, I resolved to be bold,
>   And make a suit unto him to afford
> A new small-rented lease, and cancell th' old.
> In heaven at his manour I him sought:
>   They told me there, that he was lately gone
>   About some land, which he had dearly bought
> Long since on earth, to take possession.
> I straight return'd, and knowing his great birth,
>   Sought him accordingly in great resorts;
>   In cities, theatres, gardens, parks, and courts:

At length I heard a ragged noise and mirth
  Of theeves and murderers: there I him espied,
  Who straight, *Your suit is granted,* said, and died.

These are the last four stanzas of Taylor's "Meditation":

God's Judge himselfe: and Christ Atturny is,
  The Holy Ghost Regesterer is founde.
Angells the sergeants are, all Creatures kiss
  The booke, and doe as Evidences abounde.
  All Cases pass according to pure Law
  And in the sentence is not Fret, nor flaw.

What saist, my soule? Here all thy Deeds are tri'de.
  Is Christ thy Advocate to pleade thy Cause?
Art thou his Client? Such shall never slide.
  He never lost his Case: he pleads such Laws
  As Carry do the same, nor doth refuse
  The Vilest sinners Case that doth him Choose.

This is his Honour, not Dishonour: nay
  No Habeas-Corpus gainst his Clients came
For all their Fines his Purse doth make down pay.
  He Non-Suites Satan's Suite or Casts the Same.
  He'l plead thy Case, and not accept a Fee.
  He'l plead Sub Forma Pauperis for thee.

My case is bad. Lord, be my Advocate.
  My sin is red: I'me under Gods Arrest.
Thou hast the Hint of Pleading; plead my State.
  Although it's bad thy Plea will make it best.
  If thou wilt plead my Case before the King:
  I'le Waggon Loads of Love, and Glory bring.

There are many points of contrast between Herbert's poem and Taylor's. The aristocratic Anglican thinks of the feudal relationship between poor peasant and generous lord, and the theocratic Calvinist pictures a court of law in which man stands a guilty pauper before the divine Judge until spared by the legal pleading of his unpaid Advocate. The sonnet form concentrates Herbert's language where Taylor can proceed discursively simply by piling one stanza on another. Herbert's conceit unfolds briskly with narrative detail, reaching a climactic reversal and conclusion in the last line and a half. The narrative is itself the metaphor, so that the other set of terms in the metaphor can remain delicately implicit and the point can be conveyed without being drawn. Once Taylor has set up his conceit, he fills it out slowly and, by comparison with Herbert, ploddingly, through an accumulation of detail, building from point to point to the personal plea in the final stanza. If the Father is Judge and the Son Advocate, then Taylor's heavy-handed thoroughness requires that the Holy Ghost be found a role in the court. And since the court meets in heaven, angels would logically be present, and then earthly creatures give evidence as witnesses, and so forth. Taylor enjoys wielding his technical knowledge of legal terms, but speaking at the end as simple criminal before the bar, he drops the level of speech to offering humble "Waggon Loads of Love" as fee. Where Herbert's verse is supple and light-stressed with many run-on lines and rich variety in the pentameter, Taylor's pentameters tread with stronger and more regular emphasis, and a preponderance of end-stops. Though these passages show Herbert the defter poet, the immediate point is to illustrate how different the language and so the sensibility of the two poets are.

Not that the differences always work to Herbert's advantage, as the following poems, even more directly paired, illustrate. The refrain of Herbert's "The Sacrifice"—"Was ever grief like mine?" —became the erratic refrain "Was ever Heart like mine?" in Taylor's 40th Meditation of the First Series. The first four stanzas of each will give a good sense of the poem. First Herbert:

Oh all ye, who passeby, whose eyes and mind
To worldly things are sharp, but to me blind,
To mee, who tooke eyes, that I might you finde.
    Was ever grief like mine?

The Princes of my People make a head
Against their Maker: they doe wish me dead,
Who cannot wish, except I give them bread:
    Was ever grief like mine?

Without me each one, who doth now me brave
Had to this day bin an Egyptian slave.
They use that power against me, which I gave.
    Was ever grief like mine?

Mine owne Apostle, who the bag did beare,
Though he had all I had, did not forbeare
To sell me also, and to put me there.
      Was ever grief like mine?

Then Taylor:

Still I complain; I am complaining still.
  Oh, woe is me! Was ever Heart like mine?
A sty of Filth, a Trough of Washing-Swill
  A Dunghill Pit, a Puddle of mere Slime.
  A Nest of Vipers, Hive of Hornets, Stings.
  A Bag of Poyson, Civit-Box of Sins.

Was ever Heart like mine? So bad? black? Vile?
  Is any Divell blacker? Or can Hell
Produce its match? It is the very Soile
  Where Satan reads his Charms, and sets his Spell.
  His Bowling Ally, where he sheeres his fleece
  At Nine Pins, Nine Holes, Morrice, Fox and Geese.

His Palace Garden where his courtiers walke.
  His Jewells Cabbinet. Here his Caball
Do sham it, and truss up their Privie talk
  In Fardells of Consults and bundles all.
  His shambles, and his Butcher's stale's herein.
  It is the Fuddling Schoole of every sin.

Was ever Heart like mine? Pride, Passion, fell.
  Ath'ism, Blasphemy, pot, pipe it, dance
Play Barlybreaks, and at last Couple in Hell.
  At Cudgells, Kit-Cat, Cards and Dice here prance.
  At Noddy, Ruff-and-trumpt, Jing, Post-and-Pare,
  Put, One-and-thirty and such other ware.

Herbert's polished paradoxes and fine workmanship become tiresome when prolonged to the full 63 stanzas, nor does the decorous composure of the surface suggest real grief or sacrifice. By contrast, Taylor's syllabic density and strong emphasis here work to sustain the accumulation of graphic detail—the heart's sty, the devil's games, the catalogue of sins—as each question and phrase adds to the tough and mounting self-accusation.

    Although Taylor was working in the mode of metaphysical

poetry and although the echoes and references to Herbert's verse indicate that Taylor knew and liked Herbert best among the poets who influenced him, Isaac Watts, the best and most widely known dissenter-poet of his day and with the possible exception of Charles Wesley the finest of British hymn-writers, provides in many ways a closer point of comparison than the aristocratic, Anglican Herbert.[15] Watts was roughly contemporary with Taylor, born about thirty years after him but poetically active during the same years as Taylor, before and after 1700. Both were dedicated nonconformist pastors, and their writing—both verse and theological exposition—grew out of their ministering. Watts' *Hymns and Spiritual Songs,* which went through many editions between its initial appearance in 1707 till Watts's death in 1748 (and of course through many editions since), sorted out the hymns into three categories: Book I, Collected from the Holy Scriptures (that is, paraphrased or adapted from biblical passages); Book II, Composed on Divine Subjects; and Book III, Prepared for the Holy Ordinance of the Lord's Supper. One of Watts's favorite biblical sources, as was Taylor's, was *The Song of Solomon;* 13 of the 150 hymns in Book I derive from the *Song* with its richly exotic imagery and impassioned tone.

The parallels between Watts and Taylor are so striking that we begin to wonder whether they were not proceeding quite independently from a common sensibility shared by dissenters of the late seventeenth and eighteenth centuries. If so, their particular expression of that sensibility is significantly different. Watts did publish a book of lyrics called *Horae Lyricae,* but his major work is *Hymns and Spiritual Songs.* Written for public performance in church by a mixed congregation, the hymns had a collective purpose: to combine words and melodies, often traditional melodies, in order to move the affections and commit the community to religious truth with emotional conviction. The hymns employed a variety of simple quatrains (the dissenters' hymn-meters which Emily Dickinson would find at hand to use more than a century later) and a simple but eloquent declarativeness of style. By contrast, Taylor's poems were private meditations, written with no intention of publication in the secrecy of heart and conscience, the contortions of self-accusation, penitence, and exaltation testing and cleansing the pastor for the administration of the Sacrament.

Consequently, everything in Taylor's *Preparatory Meditations*—the stanza structure, the sound texture, the diction and imagery and conceits, and, underlying all these technical matters, the quality of emotional and psychological experience—is more complex and idiosyncratic.

Here, for example, are poems by each on the image of Christ as the Bread of Life, from the sixth chapter of St. John's Gospel. Watts' hymn is the fifth in Book III:

> Let us adore th' eternal Word,
>   'Tis he our Souls hath fed;
> Thou art our living Stream, O Lord
>   And thou th' immortal Bread.
>
> The *Manna* came from lower Skies,
>   But *Jesus* from above,
> Where the fresh Springs of Pleasure rise,
>   And Rivers flow with Love.
>
> The *Jews* the Fathers dy'd at last
>   Who eat that heavenly Bread;
> But these Provisions which we taste
>   Can raise us from the Dead.
>
> Blest be the Lord that gives his Flesh
>   To nourish dying Men;
> And often spreads his Table fresh
>   Lest we should faint again.
>
> Our Souls shall draw their heav'nly Breath
>   While *Jesus* finds Supplies;
> Nor shall our Graces sink to Death,
>   For *Jesus* never dies.
>
> Daily our mortal Flesh decays,
>   But *Christ* our Life shall come;
> His unresisted Power shall raise
>   Our Bodies from the Tomb.

Now the last three stanzas of Taylor's Meditation 8 of the First Series:

> In this sad state, Gods Tender Bowells run
>   Out streams of Grace: And he to end all strife

The Purest Wheate in Heaven, his deare-dear Son
    Grinds, and kneads up into this Bread of Life.
Which Bread of Life from Heaven down came and stands
    Disht on thy Table up by Angells Hands.

Did God mould up this Bread in Heaven, and bake,
    Which from his Table came, and to thine goeth?
Doth he bespeak thee thus, This Soule Bread take.
    Come Eate thy fill of this thy Gods White Loafe?
    Its Food too fine for Angells, yet come, take
    And Eate thy fill. Its Heavens Sugar Cake.

What Grace is this knead in this Loafe? This thing
    Souls are but petty things it to admire.
Yee Angells, help: This fill would to the brim
    Heav'ns whelm'd-down Chrystall meele Bowle, yea
        and higher.
    This Bread of Life dropt in thy mouth, doth Cry.
    Eate, Eate me, Soul, and thou shalt never dy.

The following stanzas from the seventy-fourth hymn of Book I, one of Watts' finest, adapts verse from *The Song of Solomon*; since it uses many of the images and metaphors which Taylor derived from the same biblical source and which we will study in the next section of this chapter, it deserves comparison with Taylor's stronger, quirkier, more enraptured development in the passages cited later:

We are a Garden wall'd around,
Chosen and made peculiar Ground;
A little Spot inclos'd by Grace
Out of the World's wide Wilderness.

Like Trees of Myrrh and Spice we stand,
Planted by God the Father's Hand;
And all his Springs in Sion flow,
To make the young Plantation grow.

Awake, O heavenly Wind, and come,
Blow on this Garden of Perfume;
Spirit Divine, descend and breathe
A gracious Gale on Plants beneath.

Make our best Spices flow abroad
To entertain our Saviour-God:

And faith, and Love, and Joy appear,
And every Grace be active here.

Let my Beloved come, and taste
His pleasant Fruits at his own Feast.
I come, my Spouse, I come, he crys,
With Love and Pleasure in his Eyes.

Taylor's poems bespeak a vigorous, passionate, and learned mind shaping its apprehensions and speech without the chastening refinements which a sophisticated society of poets and readers would have bred in him: a society open to and assumed by both Herbert and Watts. Emerson once remarked in his *Journal* that "the literary man in this country has no critic," and that fact is both a grumble and a boast. Taylor wrote poetry more like an Anglican, but to that poetic tradition he brought a Puritan sensibility articulating his self-examination on the frontier eccentrically, crankily even, but always boldly. And in these accents we can hear the first intimations of a distinct poetic idiom, as the circumstances of the poet in America, almost surely without reflection or conscious intention on his part, began to separate him from the British tradition. Taylor's qualities suggest the advantages and difficulties of independence: honesty which lacks tact and finish, self-involvement which can snarl itself in knots and crotchets, fresh energy which can move into clumsiness, a complex personal idiom ready to sacrifice conventional clarity; and these are the characteristics which will mark the American strain as it splits away from the British. In 1913 Ezra Pound, contrasting *Leaves of Grass* to the Anglo-Saxon "Seafarer" as a way of placing himself as an American poet, specified the American quality:

It is, as nearly as I can define it, a certain generosity; a certain carelessness, or looseness, if you will; a hatred of the sordid, an ability to forget the part for the sake of the whole, a desire for largeness, a willingness to stand exposed.
'Camerado, this is no book;
Who touches this touches a man.'
The artist is ready to endure personally a strain which his craftsmanship would scarcely endure.
Here is a spirit, one might say, as hostile to the arts as was the Anglo-Saxon objection to speaking at all.

Yet the strength of both peoples is just here; that one under-
takes to keep quiet until there is something worth saying, and the
other will undertake nothing in its art for which it will not be in
person responsible.[16]

An uncanny amount of what Pound identifies as "our American
keynote" is prefigured in the poetry of Edward Taylor, and suddenly the three centuries of American poetry—at least our most
distinctive and original work—fall into place. Edward Taylor
was the most original American poet until Poe and Emerson. Intervening poets such as Freneau, Barlow, and Dwight—like such
later poets as Longfellow, Lowell and Tuckerman—were still
seeking their models abroad, so that even those poems which use
American scenes and materials strike the mind and tongue and
ear as, for the most part, tepid imitations of English examples.
With Taylor, however, the split had opened, and in time poets
like Emerson and Dickinson, Whitman and Williams would come
to widen the breach and establish an ocean between poets here
and poets there. It is a noteworthy and perhaps symbolic fact that
the only poetry in English in Taylor's immense library was a
volume of Anne Bradstreet.

2

Taylor was no crude and misplaced shadow of Herbert.
There is nothing in English metaphysical poetry like either *God's
Determinations* or the two Series of *Preparatory Meditations*. In
fact, it is the first instance of what may be a distinctly American
genre: the open-ended poem written over years, perhaps even
over a lifetime, in separate but interacting segments. At any rate,
there is nothing like Taylor's *Preparatory Meditations* until Whitman's *Leaves of Grass*, Pound's *Cantos* and Williams' *Paterson*.
For all the uneven quality of the particular poems and all the
repetitiousness in theme, tone, and imagery, Taylor remains a
poet of power and scope, not only in the excellence of particular
poems and passages but in the huge harmony of the whole work,
and the same is true of Whitman, Pound, and Williams. It is a
corpus because its slow progression formulates the terms for
translating a vision of reality into a coherent poetic creation. Religious and moral convictions do not make an artist; only the

ability to find the symbols for one's convictions lifts utterance into art. Each Meditation elaborates a generating idea or conceit to a personal application at the end. The poetic vitality arises from the metaphorical imagery: not so much from single or individual metaphors (many of which are usual enough) as from the patterns they assume. Certain key metaphors, repeated until they become related, gather themselves into clusters and designs of clusters, evolving a dynamic structure within the uniform regularity of the stanza and the uniform structure of the poems.[17] Images recur and begin to associate themselves with other recurrent images until they accrete as focal symbols which in concert with one another make a kind of figurative *pointillisme.* Point by related point, image by reiterated image, context by analogous context, Taylor draws out the imaginative correlatives for his sense of things. Pound wrote in an early essay, in his own effort to define himself as a poet, that out of the discovery of his unique quality and virtù "the artist may proceed to the erection of his microcosms"[18]—a very American notion.

The forty-nine poems of the First Series of *Meditations* comprise a manageable yet broad enough field to illustrate Taylor's metaphorical method, and they are a unit which the poet himself marked off.*

The first stanza of the First Meditation immediately announces the controlling paradox of the poem—and of existence itself:

> What Love is this of thine, that Cannot bee
>   In thine Infinity, O Lord, Confinde,
> Unless it in thy very Person see,
>   Infinity, and Finity Conjoyn'd?
>   What hath thy Godhead, as not satisfide
>   Marri'de our Manhood, making it its Bride?

Godhead moving into hypostatic union with humanity in Christ; creation as the divine Incarnation: both mysteries of Infinity and Finity not just joined but conjoined reciprocally and mutually.

*Forty-nine is the squaring of seven, a number of "Rich Mystery" not only in the occult tradition but in Christianity as well, as the 21st Meditation of the Second Series testifies: "Thou [God] makest to entertain thy Guests most dresst/ In dishes up by SEVENS which afford/ Rich Mystery under their brims expresst."

Christ's Person unites man and God, and so by extension all creation is a projection of Godhead into Manhood, Spirit into Matter: the sublime and daily paradox. The imagery of the rest of the poem develops this paradox through the antithetical but primary elements of fire and water, telling the same mystery in terms of interdependent opposites. The second stanza uses liquid images and mentions hellfire in the last line; the third and final stanza repeats the water imagery in the first line but goes on to pray for the flame of love:

> Oh, Matchless Love! filling Heaven to the brim!
>   O're running it: all running o're beside
> This World! Nay Overflowing Hell; wherein
>   For thine Elect, there rose a mighty Tide!
>   That there our Veans might through thy Person bleed,
>   To quench those flames, that else would on us feed.
>
> Oh! that thy love might overflow my Heart!
>   To fire the same with Love: for Love I would.
> But oh! my streight'ned Breast! my Lifeless Sparke!
>   My Fireless Flame! What Chilly Love, and Cold?
>   In measure small! In Manner Chilly! See
>   Lord blow the Coal: Thy Love Enflame in mee.

Taylor wrote the Meditations as a spiritual and emotional preparation for receiving and administering the Lord's Supper in his church. The Sacrament memorialized the Divine Presence in the individual and joined him thereby to the Communion of Saints—that is, in Calvinist terms, to the Community of the Elect. But that determination rested on personal, subjective confirmation. Consequently, before his appearance at the altar in front of his flock the pastor wrote poems in secret. His only surviving prose is a sequence of sermons called *Christographia* propounding from Scripture and doctrine the significance of the Word's dual nature, God and man, for our mixed existence, body and soul. By extension, in searching his inner heart his words return again and again to the fundamental question that lies beyond question: "But how it came, amazeth all Communion./God's onely Son doth hug Humanity,/Into his very person" (I, 10); "Shall Mortall, and Immortall marry? nay,/Man marry God?

God be a Match for Mud?" (I, 23).* The answer is incredible Truth: "Thy Maker is thy Husband. Hearst thou this?"

Marriage, hugging embrace, manhood wed as bride—from the start Taylor describes the incarnational mystery in sexual terms. He is, of course, working from a long tradition; the great mystics and religious poets have always invoked sexual passion as the closest human analogue for the impossible but experienced union of opposites. But the sexual mystery is more complex than that; it works both ways. It is not only that man cites the most ecstatic natural union as his inadequate-best way of talking about something more-than-natural. From the human perspective we are faced with the sublime paradox of Spirit freely choosing to express Himself in the human body. Without surrendering transcendental unity He projected Himself into division, submitting to the rhythm of time-space; He entered the sexual dimension and turned us towards the wholeness which is Himself. Time-space moves by the beat of the clock, the pulse of the pendulum, and God is the force beating in every pulse. Once God had become flesh, the duality which is the law of matter and of human sexuality could be resolved, by His own design, only in our integration and perfection as human beings.

Taylor's theology was a firmly founded intellectual structure, but his emotional life was just as strong and just as surely based. For the Christian the paradox of the Incarnation is further complicated by the fact that human nature is fallen, and either the cause or the result of the fall is sexual temptation and sexual sin. Passionate and sensual by nature, even more passionate and sensual than most men (the poetry would suggest), Taylor had constantly to remind himself that the body was, in itself, the unregenerate corpse of fallen man; the opening lines of many poems dwell on the filth, diseases, and vices that afflict the flesh. However, a radical and pervasive sense of the Incarnation such as his would not lead him to rest in a manichaean opposition of body and spirit; precisely to the contrary, he would want to see

---

*Throughout this chapter citations of lines will be provided in the text from Professor Stanford's edition. The roman numeral indicates the First or Second Series of *Meditations*; the arabic numeral indicates the number of the poem within the Series.

them as "conjoyn'd" and thereby redeemed. Even an orthodox Calvinist had to distinguish between the corruptible body, weak and prone to sin, and the glorious body, rapturous in ecstasy, which the Incarnation made possible.

Seventy-six of the *Meditations*, including all written between 1714 and 1720 and between 1722 and 1725, take as their scriptural text verses from *The Song of Solomon*, which Taylor refers to as *Canticles*. Its explicit sexuality and erotic imagery have always made fastidious exegetes nervous, but Taylor takes the *Song* as the chief biblical source for his poetry. For Solomon's love-song is not just a spiritual allegory for the marriage of Christ the Bridegroom to His Church, long before His birth; it celebrates the fact that spiritual rapture possesses us not despite the flesh but in the flesh, and the consequent fact that true erotic love is a movement of the spirit. Taylor's Communion meditations do not explore this second proposition, as Whitman's poems would, but they are based on the first conviction. Far from denying Eros, Jesus incorporates and inspires Eros; therein lies the distinction between the sexless angels on the one hand and men and women on the other. We experience all things, including redemption, in the terms of our humanity.

Earlier in the chapter we heard the Puritan concern that "the senses are seduced by Objects, these help to abuse Imagination, which excites disorders in the inferior parts of the soul, and raiseth Passions"; that scruple enforced the plain style. Aware as Taylor was of human frailty and the effects of original sin in the absence of grace, he emphatically agreed with these prohibitive words in most situations. But not in the context of grace and in the privacy of the heart rapt by God; there inhibitions could signify the heart's obdurate coldness. If God chose to come to us, it could only be to possess us in the totality of our human nature, and we ought to strive to respond in the totality of our human nature. So, with *The Song of Solomon* providing the rubrics, Taylor joined the Christian poets who saw their manhood broken by God's holy lust: a line extending in modern poetry from John Donne to a contemporary like William Everson (Brother Antoninus). Donne ended the fourteenth Holy Sonnet with "I,/ Except You enthrall me, never shall be free,/ Nor ever chaste, except Thou ravish me"; Everson prayed, "Annul in me my man-

hood, Lord, and make / Me woman-sexed and weak," and wrote
a poem titled "The Song the Body Dreamed in the Spirit's Mad
Behest," which opens "Call Him the Lover and call me the Bride"
and concludes "His great Godhead peels its stripping strength /
In my red earth."[19] What links these vastly different poets, one so
British and the other so American in sensibility and speech, is the
incarnational conviction that in the human fusion eros and agape
are inseparable and that man is woman before God.

It is true that Taylor's imagination was restrained by the
Calvinist distrust of the unregenerate body and that a poet like
Everson, coming after Whitman as well as after Freud and Jung,
is blunter and freer because of a deeper, more open engagement
with sexuality. As a result, Taylor translates much of the erotic
dimension of his imagination into metaphors less overtly sexual
and often derived from his reading in Scripture, literature, and
science. Nevertheless, the sexual implications are there, felt and
admitted, and the strategy of Taylor's first Meditation is to establish the sexual basis for the subsequent figures of speech depicting his experience of grace.

The second poem introduces the metaphor of boxes and
containers, images which will be familiar by the end of the
Series:

> Oh! that my Soul, Heavens Workmanshop (within
>   My Wicker'd Cage,) that Bird of Paradise
> Inlin'de with Glorious Grace up to the brim
>   Might be thy Cabbinet, oh Pearle of Price.
>   Oh! let thy Pearle Lord, Cabbinet in mee.
>   I'st then be rich! nay rich enough for thee.
>
> My Heart, oh Lord, for thy Pomander gain.
>   Be thou thyselfe my sweet Perfume therein.
> Make it thy Box, and let thy Pretious Name
>   My Pretious Ointment be emboxt therein.
>   If I thy box and thou my Ointment bee
>   I shall be sweet, nay, sweet enough for thee.

And later: "Yet may I Purse, and thou my Mony bee./I have
enough. Enough in having thee." The body cages the soul, its bird
of Paradise, but the bird is itself filled with grace, which is like
the precious pearl in the soul's cabinet. And so with the poman-

der and the perfum, the box and the ointment, the purse and the money. Many other Meditations repeat these and related images: castles enclosed by ramparts, cities encircled by walls, man's images for the New Jerusalem which is the City of God.

Why such profuse imagery of containing and being contained? As the pattern builds from poem to poem, the accumulation of images begins to suggest that for Taylor each thing must exist within fixed bounds and limits, that finally the cosmos itself is clasped round in an order which fulfills the creatures it holds in place. God is the absolute who completes each circumference—the self, its sphere of activity, at last the entire system of spheres—yet God is the center of each sphere as well. Man's lot is to contain God by being contained by Him; the omnipotent Deity must come to possess, sometimes by force, his sometimes fractious creatures. Each creature is cast in the archetypally feminine role: the vessel (container, box, walled city, and so on) which opens for entrance in order to close round the quickened life.

Often this conception is worked out specifically in terms of opening and closing, locking and unlocking boxes. In the fourth Meditation Taylor puns on the word "chest" as the heart's box:

> My Silver Chest a Sparke of Love up locks:
> And out will let it when I can't well Use.
> The gawdy World me Courts t'unlock the Box. . . .

In these lines the poet resists the advances of the "gawdy World" and unlocks his Love only when he has made a pilgrimage to the Rose of Sharon, which envelops the love-spark into itself: "Her Chest Unlocks; the Sparke of Love out breaths/ To Court this Rose: and lodgeth in its leaves." The poet's feminine heart ("Her Chest") takes the man's role in courtship, but by inversion the situation quickly doubles on itself so that each contains the other: "Shall not thy Rose my Garden fresh perfume? . . . Enthrone thy Rosy-selfe within Mine Eyes" (I, 4); "Lord make my heart thy bed, thy heart make mine./ Thy Love bed in my heart, bed mine in thine" (I, 35). Or again in the penultimate poem of the Series: "And let thy Joy enter in mee before/I enter do into my masters joy" (I, 48).

Other poems repeat this interaction of containment: "Open thy Casement wide, let Glory in,/ To Guild thy Heart to be an Hall for him" (I, 18); "Thy Milke white Hand . . . opes this Gate, and me conducts into/ This Golden Palace" (I, 24); "Untap thy Cask. And let my Cup Catch some" (I, 28). Toward the end of the Series, in the 42nd poem, the box-lock-key conceit receives full treatment; here are two stanzas:

> Such is my Lord, and more. But what strang thing
>   Am I become? Sin rusts my Lock all o're.
> Though he ten thousand Keyes all on a string
>   Takes out, scarce one, is found, unlocks the Doore.
>   Which ope, my Love crincht in a Corner lies
>   Like some shrunck Crickling: and scarce can rise.
>
> Lord ope the Doore: rub off my Rust, Remove
>   My Sin. And Oyle my Lock. (Dust there doth shelfe).
> My Wards will trig before thy Key; my Love
>   Then, as enliven'd, leap will on thyselve.
>   It needs must be, that giving handes receive
>   Again Receivers Hearts furld in Love Wreath.

This "Holy Huswifery" will bring the poet to birth as the new man sired in him by God; clothed in "royall Robes," he will emerge from his present "Peephole" into the heavenly city "enwalld with jems," "Rim'd with Glory round."

Thus enclosing walls do not make a prison, nor is a prescribed universe merely static. In time–space the order is gestative process: a budding and a becoming. The third poem of the Series draws together enforced order and natural process and grounds them in the sexual link: "Guarded, engardened, nay, Imbosomed bee." If the garden is walled, the walls enwomb a garden; if the course of things is set, it is a process of realization. In fact, the enclosure is necessary for ordered and controlled growth; unlike the wilderness, the garden grows within the City of God, trimmed and tended by the gardener's care. The garden, especially the walled and castled garden, recurs in many poems and is summed up as "Christ's Curious Garden fenced in/ With Solid Walls of Discipline/ Well wed, and watered, and made full trim" ("The Soule Seeking Church-Fellowship" in *God's Determinations*).

Another version of organic growth within containment is the grafting conceit, adapted from Saint Paul. In Meditation 29 the poet, as the withered twig, receives his potency and fruition from being implanted in the trunk of the living tree: an emblem, at once masculine and feminine, of the life-energy in God's garden, which, as above, quickens the masculine into birth.

> Thou! thou! my Deare-Deare Lord, are this rich Tree
>   The Tree of Life Within Gods Paradise.
> I am a Withred Twig, dri'de fit to bee
>   A Chat Cast in thy fire, Writh off by Vice.
>   Yet if thy Milke white-Gracious Hand will take mee
>   And grafft mee in this golden stock, thou'lt make mee.
>
> Thou'lt make me then its Fruite, and Branch to spring.
>   And though a nipping Eastwinde blow, and all
> Hells Nymps with spite their Dog's stocks threat ding
>   To Dash the Grafft off, and it's fruits to fall,
>   Yet I shall stand thy Grafft, and Fruits that are
>   Fruits of the Tree of Life thy Grafft shall beare.

In the Mystical Body of the Church, the measure is: "By their fruits you shall know them." At the same time, the harsh sound and movement of these lines, which has many parallels in other *Meditations*, indicate the hellish attempts to interfere with the rhythmic process of bearing.

The lines cited above from *God's Determinations* depict the walled garden as "made full trim" by being "well wed, and watered." Often animating grace is seen as moving waters making the flowers spring up. The poems abound in images of fertility: liquid pouring, flowing, overflowing from a "sea of Grace," an untapped Cask (I, 28). Sometimes baptismal water becomes wine, or blood, or Sacramental wine-blood. To cite from many examples: "streams of Grace" "run" from God to the poet (I, 8); Christ's veins spout into his wine-beaker (I, 10). With moisture gardens also need the "flowering rays" of the sun (I, 19). As in the introductory poem, fire and water, those seemingly contradictory elements, work together in the organic dynamism of growth and realization. Christ is explicitly the "Sun of Righteousness" (I, 19) and elsewhere a flame, sometimes the "Candle" irradiating a blackened world. So "I'll at thy Glory my dark Candle light" (I, 21), and, reciprocally, "Lord ting my Candle at thy Burning Rayes" (I, 16). Several times Taylor calls this interchange "mutual propriety"; the word "propriety" suggests both the distinct natures of God and man and also their suitability to each other, and the pun "mutual propriety" sums up once more the double mystery of the painful disjunction and glorious conjunction between the human and the divine.

There are other images of moving down a fixed course. Flowing containers like pipes, gutters, conduits, and channels span the gap between orders of being, and again the image takes on erotic overtones:

> Had not my Soule's thy Conduit, Pipes stopt bin
>   With mud, what Ravishment would'st thou Convay?
> Let Graces Golden Spade dig till the Spring
>   Of tears arise, and cleare this filth away.
>   Lord, let thy spirit raise my sighings till
>   These Pipes my soule do with thy sweetness fill.   (I, 4)

(The various strains of metaphor become so closely associated with one another in the *Meditations* that this same poem also speaks of flames, an overflowing cup, locks and keys, flooding streams, sunbeams, and a rose garden.) A variation of the pipe conceit is the distillation of grace from God to man; one instance among several is the 7th poem, which describes Jesus' body as the apparatus and vessels of a distillery. In an even more extreme conception, Christ's veins become "Golden Pipes" and "gutters" for transmitting the distilled "Red wine" (I, 10; see also I, 32). Through distillation the mystical science of alchemy—which exerted such power over the seventeenth- and eighteenth-century imagination—hoped to sublimate matter so that its sexual oppositions would reveal themselves as resolved in a divine *conjunctio oppositorum*, called often the *hieros gamos*, or holy marriage. References to alchemy and to alchemical jargon indicate Taylor's interest in the subject, but what he does here, without straying into the dubious ways of the occult, is to develop a heavily theological, Christocentric version of the process which spiritualizes matter.

At the same time, a Calvinist version of the *conjunctio oppositorum* is the goal of the poems. Our human nature is dual and paradoxical, but by His own choice God entered a dual existence. In His person the paradox is resolved, and by extension the paradox of our existence can be individually resolved. With the imagination anticipating and responding to grace, Taylor's poems represent his attempt to pitch himself beyond the paradoxes and divisions of our natural experience, epitomized in the sexual polarity, into a transpolar, transsexual, androgynous wholeness of mind and heart and soul posited in the images of God husbanding human nature and manhood brided to Godhead: "Shall Mortall, and Immortall marry?" Consequently the busy kinetics of the poems, the stresses and tension of the language, move toward a still completion, often depicted as a meal or feast bestowed on a starving man. There are many poems on the theme of fullness, and in the 27th, which stems from the scriptural text "In Him shall all Fulness dwell," Taylor substantiates the abstract notion by linking it with several of the principal metaphorical patterns of the Series: a box of gold, a case of rubies, a cabinet of pearls, golden pipes spilling to clay vessels, fire, streams, flowers.

Even this brief sketch of the interwoven metaphors in the *Meditations* should demonstrate that the texture of the verse is carefully and richly wrought beyond anything the plain style would tolerate. Why would a conservative Puritan divine embroider a tapestry more splendid by far than the "cloth of gold . . . stuck with as many jewels as the gown of a Russian ambassador," a style which Cotton Mather was also so bold as to sanction? To begin with, the stereotype of the Puritan as a clammy and sexless creature will not bear close examination: Anne Bradstreet was no frigid woman nor Taylor afraid of his senses. Moreover, his mighty sense of the Incarnation makes him perceive spirit immanent in flesh and matter. Even so, why should Taylor's fancy turn so frequently to gold, gems, perfumes, liquors, brocades, incense—things which were clearly not part of his life at Westfield? The question implies the answer: exactly because his rich and convoluted imagination dwelt in a wilderness. Because neither the forest filled with beasts and Indians nor the grim austerity of the Westfield community represented to his imagination the garden in the City of God, his imagination compensated from its own resources. The insufficiencies of nature and society drove him into the privacy of his imagination where his passionate nature could articulate the Puritan vision of the city on the hill which John Winthrop had voiced to the first ship-load of Puritans in the misery and anxiety of their earthly condition.

Behind Taylor's poems lies a theological framework, but the poems record the budding of his spiritual life: the walled garden again. The recurrence of metaphorical images makes up the fiber and texture of the sequence. By circling back again and again, they envision a world which is, microcosmically as well as macro-cosmically, predestined yet creatively in process. Taylor is a poet adequate to his vision, and his achievement lies at last not in particular poems, even the better or best poems, but in the corpus. All the elements of the First Series of *Meditations* are given in the first poem or poems; then the poet associates, elaborates, builds, connects, spatializing the implications of the initial vision. There is little or no temporal development from one point to another, as there is in much of Donne's and some of Herbert's verse; the movement is not linear and progressive but circular and self-defining. The analogy has already been made between the *Meditations* and other American open-form poems like *Leaves of Grass* and the *Cantos*. In some ways—certainly in religious vision and in the sense of a structured cosmos—a better analogy is Eliot's *Four Quartets*, whose circular movement brings us to the point of recognizing that "the end of all our exploring/ Will be to arrive where we started/ And know it for the first time." In fact, there will be nothing like Taylor's poems of Christian meditation in our poetry until the *Quartets*. Like Eliot's, Taylor's poems embody the process of realization; the conclusion of the work returns by circuitous indirection to the point of origin: "Infinity, and Finity Conjoyn'd," the mystery itself fleshed in his experience and figured forth in his imaginative symbols.

3

It was Taylor's passionate belief in the Incarnation which sustained his finding images for the spiritual life in even secular objects, and it is revealing of how deep-rooted the mystery of Communion is in the New England (and so to some extent the

American) consciousness to note Emerson, over a century later
and much further along in the evolution of the New England
mind, celebrating the poetic spirit of pagan "Bacchus" in imagery
of bread and wine. Emily Dickinson began a poem with "A Word
made Flesh" and maneuvered a declension of incarnation from
the Divine Word to the last lines, "this consent of Language/
This loved Philology." Even so crusty a skeptic as Robert Frost
selected these lines to preface his final volume:

> But God's own descent
> Into flesh was meant
> As a demonstration
> That the supreme merit
> Lay in risking spirit
> In substantiation.
> Spirit enters flesh
> And for all it's worth
> Charges into earth
> In birth after birth
> Ever fresh and fresh.
> We may take the view
> That its derring-do
> Thought of in the large
> Is one mighty charge
> On our human part
> Of the soul's ethereal
> Into the material.

Taylor was a Christian as Frost was not; but then Frost was a
New Englander, no matter how many stages of belief later. John
Livingston Lowes once suggested that all religious poetry was
informed by some notion of Incarnation:

> . . . the essential element of all poetry which has religious
> significance is precisely that imaginative transformation of the
> unseen which is felt to be eternal into terms of things which we
> have heard, which we have seen with our eyes, which we have
> looked upon, and our hands have handled.[20]

In Frost's lines God's descent into flesh is reenacted in the
mighty charge of each human spirit into its material ambience.
Taylor would have emphasized God's mighty charge into the

material and human sphere, but exactly that incarnational sense justified—indeed sanctified—for Taylor (as man's charge was to justify for Frost) his intention of using the external world as tropes for his inner experience. So his acts of self-examination and self-comprehension were acts of divine worship; many of them conclude with a plea for inspiration so that the poet can "serve thy Sacred selfe with Sacred art" (II, 36).

Time and again, however, Taylor is struck by how paltry the proliferating language of fancy is for the sublime reality which it strains to voice. "My Quaintest Metaphors are ragged Stuff/ Making the Sun seem like a Mullipuff" (I, 22); "sparkling Metaphors . . . would bee/ A Pack of guilded Non-Sense to thee" (II, 35); "My Metaphors are but full Tacklings tag'd/ With ragged Non-Sense" (II, 36). Just rags and tatters, not the whole cloth; the refrain sounds through the poems. What finally justified spinning out scraps of tropes was the conviction that a more direct expression of truth underlay the tropes in a typology manifest in nature and human nature. Typology, a technical term used here in an applied sense, needs explanation, but the distinction—and relation—between types and tropes have far-reaching implications not just for Taylor's poetry but for the course of American poetry.

Types were a special kind of symbol, and the notion of typology began as a way of interpreting Scripture. Since very early in the Christian tradition the Old Testament has been read as a sacred history designed to anticipate the New Dispensation. The Old and the New, then, demonstrated not the division splitting history but the unified continuity of human experience. The marvelous account of Jonah and the whale, for example, became a symbolic prefiguration of Christ's passion and resurrection. Jonah was called the "type" of Christ, who was called technically the "antitype," the reality behind the type, to which the type points and in which the type is fulfilled. Abraham's son by his wife was a type of the elect; his son by the slave, a type of the damned. The technical terminology is misleading, because the anti-type is really the positive expression of the prefigurative type. Thus in a typological reading of the Bible, Abraham, Jacob, Moses, and the line of Prophets were types of the Messiah; their meaning was only completed in the supreme Prophet, and the antitype was the absolute reality behind, the end and fulfillment of these imperfect foreshadowings and reflections. Typology was, therefore, a way of revealing the spiritual truth in the historical occurrence, of perceiving the eternal plan in the contingencies of time. The type was intentional; God meant the person or event to symbolize His truth, and the connection between type and antitype was real and primary.

Taylor's abiding sense of typology expressed itself in the poems which begin the Second Series of *Preparatory Meditations.* However, when in the midst of explicating biblical types Taylor speaks of himself in feminine-sexual terms as "Impregnate with a Sparke Divine" (II, 3), he is suggesting a sense of Incarnation which predicates an extended notion of typology. If the Incarnation was not a single past event but is a continuous charge of spirit into matter, then it is ever-operative in us and in our world, and individual human experience opens up a wholly new constellation of possibilities. This pervasive sense of types radically affects every aspect of the mutual relationship between the self and the world. Revelation is not just Scripture unriddled exegetically in the plain style, but the pattern of everyday experience. God so manages the world as to make it a personal revelation to each man (or at least to each of the elect). Then nature is also the book of types, and poetry is indeed a "Sacred art" in a precise sense: a record of experiential revelations.

The Puritans had always sought to read sermons in stones and intentional significance in the smallest occurrences, as their histories, journals, and diaries attest. Anne Bradstreet was impressed by the "hourly mementos" which present "emblems" to men; so vitally related were the material order and the spiritual order that she could feel tempted to identify the type and antitype in a pantheistic unity, as in these lines addressed to the sun as the "universe's eye," almost as Emerson or Thoreau would:

> Soul of this world, this universe's eye,
> No wonder some made thee a deity.
> Had I not better known, alas, the same had I.[21]

Taylor's first *Meditation* of the Second Series proclaims how man may come to perceive types if his human fallibility be transfigured and completed by grace:

My Stains are such, and sinke so deep, that all
    The Excellency in Created Shells
Too low, and little is to make it [my dull heart] fall
    Out of my leather Coate wherein it dwells.
    This Excellence is but a Shade to that
    Which is enough to make my Stains go back.

The glory of the world slickt up in types
    In all Choise things chosen to typify,
His glory upon whom the worke doth light,
    To thine's a Shaddow, or a butterfly.
    How glorious, then, my Lord, art thou to mee
    Seing to cleanse me, 's worke alone for thee.

The glory of all Types doth meet in thee.
    Thy glory doth their glory quite excell:
More than the Sun excells in its bright glee
    A nat, an Earewig, Weevill, Snaile, or Shell.

Just as the sun surpasses such tiny creatures as gnats and ear-wigs, so God's essential Being excels all "Created Shells," and yet creatures, "chosen" to reflect Him, reveal his multiple Excellency to eyes opened by grace. Since man cannot "view/ This excellence of thine, undazled," he must view it through a "world slickt up in types," and yet since all types "meet in thee," perception opens on a panorama of divine evidences. So while man can never know "Godhead Fulness, thine essentially," he can come to glimpse its manifestation in "All Created Fulness," because God distills his Life "like golden Spirits" "to ery member of thy Mystick Selfe" (II, 47) and "fills my Shell" (II, 5). By this action His visible saints constitute types of Him, like stars that "dance/ A Galliard, Round about the Sun" (II, 4). Man's wilful and sinful stains place him lower than unconscious creatures who spontaneously express God, but paradoxically (as Coleridge would note again in the next century) man's powers of reflection and will make him capable through grace of comprehending God's revealed splendor and rendering conscious expression of it—and therein lies the exaltation of the poet's tongue and the sacredness of his song.

    Jonathan Edwards' philosophical mind would state the point more abstractly again and again in *Images or Shadows of Divine*

Things:* "The things of this world are ordered [and] designed to shadow forth spiritual things," for God "makes the inferiour in imitation of the superiour, the material of the spiritual, on purpose to have a resemblance and shadow of them."[22] Consequently "the system of created beauty may be divided into two parts, the typical world, and the antitypical world. . . . Thus the material and natural world is typical of the moral, spiritual, and intelligent world, or the city of God."[23] It is not a long step from this conviction to Emerson's statement in *Nature* that since "particular natural facts are symbols of particular spiritual facts," "Nature is symbol of Spirit."

The poet's task, then, was to apprehend the types in his own experience in order to say how Nature reflects Spirit. The poet could resort to his own poor devices of articulation; if God spoke in types, tropes were often the human response, our ragged attempts at articulation. Even the plain style allowed the writer within severe limits to draw analogies and similitudes as illustrations and intensifications of the meaning, but these tropes remained rhetorical strategies. However, Taylor's sense of poetic Truth ran too deep to regard tropological "fictions," to use Wallace Stevens' word, with the final seriousness that Stevens had to confer on them. A century later Samuel Taylor Coleridge would discriminate the tropes of fancy from the insights of Imagination. They were different modes of perception; more than that, they proceeded from different faculties of perception: Imagination, godlike and God-given, sees into the life of things, while imagination or fancy merely patterns fragments in the mind through the association of images. Fancy is an aspect of the Understanding, as it operates on material phenomena in time and space; Imagination is an aspect of transcendental Reason, which sees the universal in the particular. No Romantic psychologically and emotionally, Taylor made the same distinction with a more muddled vocabulary. He sometimes used "fancy" in the Coleridgean sense as the faculty which supplied figures of speech to "varnish" and "decorate" with "secular Glory," but sometimes he said "imagination" for Coleridge's "fancy"—for example,

---

*Taylor calls the type a "shadow" (II, 1), an "image" (II, 7), a "looking glass" and "map" (II, 9). He also associates types with several of the metaphors we have discussed: "flowering types" (II, 10), "typic beams" (II, 12), a "Box" of types (II, 50).

when in *Christographia* he spoke of the "figments" of "Fictitious imagination."[24] But if some metaphors were fictitious, Taylor did see that there was another kind of metaphor, which today we would call a symbol. Thus, in *Christographia* again, there is a "life Metaphoricall" different from but related organically to the "Life Essentiall"; by embodying this "Life Essentiall" and "Eternall," temporal objects became "Metaphoricall" in a profound sense that pertains to their very reality. And it is exactly the difficulty of penetrating to the typological significance of this "Life Metaphoricall" which makes poets fall back on merely tropological metaphors as enlivening analogies supplied by their own wits and observation. The distinction always obtained however; a trope, while not "a lying form of Speech," "never was expected to be literally true," and amounted to no more than "a neate Rhetoricall, and Wise manner of Speaking."[25]

In much the same manner as Taylor and from the same presumptions about types and tropes, Edwards discriminated between "flowers of rhetoric" and the "naked idea" of an object: "Seeing the perfect idea of a thing, is, to all intents and purposes, the same as seeing the thing. It is not only equivalent to seeing it, but it is the seeing of it; for there is no other seeing but having an idea. Now, by seeing a perfect idea, so far as we see it, we have it."[26] In the perception of a type, phenomenological object and essential idea were one and the same, and this is the only true "seeing." Perry Miller's "Introduction" to the notebook he published as *Images or Shadows of Divine Things* summarizes the argument:

> In the type there must be evidence of the one eternal intention;
> in the trope there can be evidence only of the intention of one
> writer. The type exists in history or temporal experience and its
> meaning is factual that is, objective. . . . By contrast, the allegory,
> the simile, and the metaphor have been made according to the
> fancy of men, and they mean whatever the brain of the begetter
> is pleased they should mean. In the type there is a rigorous
> correspondence, which is not a chance resemblance, between the
> representation and the antitype; in the trope there is
> correspondence only between the thing and the associations it
> happens to excite in the impressionable . . . senses of men.[27]

Edwards kept the notebook in order to jot down nature descriptions and meditations with the intention of writing a philosophical treatise; although he did not write the treatise, the notebook stands as his typological reading of nature.

Taylor's figurative speech, then, is intended always to support an intuited relation between nature and man; his highly tropological style rests on a typological vision which is the heart of the miscellaneous pieces as well as the sequences. "Upon a Wasp Child with Cold" demonstrates the relation between types and tropes. The poet describes the insect minutely, lining out similes and metaphors which associate the wasp with the human form and faculties, and these tropes, at first playful, finally become strategic in seeing the wasp as a woman:

> Her petty toes, and fingers ends
> Nipt with this breath, she out extends
> Unto the Sun, in greate desire
> To warm her digits at that fire.
> . . . .
> As if her velvet helmet high
> Did turret rationality.
> She fans her wing up to the Winde
> As if her Pettycoate were lin'de,
> With reasons fleece, and hoises sails
> And hu'ming flies in thankfull gails
> Unto her dun Curld palace Hall
> Her warm thanks offering for all . . . .

The wit resembles the joshing seriousness of Frost's couplets such as "Departmental" or "A Considerable Speck," which are both also about insects. Taylor's fancy makes the wasp into a well-dressed lady and then confers masculine reason and spirit on her "Corporation." But all this inventiveness points to a more essential connection between creatures high and low in the scale of being. The poem moves, as Frost's skeptical poems generally cannot, through a process of deepening insight, so that the last lines identify the wasp, small as it is, as a type of the organic continuity of insect and man and God:

> Lord cleare my misted sight that I
> May hence view thy Divinity.
> Some sparkes whereof thou up dost hasp
> Within this downy little Wasp
> In whose small Corporation wee

A school and schoolmaster see
Where we may learn, and easily finde
A nimble Spirit bravely minde
Her worke in e'ry limb: and lace
It up neate with a vitall grace,
Acting each part though ne'er so small
Here of this Fustian animall.
Till I enravisht Climb into
The Godhead on this Lather [Ladder] doe.

The tiny body encloses Godhead just as larger creatures do, and so becomes a classroom and teacher wherein we can read in miniature the lesson of Incarnation. In an ascending scale experience discloses to the increasingly "enravisht" pupil the divine manifestations in matter.

Although the poet may—as in the lines above—employ both types and tropes in the same poem, although types and tropes coexist in the poetic statement, it is useful for the critic to differentiate between them. Types and tropes arise from fundamentally different relations between the poet and the language he uses and the meanings his language makes; there is a different source for the image and a different kind of connection which it makes. All poets employ tropes, but only some see types. One way in which a poet strives to comprehend experience in poetic form is to render it in concrete images, to make relations and associations—sensory, emotional, conceptual, moral—in metaphors and figures. Through such tropes the poet can synthesize and pattern his experience by sensing—or making—connections between elements of his experience. The poet makes his own meanings and finds his own words. Another way in which some poets have at times come to see and order experience is through what Emerson would call "a very high sort of seeing," a flash of penetration into the absolute significance of what has happened to him. Sense impressions yield the true relation of beings under Being itself. Insight into such "types" brings to light the pattern in the natural order.

The difference between types and tropes, therefore, is not mere logic-chopping; it makes a distinction between metaphor as figure of speech and metaphor as symbol, between imagination (or fancy) and Imagination. Types and tropes proceed from different processes of perception, constitute different acts of perception, and assume a different balance between poet and experience. Not that the poet must choose one or the other; the usefulness of the distinction lies in its providing the terms for sorting out the uses of language, even in a single imaginative act. Any attempt to forge "a closer alliance between the two realms of being, the object in nature and the thesis in the mind"[28] (as Edwards stated the problem), makes that act of perception a tricky exchange between subject and object. The perceiver must strike a balance each time, and the fulcrum will shift, depending at the given moment on the state of the individual's mind and the quality of the experience. The balance point of perception lies somewhere between the extremes of objectivity and subjectivity, and the point of relation is the point of tension determined by the interplay of forces— that is, by the relative counterweights or counterpressures on both sides for the particular poet writing that poem, or stanza, or phrase at such and such a moment.

At the same time, over a career of writing, in which the poet establishes that point of balance again and again, he tends to take a position or range of positions which identifies his characteristic way of striking the balance. The poet who has little or no typological sense will have to order experience into art through the innate, unaided powers of his craft and his imaginative scope; the form and meaning of the poem are a matter of mind moving tongue. The poet who has a strong and operative sense of types will respond to the sign and speak as a medium or seer. Taylor and Edwards would have identified such a vessel with the elected man of grace, but as the Puritan theocracy crumbled to a more diverse and secular American society, the religious seer became the poet—or at any rate one conception of the poet.

The religious, moral, and literary attitudes of poets became very much more complex and ambiguous through the nineteenth century and into the twentieth; the sharp contrast between "type" and "trope" has become blurred, and other critical terms have evolved, more accurate for an explication of modern texts. However, "type" and "trope" do suggest divergent tendencies in the psyche. Behind the type and the trope lie different relations between the poet and experience on the one hand and between the poet and the medium of language on the other. A poet cannot

will types, or his seeing types; he can only remain open and receptive to a world which is itself open to receive him, though perhaps only after much pain and waiting. A poet wills tropes, or at
any rate makes them from himself for himself. In this instance
the world—separate certainly, alien perhaps, even hostile—does
not yield itself spontaneously in revealed meaning. It will only
yield to the active probing of the poet's imagination; or, more
bleakly, it will only yield up the fragments from which the poet
can make his own meaning (or statement of nonmeaning) and
compose an artificial, fictional world. The typological poet enters
his world and participates in it; the tropological poet manipulates
or resists the otherness through which he moves. It is not categorically true that typological poets are believers and visionaries,
whereas tropological poets are stoics, skeptics, or tragedians; but
those are the strong proclivities. In religious and moral terms, the
typological poet has less sense of original sin and the imperfect-
ability of life, and the tropological poet has a stronger sense of
evil; in psychological terms, the typological poet has a greater
trust in the unconscious for relationship, integration, and transcendence, and the tropological poet a consciousness of alienation,
guilt, and solipsism; in aesthetic terms, the typological poet tends
to employ open forms which he sees as organic, and the tropological poet tends to depend on closed forms to impose coherence on
the medium as on experience. There are exceptions to every one
of these generalizations, and none can stand unqualified, especially when applied to particular poets. For example, Taylor's
typological sense, enforced by the stylistic assumptions of his day,
led him to use stanza, meter, and rhyme, however individualis-
tically, to render his belief in a universe of forms within forms,
all things governed by divine ordinances of growth.

Nevertheless, if the critic proceeds with sufficient caution
about these oversimplifications, he can begin to distinguish loose
and meandering lines of connection which define the underlying
dialectic of the American tradition: on the more tropological side,
from Edgar Allan Poe to Wallace Stevens, Robert Frost, and John
Crowe Ransom to such contemporaries as Robert Lowell, J. V.
Cunningham, and W. D. Snodgrass; on the more typological side,
from Taylor through Emerson and Whitman to Pound and Williams to Charles Olson and Denise Levertov, Allen Ginsberg and

William Everson. Many poets are difficult to place in this schema, and even the poets placed above present problems and complications; but the ambivalences and complications are themselves part of the dialectic.

Even if one should discount the usefulness of the terms "types" and "tropes" for twentieth-century poetry, there can be no doubt that the Puritan distinction dramatized a fundamental question for the imagination which nineteenth-century poets had to answer in religious, aesthetic, and social contexts that were increasingly complex and uncertain. Moreover, Samuel Taylor Coleridge, that exquisitely tuned antenna to the intellectual life of the nineteenth century, reiterated the commonly accepted distinction between two sorts of philosophical and psychological relationships between the poet and the world which makes for two kinds of poetic image (and for which "type" and "trope" are one formulation):

> Nature has her proper interest; & he will know what it is, who believes & feels, that every Thing has a Life of it's own, & that we are all *one Life*. A Poet's *Heart* & *Intellect* should be *combined*, *intimately* combined & *unified*, with the great appearances in Nature—& not merely held in solution and loose mixture with them, in the shape of formal Similies. I do not mean to *exclude* these formal Similies—there are moods of mind, in which they are natural—pleasing moods of mind, & such as a Poet will often have, and sometimes express; but they are not his highest, & most appropriate moods.[29]

All the poets discussed in subsequent chapters would have recognized without question the discrimination which Coleridge was making, even when those "highest, & most appropriate moods" seemed beyond realization, as at times they seemed to Coleridge himself.

III

RALPH WALDO EMERSON:
The Eye of the Seer

By the early 1820s, when Ralph Waldo Emerson began to write in his journal and to versify about "The Poet and the Poetic Gift," the figure of the American poet—indeed, the arrival of the American poet—was a matter of concern for everyone hopeful for the future of American civilization. Among the early entries in that prodigious journal whose leaves would generate the essays and poems of a lifetime, Emerson wrote with a grandiloquent and purposeful flourish:

DEDICATION

Boston July 11 [1822]

I dedicate my book to the Spirit of America.
. . . With a spark of prophetic devotion, I hasten to hail the Genius, who yet counts the tardy years of childhood, but who is increasing unawares in the twilight, and swelling into strength, until the hour, when he shall break the cloud, to shew his colossal youth, and cover the firmament with the shadow of his wings.[1]

The full-grown poet magnified by "the Spirit of America" could confront the new and seemingly prosaic facts of a booming country and transfigure them. Through visionary eyes, the ragged line of the frontier crawling across the continent would come to be seen not as the vanquishment of nature by men but as the spiritual assimilation of Americans to their land. Robert Frost would look back in "The Gift Outright" to observe that

The land was ours before we were the land's.
She was our land more than a hundred years
Before we were her people.

The danger, which Emerson could already see, was that possession would become exploitation, become rape. So he asserted that "art" had to elevate and transcendentalize even the scientist's laboratory, the appalling forces of the engine, and the economic machinery of capitalism itself; for it is the "instinct" of genius

to find beauty and holiness in new and necessary facts, in the field and road-side, in the shop and mill. Proceeding from a religious heart it will raise to a divine use the railroad, the

insurance office, the joint-stock company; our law, our primary
assemblies, our commerce, the galvanic battery, the electric jar,
the prism, and the chemist's retort; in which we seek now only an
economic use.[2]

The imperative challenge was as modern as the materials:

Readers of poetry see the factory-village and the railway, and
fancy that poetry of the landscape is broken up by these; for
these works of art are not yet consecrated in their reading; but the
poet sees them fall within the great Order not less than the
beehive or the spider's geometrical web.[3]

Through the years Emerson insisted to his readers and audiences,
as in this late piece on "Poetry and Imagination," that the poet's
mission was "to point out where the same creative force is now
working in our own houses and public assemblies [as in our
private communion with Nature]; to convert the vivid energies
acting this hour in New York and Chicago and San Francisco,
into universal symbols."[4] He had to be hardy and resilient enough
to make the imaginative leap from the Atlantic to the Great Lakes
to the Pacific in order to confer on the sprawling confusion of
America moral and psychological coherence. The expansiveness
demanded of the poet was an urgent, in some ways desperate,
stratagem to control and elevate the materialistic drive which
social institutions too often seemed to sanction. Only so gigantic
a "hero" (one of Emerson's favorite words, as it was one of
Carlyle's) would be capable of matching commercial enterprise
with spiritual ideals and thereby invest the westward march with
moral energy and civilized aims. The poet would have to come as
a kind of noninstitutional (and anti-institutional?) savior; his
long-awaited advent would redeem "America," or the "Spirit of
America," from the grasping, wasteful hands of the Americans.

Like all the others, Emerson had to be vague about how the
poet would make a "factory-village" like Lowell, Massachusetts,
into a work of art or consecrate the railway as it hurtled west
and east with people and products. His imprecision, in fact,
masked ambivalence. With many others, he was convinced that
"our whole history appears like a last effort of the Divine Providence in behalf of the human race," and yet the blatant exploita-

tion which spoiled cities and the frontier—the capitalists' profits, the sweat-shop of the workers, the land-grab of the pioneers— seemed to make our actual development, even at times to Emerson, a "historical failure on which Europe and America have so freely commented."[5] If our economic growth and technical accomplishments stifled the imagination and crippled those who wanted to free it, Emerson's response was unequivocal: "Let there be worse cotton and better men." But again and again he noted the harsh truth in his journal: "In America I grieve to miss the strong black blood of the English race: ours is a pale diluted stream"; "Wordsworth, Coleridge, Tennyson, Carlyle, and Macaulay cannot be matched in America"; "all [the American geniuses] lack nerve & dagger."[6] Reviewing our meager cultural achievement in 1863 in the midst of a self-destructive war, he posed the question in his journal as damningly as Sydney Smith had forty years before:

> Why is there no genius in the Fine Arts
> in this Country?
>   In sculpture –   Greenough is picturesque
>   In painting –   Al[l]ston
>   In Poetry   Bryant
>   In Eloquence –   Channing
>   In Architecture –
>   In Fiction   Irving, Cooper
>   In all feminine, no character*

He could summarize his answer under two large headings: "1st reason: Influence of Europe mainly of England. . . . 2nd reason. They [artists] are not called out by the necessity of the people. . . . The mind of the race has taken another direction— Property."[7]

The crushing weight of cultural tradition could only be lifted off the literary situation on the shoulders of a powerful American genius. But would a people hell-bent on Property produce and then permit the savior who would deliver their best self from their worst self? So indeterminate was the present prospect that

---

*Emerson omitted Poe, Hawthorne, and Melville (who drew too strongly on "the power of blackness") and Whitman (who presented difficulties discussed in a later chapter). The sexist bias of the last remark contrasts with his later linking of genius with the feminine.

in self-defense many sensitive, intelligent, religiously inclined young people could only "withdraw themselves from the common labors and competitions of the market and the caucus, and betake themselves to a certain solitary and critical way of living." They had to "hold themselves aloof" from society because of "the disproportion between their faculties and the work offered them." Emerson's attempt to explain and justify "The Transcendentalist" to the proper Bostonians of the 1840s describes in general but surprisingly accurate detail that persistent segment of Americans, from the Transcendentalists to the Beats of the 1950s and much of the counter-culture of the 1960s and 1970s, who felt betrayed by the organized, productive society of their day and said NO to the prevailing mores in the name of an individualistic search for mystical unity. As the herald and public apologist for more Americans than he knew, Emerson ironically rehearsed their "offenses" to the bourgeois audience gathered in the Boston Masonic Temple in 1842:

> They are not good citizens, not good members of society; unwillingly they bear their part of the public and private burdens; they do not willingly share in the public charities, in the public religious rites, in the enterprizes of education, of missions foreign and domestic, in the abolition of the slave-trade, or in the temperance society. They are inactive; they do not even like to vote. The philanthropists inquire whether Transcendentalism does not mean sloth. They had as lief hear that their friend is dead, as that he is a Transcendentalist.[8]

Emerson always saw the choice as lying between the dead grasp of the past and the open future; "there are always two parties . . . the Establishment and the Movement." The religious and moral dissent of the Transcendentalists is by no means identical in quality or ends with that of the Beats and hippies. The Transcendentalists would have been shocked by the promiscuity and drugs and outrageous behavior which gave notoriety to much of the cultural underworld, but not by their deepest instincts and promptings; for both "Movements," considered disruptive by their contemporary "Establishments," assert Idealism against Materialism and deny economic norms for personal fulfillment. Emerson's conclusion: "Whoso would be a man, must be a nonconformist." Consequently, the Transcendentalists' nonconformity, though "lonely," "does not proceed from any whim" but came to be

> chosen both from temperament and from principle; with some unwillingness too, and as a choice of the less of two evils; for these persons are not by nature melancholy, sour, and unsocial, —they are not stockish or brute,—but joyous, susceptible, affectionate; they have even more than others a great wish to be loved.[9]

Emerson reached no satisfactory reconciliation of the poet's public and private responsibilities. The two impulses seemed contradictory: the one would constrain the poet to join city to country, sea to sea in a feat of imaginative absorption; the other would constrain him to resign from society in order to guard his gift from that corruptive touch. The essay on "The Poet" concludes with the commandment: "Thou shalt leave the world, and know the muse only. Thou shalt not know any longer the times, customs, graces, politics, or opinions of men, but shalt take all from the muse."[10] But it was not simple in practice; as the poem "Days" indicates, he could turn the mocking scorn on himself for his disdaining the larger opportunities and social responsibilities and satisfying himself with only "a few herbs and apples" in the retirement of his "pleached garden."

Was his restraint wisdom or diffidence? To what extent could a poet have public responsibility or involve himself in public issues? Emerson had rallied the American Scholar to ripen his thought in action, but he himself would find that involvement difficult and draining. He did have strong feelings about political and social issues and sometimes spoke them out from the platform. However, he gave a more characteristic response when W. H. Channing, his friend and "the evil time's sole patriot," pressed him to take a more active role in public affairs, for example for Abolition and against the Mexican War:

> I cannot leave
> My honied thought
> For the priest's cant,
> Or statesman's rant.
> If I refuse
> My study for their politique,

Which at the best is trick,
The angry Muse
Puts confusion in my brain.

If it came to a choice, the poet's calling committed him to "the Spirit of America" rather than to political action; otherwise the rejected Muse would retaliate by befuddling the imagination. So the poet had to ply his lone course closer to Nature than to the people who inhabited and devastated it:

The God who made New Hampshire
Taunted the lofty land
With little men....[11]

Perhaps by its very separateness, its concentration on its own values, poetry could best infuse into the "little men" a spirit more worthy of "the lofty land." Perhaps the poet could most practically change America by doing his own work (as Wallace Stevens would also say to the Marxists and activists of his day): "The public can get public experience, but they wish the scholar [here as elsewhere in Emerson synonymous with writer] to replace to them those private, sincere, divine experiences, of which they have been defrauded by dwelling in the street."[12] Consequently, acutely aware of the forces which ran the social machinery before and after the Civil War, Emerson chose to combine the private muse with the public platform—indeed to preach the private muse in the lyceums across the land. If his precepts could project the notion of an American bard and arouse the bard himself, if he could begin to realize some of these qualities in his own writing, then he would have released the artist from the bonds of the English tradition and unleashed on a nation ruled by the law of things a miraculous force subversive beyond calculation. He would have activated "the Spirit of America" to the work of "metamorphosis" (he used the word over and over); he would have brought into concord the poet and his people, the people and their land, the crude facts and noble aspirations of American society. Although Emerson did not finally resolve all contradictions, his presence loomed so large and so long down the nineteenth century that he is an irreducible part of the landscape: a kind of watershed in American literature. His measure is no less immense; other writers would agree or quarrel with his premises and conclusions, but in some way he had to be reckoned with when the hand took up the pen. They could follow or oppose or qualify, but they could not ignore Emerson. The unifying theme of his lectures and poems is the activity of genius—its sources and goals—and this inculcation of the poetic genius gave him a place in American letters fully as commanding as the position of Wordsworth in England during the nineteenth century.

2

William Cullen Bryant, whom Emerson cited as the only notable American poet, had come to be known as the "American Wordsworth." The gentle Bryant chafed somewhat at the epithet, understandably so when one considers his deliberate use of native materials and his advocacy of an American poetry. The landscapes of his nature poems extended from the mountains and valleys of the Berkshires west to the great prairies dotted with Indian and buffalo. In fact, the easy tag did gloss over the substantive differences in tone and attitude which make Bryant at least as much a pallid survival of a previous faith as the pioneer of the Romantic vision in America.

A comparison of "Inscription for the Entrance to a Wood," one of Bryant's best and most characteristic poems, with a Wordsworth poem like "Simplon Pass" or "Tintern Abbey" or "Nutting," emphasizes the difference. The virtues which nature offers to Bryant are mostly negative in import and feeling: "calm," "contentment," and "tranquility" to heal the "sick heart"; deliverance from the "sorrows, crimes, and cares" of urban living into a happy solitude; escape from "the haunts of men" into "the haunts of Nature" (the word "haunts" itself suggests spookily a dead past). The reason that nature is relatively healthier and happier than man is presented in Calvinist terms: nature fell by man's sin, but nature is blamelessly fallen from paradise, while man's guilty consciousness deserves the punishment it endures.

> The primal curse
> Fell, it is true, upon the unsinning earth,
> But not in vengeance. God hath yoked to guilt
> Her pale tormentor, misery. Hence, these shades
> Are still the abodes of gladness; the thick roof
> Of green and stirring branches is alive
> And musical with birds, that sing and sport
> In wantonness of spirit; while below
> The squirrel, with raised paws and form erect,
> Chirps merrily.

There is nothing in Bryant remotely analogous to Wordsworth's "Simplon Pass":

> —Brook and road
> Were fellow-travellers in this gloomy Pass,
> And with them did we journey several hours
> At a slow step. The immeasurable height
> Of woods decaying, never to be decayed,
> The stationary blasts of waterfalls,
> And in the narrow rent, at every turn,
> Winds thwarting winds bewildered and forlorn,
> The torrents shooting from the clear blue sky,
> The rocks that muttered close upon our ears,
> Black drizzling crags that spake by the wayside
> As if a voice were in them, the sick sight
> And giddy prospect of the raving stream,
> The unfettered clouds and region of the heavens,
> Tumult and peace, the darkness and the light,—
> Were all like workings of one mind, the features
> Of the same face, blossoms upon one tree,
> Characters of the great Apocalypse,
> The types and symbols of Eternity,
> Of first, and last, and midst, and without end.

Here are the last lines of Bryant's "Inscription" and of Wordsworth's "Nutting," both blank-verse reflections on going to the woods:

> Softly tread the marge,
> Lest from her midway perch thou scare the wren
> That dips her bill in water. The cool wind,
> That stirs the stream in play, shall come to thee,
> Like one that loves thee nor will let thee pass
> Ungreeted, and shall give its light embrace.
>
> ("Inscription," ll. 37–42)

> Then up I rose,
> And dragged to earth both branch and bough, with crash
> And merciless ravage: and the shady nook
> Of hazels, and the green and mossy bower,
> Deformed and sullied, patiently gave up
> Their quiet being: and unless I now
> Confound my present feelings with the past,
> Ere from the mutilated bower I turned
> Exulting, rich beyond the wealth of kings,
> I felt a sense of pain when I beheld
> The silent trees, and saw the intruding sky—
> Then, dearest Maiden, move along these shades
> In gentleness of heart; with gentle hand
> Touch—for there is a spirit in the woods.
>
> ("Nutting," ll. 43–56)

Not only is Wordsworth's poem active, even explicitly sexual, where Bryant's is not; there is in Bryant no such humbling yet exalting confrontation of the arrogant ego with the life-force immanent in Nature as Wordsworth presents here. Quickened by spirit, Nature was, to the male poet, not just mother but, before that, virgin to be loved but not raped.

Wordsworth, more than any other British poet, broached a new perception of the pervasive divinity of Nature. Bryant was closer in spirit and diction to Wordsworth's more conventional and sentimental nature poems than to Wordsworth at his most original and even closer perhaps to Wordsworth's eighteenth-century predecessors, James Thomson and William Cowper, for whom the God of Nature was still relatively remote and static. Nature led Bryant to a peaceful haven untainted as yet by man, not to the activating source of energy which the early Wordsworth often encountered. Bryant's sense of the "primal curse" of original sin which fell even on "unsinning nature" shows him to be at heart a Christian (however diluted from seventeenth-century Puritanism) as the author of the *Lyrical Ballads* was not. Consequently, in a sense which Bryant did not intend, he was correct in preferring to think of himself not as an imitation Wordsworth but as a native product whose deepest instincts were rooted in the older mind and spirit of New England. His ancestors had been strict Calvinists; his father became a Unitarian; and he became a nature poet. That sequence of vocations in the single line implies a great deal of the history of the New England mind (as does the progression from Taylor and Edwards to William Ellery Channing to Emerson).

The Calvinist spirit haunts "To a Waterfowl," perhaps Bryant's finest lyric:

> Whither, midst falling dew,
> While glow the heavens with the last steps of day,
> Far, through their rosy depths, dost thou pursue
> Thy solitary way?
>
> Vainly the fowler's eye
> Might mark thy distant flight to do thee wrong,
> As, darkly seen against the crimson sky,
> Thy figure floats along.
>
> Seek'st thou the plashy brink
> Of weedy lake, or marge of river wide,
> Or where the rocking billows rise and sink
> On the chafed ocean-side?
>
> There is a Power, whose care
> Teaches thy way along that pathless coast—
> The desert and illimitable air—
> Lone wandering, but not lost.
>
> All day thy wings have fanned,
> At that far height, the cold, thin atmosphere,
> Yet stoop not, weary, to the welcome land,
> Though the dark night is near.
>
> And soon that toil shall end;
> Soon shalt thou find a summer home, and rest,
> And scream among thy fellows; reeds shall bend,
> Soon, o'er thy sheltered nest.
>
> Thou'rt gone, the abyss of heaven
> Hath swallowed up thy form; yet, on my heart
> Deeply has sunk the lesson thou hast given,
> And shall not soon depart.
>
> He, who, from zone to zone,
> Guides through the boundless sky thy certain flight,
> In the long way that I must tread alone,
> Will lead my steps aright.

The incident becomes a type of Providence guiding the individual through the difficulties of life to his final resting place; bird and man are linked in having a shelter at the end of the arduous journey. The poet was reading "the language and lessons of Nature," to use Edwards' phrase, just as Puritans had done from the outset. But this affirmation is not what is most memorably conveyed by the language of the poem. It is the bird's flight which transfixed Bryant and moved him deeply; what we remember is the lone bird on its far flight through the cold, thin air to some unknown destination, obliterated at last glimpse in the dark abyss of night. The conclusion states a correspondence between man and bird under God's Providence, but the imagery of the poem emphasizes the uncertainty which, as more real to the poet, is more realized in the poem. Bryant almost surely did not recognize that the connotations of his language contradicted the denotation or at any rate pointed away from the intended statement; but if this is a type, it is dimly perceived and wrung from the situation only with great determination. Bryant wanted to affirm a reassuring "Power" against the encroachment of darkness, but all that was left him was the pale vestige of the Calvinist God. For all his good intentions and good poems, for all his encouragement to the American Muse, Bryant represented what remained of Puritanism, with little of the vigor of Taylor and Edwards and little of the Romantic energy which would allow Wordsworth to feel afresh the "Power" that rolls through all things.

It was Emerson who carried forward Edwards' typological sense and revitalized it with the energies of Transcendentalism, which Wordsworth, along with Coleridge and Carlyle, had helped to channel overseas to the New World. Because both Wordsworth and Emerson saw in Nature "the types and symbols of Eternity," there is a more essential relationship between them than between Wordsworth and Bryant. Both Wordsworth and Emerson have strong links with the previous century, but they were able to make the transition into the nineteenth; indeed were in large measure the transition into the nineteenth for their respective cultures. Emerson's trip to England in the early 1830s was in part a pilgrimage to meet and converse with Wordsworth, Coleridge, and Carlyle. Although from beginning to end Emerson remained the

New Englander, he was a new breed, who could stand on the conviction that

> It is not in the power of God to make a communication of his will to a Calvinist. For to every revelation he holds up his silly book [that is, the Bible]. . . . There is a light older than intellect, by which the intellect lives & works, always new. . . . This light, Calvinism denies, in its idolatry of a certain past shining.[13]

The false wall of security which "idolatry" of Christ erected around men closed them off from fresh springs of revelation. Even contemporary Unitarianism, which had splintered off from the old Congregationalism, was too old-fashioned and "corpse-cold" for Emerson. Unlike Taylor, who wrote his poems in preparation for the Sacrament of Communion, Emerson resigned his pulpit because he could no longer administer the Lord's Supper in conscience: "I have no hostility to this institution; I am only stating my want of sympathy with it. . . . I am not interested in it." Christ's coming was not for him a fact which changed history but merely a signal instance of the perfection of human possibilities. The "open eye" of Christ's humanity most fully "saw that God incarnates himself in man, and evermore goes forth anew to take possession of his world." Emerson took the Christian commitment to be ethical rather than theological, "not forms, but duties": "If I understand the distinction of Christianity, the reason why it is preferred over all other systems and is divine is this, that it is a moral system." He discarded the historical doctrine of the Incarnation in order to live it out again as best he could in his own person; he shed the shell of Calvinist theology in order to set his own course as a self-reliant philosopher-poet. "The Problem" presented his decision in verse:

> I like a church; I like a cowl;
> I love a prophet of the soul;
> And on my heart monastic aisles
> Fall like sweet strains, or pensive smiles;
> Yet not for all his faith can see
> Would I that cowlèd churchman be.

Emerson's manifesto, *Nature* (1836), summoned each person to make "an original relation to the universe," in both senses of the word "original": individual and primary, at and from the source. That penetration to the heart of Nature would disclose experientially absolute Beauty, Truth, and Virtue.[14]

Although Emerson published only two volumes of verse, he insisted that in all his thinking and writing he was a poet, and his notion of the aim and activity of the poet so splendidly epitomized the idealistic strain in the American character that his words blazed a path for others to explore, extend, and depart from on their own excursions. At the beginning of *Nature* a simple statement carries momentous psychological, moral, and aesthetic implications: the poet is "he whose eye can integrate all the parts." The poet as "eye" is far more than a naturalist observing phenomena in minute detail like Frederick Goddard Tuckerman out in Greenfield or even Emerson's friend Thoreau camping out on Emerson's ground at Walden Pond. For all of Emerson's love of the woods and lakes around Concord, Emerson would write an essay on the "Natural History of Intellect" while Thoreau was to write the "Natural History of Massachusetts." Emerson would continue to complain that naturalists, with their labels and discriminations, were always pointing to the particular instead of the universal: "Our botany is all names, not powers." In old age Emerson cited Blake's goal of seeing through the eye, not with it, but already in *Nature* (1836) he had recognized that "the eye is the best of artists" because it reveals to the imagination—not just to the senses or to the intellective understanding—"the integrity of impression made by manifold natural objects."[15] There are two kinds of seeing: with the eye and through the eye, sensory and spiritual; the second proceeds from the first but cannot be accounted for or bound by mere visual impressions:

> To speak truly, few adult persons can see nature. Most persons do not see the sun. At least they have a very superficial seeing. The sun illuminates only the eye of the man, but shines into the eye and the heart of the child. The lover of nature is he whose inward and outward senses are still truly adjusted to each other.[16]

The eye is not simply the ocular sense; the "eye" orders all the senses and faculties in a single experiential perception of the interpenetration of all things. Insight operates simultaneously as expansion and integration. Again and again the essays specify the eye as the poetic organ: the "cultivated eye"; "the wise eye"; "the world's eye"; "the comprehensive eye"; "the plastic power of the human eye"; "the supernatural eye."

The miracle of incarnation transpires not only in church sacraments but in all life, which is sacramental; Emerson used a theological term to make his point: "This contemporary insight is transubstantiation, the conversion of daily bread into the holiest symbols."[17] One of the most famous passages in Emerson is an attempt to describe this conversion; the statements are at once declarative and open-ended; they set down an experience of vision beyond analysis:

> In the woods, too, a man casts off his years, as the snake his
> slough, and at what period soever of life, is always a child. . . .
> There I feel that nothing can befal me in life,—no disgrace, no
> calamity, (leaving me my eyes,) which nature cannot repair.
> Standing on the bare ground,—my head bathed by the blithe air,
> and uplifted into infinite space,—all mean egotism vanishes. I
> become a transparent eye-ball. I am nothing. I see all. The
> currents of the Universal Being circulate through me; I am part or
> parcel of God.[18]

The punning identity of "I" and "eye" punctuates the stages of the process: I expand into the cosmos until my immensity coincides with cosmic Unity. The "eye" imagery yields not so much visual description as total kinesthetic response: the sloughing of the snake, the "head bathed by blithe air, and uplifted into infinite space," and the divine currents vibrating like electric energy through the tingling "I" which is no longer mere ego. In its apogee the ego breaks open as the deific energy completes the circuit of Being, and for that moment self-reliance, self-abnegation, and self-transcendence are one and the same. "I" as "eye" functions not as ego but as completed Self.

According to Edwards, only the man redeemed from sin could perceive "naked ideas" through the light of grace, but to Emerson such exclusive notions were constrictions of the "theologic cramp." This statement from the journals shifts the focus from theology to psychology, from the afterlife to the consciousness of the individual: "As religious philosophy advances, we will cease to say 'the future estate' & will say instead 'the whole being.' "

Ralph Waldo Emerson

"Original sin" was for him no "primal curse," as it was still for Bryant, but the first act of consciousness; it is the individual's realization that *he* exists and so exists separate among many separate beings: "It is very unhappy, but too late to be helped, the discovery we have made that we exist. That discovery is called The Fall of Man." It is, then, a fall into the self-consciousness of the isolated ego, as in "Uriel" the angel plummets from godhead to the cloudy obscurity of material nature:

> A sad self-knowledge, withering, fell
> On the beauty of Uriel;
> In heaven once eminent, the god
> Withdrew, that hour, into his cloud. . . .[19]

"Self-knowledge" forces this fundamental recognition: "Two cardinal facts lie forever at the base; the one and the two.—1. Unity, or Identity; and 2. Variety . . . . Oneness and Otherness. It is impossible to speak or think without embracing both." The perceptions of Variety and Unity are the respective functions of the different cognitive faculties of Understanding and Reason.* Experience, therefore, brings the mind to unriddle itself and embrace the two in the one; the data which the Understanding gathers concerning natural and psychological phenomena constellate in the Unity which Transcendental Reason intuits. For Emerson, Understanding and Reason are only the philosophical terms for the poet's seeing with the eye and seeing through the eye.

Consequently, Emerson would argue, the very recognition that "the world I converse with in the city and in the farms, is not the world I *think*," begins the process of assimilation, and further acts of perception begin to bind the perceiver to the per-

---

*Understanding is the logical-rational faculty which operates deductively and inductively on the data supplied by the senses; Reason is the transcendental faculty which sees intuitively universal truths in Nature. This distinction became standard as the German transcendentalist philosophers came into England and America through people like Coleridge and Carlyle. In the "Discipline" chapter of *Nature* Emerson stated it in these words: "The understanding adds, divides, combines, measures, and finds nutriment and room for its activity in this worthy scene. Meantime, Reason transfers all these lessons into its own world of thought, by perceiving the analogy that marries Matter and Mind" (*Nature, NAL, Collected Works,* I, 23.)

ceived both naturally and transcendentally. The healing of the
internal division between Understanding and Reason seals the
other breach; under the human eye concentric with "the eye of
Reason" the distinction between "me" and "not-me" disappears,
or appears superficial and illusory. Nature, then, is the medium
through which Unity is refracted and through which Uriel, fallen
in self-knowledge, strives to rise again to Unity:[20]

> shrilling from the solar course,
> Or from fruit of chemic force,
> Procession of a soul in matter. . . .

"Uriel" expresses the powers open to all despite our fallen state.
The lesions in the "double consciousness" are no more a sign of
damnation than the healing is a sign of special election. The divided man finds himself a "god in ruins," but if he be bold enough
to release the powers nascent in him, he can realise "the infinitude
of the private man"—indeed "the deity of man."[21] In this pursuit
the poet is no oddity or anomaly; he represents the ideal for all
men.

In the essay on "The Poet" Emerson extended the power of
insight into the more problematical area of articulation and
expression:

> The poet is the person in whom those powers are in balance, the
> man without impediment, who sees and handles that which
> others dream of, traverses the whole scale of experience, and is
> representative of man, in virtue of being the largest power of
> receive and to impart.[22]

The artist's "power to receive and to impart"—a double power;
vision alone is insufficient, even for the seer. "Always the seer is
a sayer" as well; his secondary but essential role is "the Namer
or Language-maker." When "the poet . . . sees through the flowing vest the firm nature, and can declare it," "the man is only half
himself, the other half is his expression."[23] Emerson is suggesting
not just that the seer has the obligation to prophesy to the less
enlightened but also that the oracle or prophet realizes what he
has blindly seen only through a reflective act like language: the
poet must write poems. Even with the insight of Imagination,

only the poet's doubling back on himself to formulate and issue his own statement can bring experience to fuller consciousness; the wordless Reason incarnates itself in natural forms, in human experience, and so in human speech.

The three axioms posited at the beginning of the "Language" chapter of *Nature* make the same point by moving in the other direction, from words to things to spirit, in a chain of correspondences:

1. Words are signs of natural facts.
2. Particular natural facts are symbols of particular spiritual facts.
3. Nature is the symbol of spirit.[24]

The tongue moves with the eye and with "the eye of Reason." Emerson's theory of language assumed that words are at root so connected with objects that the primitive meaning of all words, even abstractions, designates an object. He gave examples in the "Language" chapter and returned to the subject often, as here in "The Poet":

> For though the origin of most of our words is forgotten, each word was at first a stroke of genius, and obtained currency because for the moment it symbolized the world to the first speaker and to the hearer. . . . Language is fossil poetry.

The poet's task is to save language from dead forms—fossilization and abstraction—by constantly making it new (as Pound's phrase goes): "Every word was once a poem. Every new relation is a new word." Or should ideally be. Emerson's linguistic assumptions may be scientifically questionable, but they link his metaphysics and aesthetics. The "natural sayer" will in theory make language correspond immediately to experience by attaching words as much as possible to the objects they signify. From the same premises Thoreau says in "Walking": "He would be a poet . . . who nailed words to their primitive senses, as farmers drive down stakes in the spring, which the frost has heaved; who derived his words as often as he used them,—transplanted them to the page with earth adhering to their roots."[25]

So organic is the finding of words that the "natural sayer"

cannot rely primarily on training and discipline and practice to perfect his technique and sharpen his tools. In fact, he must be wary of the danger inherent in a mistaken trust in external arrangements. No craftsman applying his developed skills to inchoate materials, Emerson's "Language-maker" would, to the contrary, be the "receiver," the "instrument," the "bard of the Holy Ghost" "passive to the superincumbent spirit." In the open moments between the "incoming" and "receding of God," he is "nothing else than a good, free, vascular organization, whereinto the universal spirit freely flows." The poet is not the cool catalyst, as T. S. Eliot came to claim in his argument for impersonality, but the vascular tissue and living membrane; Emerson's analogy is not chemistry but biology. After the inspiration the bard's words imitate the workings of Spirit in Nature, or such is the aim:

> For poetry was all written before time was, and whenever we are so finely organized that we can penetrate into that region where the air is music, we hear those primal warblings and attempt to write them down, but we lose ever and anon a word or a verse and substitute something of our own, and thus miswrite the poem. The men of more delicate ear write down these cadences more faithfully, and these transcripts, though imperfect, become the songs of the nations.

On the highest level the poet's ingenuity and technical skill can even be an inhibitive intrusion on the creative process; to the extent that he concentrates on making language, he may be interfering with the flow of inspiration to and through the medium.[26] Paradise, Pound would repeat in *The Pisan Cantos* against Baudelaire's aestheticism, is not an artificial contrivance, but is the *tao*, or divine process of nature.

Consequently, Emerson's theory has to be of two minds about the efficacy of language. All words must be nailed to things, and yet "all the facts in Nature are nouns of the intellect, and make the grammar of the eternal language." The poet must speak, but as the essential poetry moves into language, it will be at once exalted as the "word" of God and halting as human speech. To the extent that the poet is the instrument through which Reason expresses itself, language is invaluable; to the extent that the poet speaks his own associations, language is a noisy distraction. In the first instance the poet perceives and expresses true symbols; in the second he invents decorative figures; the difference is an updated version of the Puritan distinction between types and tropes. On the one side lies Silence, on the other gibberish; and in the middle the situation is complicated by the fact that Silence can only express itself on the poet's tongue and by the fact that as the poet's tongue strives to express Silence it concentrates its many, noisy words toward a single, indiscriminate primitive syllable, like the Hindu mystic repeating "Om" until he returns to unconsciousness or pure consciousness. Is that "Om" unconsciousness or pure consciousness, wisdom or gibberish? The Hindu and the mystic say that it conveys All *and* Nothing, since the false distinction between All and Nothing exists only in human speech.

But language must negotiate that middle ground without lapsing into All or Nothing, into Silence or gibberish. For, to someone like Emerson, words are (or can be) the irreplaceable translations from the wordless sublime moving through time and space: the oracle "has only to open his mouth, and it [universal nature] speaks." Yet even the oracle's words, not to mention those of less inspired mortals, will necessarily convey only a "corrupt version" of his unspeakable meaning:* "They cannot cover the dimensions of what is in truth. They break, chop, and impoverish it." Even words rooted in things are only a gesture toward the meaning. Since the paradox of language is that "words are finite organs of the infinite mind," even the successful poem will be an incomplete articulation. Language has form, and so limits, but meaning does not; or, in the words of a couplet whose halting inadequacy is almost imitative, "The great Idea baffles wit,/ Language falters under it." At best, effort and subtle discriminations and the filing of lines and cadences can clarify a poem up to a certain point, and at worst they can break the circuit of inspiration. The "true poet" learns to acknowledge humbly that "there is a higher work for Art than the arts."[27]

Emerson's ambivalence about language seems to lead him

---

*Lao Tsu's *Tao Te Ching* begins: "The Tao that can be told is not the eternal Tao. The name that can be named is not the eternal name," trans. Gia-Fu Feng and Jane English (New York: Vintage, 1972, p. 3).

into contradiction. If words are literally the organs of the infinite mind, the poet can do no better than merely submit, but if they are his words, the poet is at some level responsible for what he says and to some extent responsible for saying it. At times Emerson writes as though inspiration were a matter of unconscious receptivity, almost of automatic writing. Yeats claimed that *A Vision* derived from his wife's automatic writing and generated images and metaphors for his poems, but he made no claim of automatic writing for himself as composer of *A Vision* or of his poems. There have been Romantic claims of more or less spontaneous creation—most notably, perhaps, Coleridge in the writing of "Kubla Khan." Even more extremely, closer to home, and farther down the line, Jack Kerouac said that he tried to open his mouth and let the Holy Ghost speak, as Jesus had urged His disciples; Ginsberg usually prepares an audience for his poems by long repetitions of "Om" and other incantatory prayers. Did Emerson really believe that a poet is a simple medium? For that matter is it simple to be a medium? Consciousness cannot be excluded by fiat, especially not in the act of writing. The inspiration may be spontaneous and unconscious, but the composition cannot be. As a practicing poet, Emerson knew this. His poems were obviously not flung on the page in an ecstatic fit; they would be on the one hand less composed and on the other hand more ecstatic. Ginsberg submits to revision the poems which he later reads after those incantations. Even something as close to automatic writing as Kerouac's "spontaneous prose" and verse appears to be is not always unrevised; *On the Road*, his most widely admired book, went through several versions.

Emerson's ambivalence is of course part of the larger Romantic dilemma. For all his vaunting claims, Shelley too acknowledged, in his *Defence of Poetry*, that the inspired poet comes to words only as the wordless inspiration is fading; the challenge to the Romantic poet is somehow to validate his inspiration. Emerson's essays and poems take a deliberately extreme position in enunciating the notion of a poetry whose source lies outside the poet but whose realization in language and form is through the agency of the poet. Coleridge too had distinguished between poetry and the made poem. The activity begins in the encounter of the poet and nature through an impulse, presumed to come from above, which emerges from the poet's psychic unconscious. He must submit to these energies breaking into consciousness as words and attend that their expression corresponds to the experience. The poem is made from the poetry as nonverbal or preverbal instinctual impulses find articulation, take direction, and cohere. "Hence," declares Emerson, "the necessity of speech and song; hence these throbs and heart-beatings in the orator, at the door of the assembly, to the end namely that thought may be ejaculated as Logos, or Word." The paradox for the prophet, whether poet or orator (and the prophetic call links the two), is that, unlike the talkers who speak *"from without*, as spectators merely,"* he must *"speak from within*, or from experience,"* making sure that the utterance published under his name coheres to tally the ejaculative, eruptive experience inside.[28]

Finally, therefore, Emerson's contradictory statements can be seen as related in the attempt to describe the gestation and birth of the poem: a process so subtle that the poet cannot sort out, in the matrix of his psyche where it all grows, unconscious intuition from deliberated choice. *Ex post facto* theory dissects what is fused in the act. The seeming contradictions are two ways of accounting for organic poetry: the paradox of its inspiration and execution. We think of the poet's Muse—a transpersonal inspiration. But since he encounters the Muse and expresses the Muse only in the forms of Nature and since the poem gestates in his mind, not hers, the process is mutually procreative. Does she shape the poem out of him, or does he shape her in the poem? Both; the father and the mother of the poem are one; the poet is Eros and Psyche.

Emerson felt impelled to take an extreme position in arguing for the mysterious sources and resources of poetry in part because of the literary situation in mid-nineteenth-century America. There were many—and Emerson had Tennyson and Poe most prominently in mind—who called themselves poets but who he believed had only technical virtuosity:

For we do not speak now of men of poetical talents, or of industry and skill in metre, but of the true poet. I took part in a conversation the other day concerning a recent writer of lyrics [probably Poe], a man of subtle mind, whose head appeared to be a music-

box of delicate tunes and rhythms,* and whose skill and command
of language we could not sufficiently praise. But when the
question arose whether he was not only a lyrist but a poet, we
were obliged to confess that he is plainly a contemporary, not an
eternal man.

"The finish of the verses" is a consequence of poetry rather than
an originating constituent. Poetry does not arise from or reside
in the poem, but vice versa; the experience is not verbal, and
language is no substitute for vision. In Emerson's mind Poe's fa-
tal mistake lay in not understanding that "it is not metres but a
metre-making argument that makes a poem." The intricacy of
Poe's forms and the musicality of his language only confirmed
him a victim of his "poetical talents." By contrast, Emerson said
of Thoreau that "his genius was better than his talent." He lacked
"lyric facility and technical skill," and his verses were often unfinished. But even when he wrote inferior poems, "he had the
source of poetry" so surely that "he held all actual written poems
in very light esteem." The difference, Emerson said elsewhere, is
the difference between the poet who speaks from character and
the poet who speaks from language. So basic is the distinction between poetry and the poem that for Emerson Poe is a bad poet
who often wrote good poems while Thoreau is a good poet who
often wrote clumsy poems.[29]

All of this is not to say that Emerson had no regard for
poetic form, but rather that he regarded poetic form with the
same ambivalence that he felt toward language, and for the same
reasons; form, like the words which comprise it, is both the received and the achieved. The poet cannot dictate the form arbi-
trarily but he has to help it define itself from within. For all his
inveighing against artifice, Emerson was by no means oblivious
to craft and structure; he was challenging Poe's notion of form
with his own. If the poem is to incarnate the experience, then
the whole poem would have to imitate the dimensions and shape
of reality. Emerson said, after all, that a metre-*making* argument
makes the poem. If a rigid and preconceived form—*forma ab
extra,* Coleridge called it—distorts words to its own shape, then

*The phrase recalls Emerson's oft-repeated epithet for Poe: "the jingle-
man."

organic form,* at least ideally, grows out of the unique experience: "a thought so passionate and alive that like the spirit of a plant or an animal it has an architecture of its own, and adorns nature with a new thing." Taylor had conceived of growth within a walled garden, contained by accepted limits; and so his poems worked themselves out in formal patterns of stanza and rhyme and in a limited number of elaborated patterns of image. By contrast Emerson wanted the inner principle of life to expand to its own natural limits so that the form of the poem would trace the growth of the generative moment. "There is no outside, no inclosing wall, no circumference to us"; before the winds of inspiration "seeming-solid walls . . . open and flow."[30]

This idea of form as internal exfoliation parallels Blake's maxim in *The Marriage of Heaven and Hell*: "Reason is the bound or outward circumference of Energy," the outward bounds being merely the demarcation which measures for consciousness the particular moment's explosive dimensions. Like each symbolic word, the "new thing" which evolves as the poet "resigns himself to his mood . . . is organic, or the new type which things themselves take when liberated." Thus while in the achieved poem "the thought and form are equal in the order of time," "in the order of genesis the thought is prior to the form." Translating a sonnet of Michaelangelo's, Emerson saw the artist's hand instinctively drawing out the form hidden but inherent in the material:

> Never did sculptor's dream unfold
> A form which marble doth not hold
> In its white block; yet it therein shall find
> Only the hand secure and bold
> Which still obeys the mind.

To the end of his life he argued that "rightly, poetry is organic. We cannot know things by words and writing, but only by taking a central position in the universe and living in its forms."[31] Words are not *about* things; they are directly related to things

*Emerson knew Coleridge's writings very well, as his contrast between *natura naturans* and *natura naturata* ("Nature" in *Essays Second Series*) and his distinction between fancy and imagination ("Poetry and Imagination" in *Letters and Social Aims*) illustrate.

and so become things in their own right. Like other things, words contain and do not contain, express and do not express, their meaning. If language incarnates Spirit, as the axiom in the "Language" chapter of *Nature* asserts, it does so only pursuant to the Spirit. The words and the form are consequent upon the seeing:

> This insight, which expresses itself by what is called Imagination, is a very high sort of seeing, which does not come by study, but by the intellect being where and what it sees; by sharing the path or circuit of things through forms, and so making them translucid to others. . . . The condition of true naming, on the poet's part, is his resigning himself to the divine *aura* which breathes through forms, and accompanying that.[32]

The present participles which stitch together all of Emerson's discussions of the poetic process indicate that it is and must be an ongoing process. Achieved forms and stated meanings become fossilized forms and dead meanings. The notion of organic form leads to what has more recently come to be called "open form" and "composition by field," and even more specifically it leads to the poet's writing not merely long poems or a long poem but a life-poem, its shape acknowledging shapelessness, its lines opening gaps, its meaning sounding the inexhaustibility and indeterminancy of meaning. This distinctly American genre is prefigured in Taylor's *Preparatory Meditations*, and Emerson's assumptions about organic form not only generated his own and Thoreau's journals but also pointed forward to Whitman's *Leaves of Grass*, Pound's *Cantos*, Charles Olson's *Maximus Poems*, Robert Duncan's *Passages* and *Structure of Rhyme* and Ginsberg's prolific notebooks in verse and prose.

Emerson spoke in strikingly modern terms of "the projection of God in the unconscious" mind of man, so that the world shows "unconscious truth . . . defined in an object" and thereby brought to expression. In "Bacchus" the poet drinks a "remembering wine" which revives "a dazzling memory" of mythic archetypes. The poetic power is linked repeatedly with instinct, spontaneous intuition, dreams, and *"dream*-power"; and "dream delivers us to dream." Images and ideas well up from and lead back to a shared source very much like the Jungian Collective Unconscious or Objective Psyche:

> What is the aboriginal Self, on which a universal reliance may be grounded? . . . The inquiry leads us to that source, at once the essence of genius, of virtue, and of life, which we call Spontaneity or Instinct. We denote this primary wisdom as Intuition, whilst all later teachings are tuitions. In that deep force, the last fact behind which analysis cannot go, all things find their common origin. . . . We lie in the lap of immense intelligence, which makes us receivers of its truth and organs of its activity.

Jung would talk about the Self in very similar terms. For him Self and ego were by no means synonymous. The Self was the totality of the psyche whose vast unconscious potentialities needed to be centralized and constellated in consciousness. The ego is the active center of consciousness but must learn to function as a constituent part of the Self, to submit to and move with the promptings of the unconscious. In "The Over-Soul" Emerson says: "All are conscious of attaining to a higher self-possession," and the context indicates that Emerson is using the word with very much the same meaning and force as Jung would, so that the activation of the Self would bring the individual into contact with that cosmic Self which is the life of the universe. For Emerson, too, individualism (Jung called the process of realization "individuation") and self-reliance meant reliance on that "aboriginal Self." Jung had a greater sense of the risks and dangers of submission to the unconscious than Emerson did, because he had a stronger sense of man's capacity for evil and violence and madness. Emerson cheerfully took it that the poet's task is to urge us to open ourselves to "Spontaneity," "Instinct," and "Intuition" because the "laws of nature . . . on the deepest level, correspond to the laws of the psyche, and vice versa." Consequently, the more deeply the poet plunges into his own mind, the more deeply he plunges into nature; and the more surely he unriddles the secrets of the Self, the more securely he touches the Truth that holds the frame of creation together. For Emerson, "the ancient precept, 'Know Thyself,' and the modern precept, 'Study Nature,' become at last one maxim."[33]

The conception of the poet as seer has, of course, a long history in Western thought from Plato and the Greeks down to the Romantics of the nineteenth century and on into the twentieth. But the poet as prophet-seer has adapted himself in particularly vigorous and bold terms to the New World, in part because Americans saw themselves as living in more personal and intimate contact with Nature, the primitive source of inspiration, and in part because the Puritans brought to Nature a strong sense of typology. Emerson came to his statement of the idea through his New England heritage—not Puritan theology but Puritan temperament; and he gave it so American a statement against American acquisitiveness that the reaction down the decades is still humming today. In fact, the Emersonian tradition is so strong and deep that Henry Miller, a writer one might think is as far removed from Emerson as possible, speaks of the artistic process in terms which constitute a resume of Emerson's principal contentions:

> Someone takes over and you just copy out what is being said. . . .
> A writer shouldn't think much. . . . I'm not very good at thinking.
> I work from some deep down place; and when I write, well, I
> don't know just exactly what's going to happen. . . . Who writes
> the great books? It isn't we who sign our names. What is an artist?
> He's a man who has antennae, who knows how to hook up to the
> currents which are in the atmosphere, in the cosmos. . . . Who
> is original? Everything that we are doing, everything that we
> think, exists already, and we are intermediaries. . . . [A writer
> should] recognize himself as a man who was possessed of a certain faculty which he was destined to use for the service of others.
> He has nothing to be proud of, his name means nothing, his ego
> is nil, he's only an instrument in a long procession.[34]

In fact, Miller knew his Emerson well enough to take as the epigraph of *Tropic of Cancer* Emerson's prediction that literature will come more and more to be an autobiographical penetration to the truth of experience.

In the September 1965 issue of *Poetry* Denise Levertov published "Some Notes on Organic Form," later included in a volume of her essays. Her remarks are instructive not just because she cites Emerson (along with Coleridge, Frank Lloyd Wright, and Robert Duncan) but because she attempts to define with greater precision than had been done heretofore this notion which is basic to the Romantic vision but which was followed out more fully by Emerson and the "open form" poets after him: Whitman in the next generation; Pound and Williams fifty years later; and in the second half of the Twentieth century, Beat poets like Ginsberg, Kerouac, and Le Roi Jones, poets of the San Francisco Renaissance like Robert Duncan and William Everson, and Projectivists like Charles Olson, Robert Creeley, and Levertov herself. With Pound and Williams and Olson, she worries about the amorphous expansiveness of Whitman and, by implication, his closest followers, and seeks to keep organic form from being equated with Whitmanian free verse. But the importance of Levertov's essay is that it draws together a century and a half of thinking about organic form and thereby describes what many critics of American poetry, including Hyatt Waggoner, have seen as the original and native strain in the American tradition. She traces out how an organic poem is written and what its sources and shape are. She cannot give rules and prescriptions, since the form of each poem is unique to the recreation of the experience—in fact is the recreation of the experience—but her comments outline the process of gestation:

> A partial definition, then, of organic poetry might be that it is a method of apperception, i.e. of recognizing what we perceive, and is based on an intuition of an order, a form beyond forms, in which forms partake, and of which man's creative works are analogies, resemblances, natural allegories. Such poetry is exploratory.

The source is "an experience, a sequence or constellation of perceptions" through which the poet "is *brought to speech.*" Contemplation and meditation are intermediate steps between experience and speech:

> To contemplate comes from "*templum,* temple, a place, a space for observation, marked out by the augur." It means, not simply to observe, to regard, but to do these things in the presence of a god. And to meditate is "to keep the mind in a state of contemplation"; its synonym is "to muse," and to muse comes from a word meaning "to stand with open mouth"—not so comical if we think of "inspiration"—to breathe in.

(We find ourselves, Emerson says, "not in a critical speculation but in a holy place.") The pressures which meditation in this sense brings to bear on the components of the experience "culminate in a moment of vision, of crystallization, in which some inkling of the correspondence between those elements occurs; and it occurs as words." Thereafter the realization leads the poet "through the world of the poem, its unique inscape revealing itself as it goes." If the poem is truly organic, rhyme, repetition, sound effects all result from connections and associations as perception takes on word-sounds, and the phrasing, cadence, line length, and groupings of lines result from the beat or pulsation or movement in the psyche as the unconscious rises to consciousness. The "intuitive interaction" of all one's faculties reproduces experience in a new form as a structure of words or, as Emerson said, *"alter idem,* in a manner totally new." One need only contrast Levertov's early poems, written in England, with those after she came to America and became an American poet to feel the dramatic shift which the Emersonian tradition, translated more immediately through Ezra Pound and William Carlos Williams, made in the substance and technique of her verse.[35]

In fact, Emerson's sense of the primacy of inspiration and his scorn for "rules and particulars" ushered the Dionysian ideal into American literature. The essay on "The Poet" describes at some length the Dionysian—powerful, original, unchained, filled with the god:

> There is a great public power on which he can draw, by unlocking, at all risks, his human doors, and suffering the ethereal tides to roll and circulate through him . . . his speech is thunder, his thought is law. . . . The poet knows that he speaks adequately then only when he speaks somewhat wildly, . . . not with the intellect used as an organ, but with the intellect released from all service and suffered to take its direction from its celestial life; or as the ancients were won't to express themselves, not with intellect alone but with the intellect inebriated by nectar.

Reeling and blinded by what he has seen, he yields to Pegasus, like "the traveller who . . . throws his reins on his horse's neck and trusts to the instincts of the animal." The essay is a litany to the poet's preternatural power: "liberating gods," "free," "drunk," "inflamed and carried away . . . holds him like an insanity," "unlocks our chains," "the ejaculations of a few imaginative men," "the conductor of the whole river of electricity." Emerson addressed a dithyrambic ode to "Bacchus," the Roman Dionysus, and often he apotheosized Pan, the demideity of Nature, as in this marvelous short piece called "Pan":[36]

> O what are heroes, prophets, men,
> But pipes through which the breath of Pan doth blow
> A momentary music. Being's tide
> Swells hitherward, and myriads of forms
> Live, robed with beauty, painted by the sun;
> Their dust, pervaded by the nerves of God,
> Throbs with an overmastering energy
> Knowing and doing. Ebbs the tide, they lie
> White hollow shells upon the desert shore.
> But not the less the eternal wave rolls up
> To animate new millions, and exhale
> Races and plants, its enchanted foam.

Actually, Emerson's poems are not nearly so wild, so drunken, so untrammeled emotionally or metrically, as his theory said that poems ideally should be. He was not Whitman, much less Hart Crane, still less Henry Miller or Ginsberg or Olson. He was too gentle and genteel, too fastidious and remote to be a full-blooded and abandoned Dionysian. As he once admitted, he had in mind only "blissful orgies," and one of the passages about Pan, here called "patient Pan," makes sure that Pan retains, though "drunk with nectar," decorum enough to tamp down the fires before they blaze out of hand; nectar is, after all, the ethereal liquor of the gods:

> Well he knows his own affair,
> Piling mountain chains of phlegm
> On the nervous brain of man,
> As he holds down central fires
> Under Alps and Andes cold;
> Haply else we could not live,
> Life would be too wild an ode.[37]

As Whitman would find out, Emerson was fastidious as well about explicit discussion of sex in public; he preferred the word "maiden" to "woman" in his verses. Critics credit Whitman with helping to make possible the direct treatment of sexual themes;

yet, in this as in so many ways, the way for Whitman was prepared by Emerson. Though Emerson did not expatiate on the
subject, he noted several times that the dualistic and compensatory process through which the Oversoul operated in time and
space found such fundamental exemplification in sexual polarity
that the polarity seemed the rhythm of life in the psyche as in
nature: "In fact, the eye,—the mind,—is always accompanied by
these forms, male and female; and these are incomparably the
richest informations of the power and order that lie at the heart
of things." The sexual mystery not only joins husbands and
wives and generates all the forms of Nature but also links body
and soul in individuals and the order of Nature with the Oversoul;
in short, it constitutes on every level "the analogy that marries
Matter and Mind." A purely scientific approach to Nature is
"barren like a single sex," but "marry it to human history, and it
is full of life."

Emerson followed the prevailing pattern of archetypal associations (whether inherent in the psyche, as some psychologists
and mythologists claim, or merely acculturated) in conceiving
Spirit as masculine and therefore as embodied in all languages "as
the FATHER." Yet when Spirit enters flesh, the masculine inter-
penetrates the archetypally feminine element, so that we all, men
and women alike, become vessels brimming with the divine wine,
wombs teeming with the divine seed. For this reason Emerson
insisted on "the feminine element . . . in men of genius"; that
feminine capacity makes them open to possession by the supernatural power operating through the sexual process of nature.[38]
Before that power, as "Ode to Beauty" has it, men are metamorphosed into women in the procreative round of nature:

> Thy dangerous glances
> Make women of men;
> New-born, we are melting
> Into nature again.

Dionysus the male androgyne is the figure of the poet as bodily
medium for the Father-Spirit.

But the interaction of masculine and feminine cannot be fixed
in this way as representing the disembodied Spirit and the carnal
passions. In another aspect of the archetype the feminine represents the individual soul leading the person beyond material limits

back to the realm of Spirit. In Emerson's own development the death of his beloved first wife, Ellen, within two years of their marriage became one of the transformative and revelatory events of his life. Her spiritual conviction and exaltation in the face of death made her afterward to him an angel, his angel confirming the reality and primacy of Spirit. Ellen became what Erich Neumann calls, in his detailed study of the feminine archetype, "the transformative anima."* The anima, which in its elementary phase is man's link to body and instincts and feelings, becomes as well in later phases the spiritualizing force freeing man from body into the transpersonal and transcendental order. The complement, but not the contradiction, of the maternal-sexual anima is Santa Sophia. There is a logical but not a psychological inconsistency to this complementarity; the archetypes express polarity as connection. Jung called this tendency of all psychological factors to metamorphose into their opposites by the Greek word "enantiadromia"; taoists see the metamorphosis written in the law of nature; alchemists sought the *conjunctio oppositorum* in the elements to draw it out in the soul; Emerson gave it a more ethical and purposive character under the Oversoul in the doctrine of Compensation.

So, for Emerson, the creative process was not simply the Spirit descending into the Dionysian poet. There was a counterthrust in Dionysus' activity, and the poem "Bacchus" allows for no misunderstanding from the very first verses: "Bring me wine, but wine which never grew/ In the belly of the grape...." Throughout the poem Emerson sets about transcendentalizing the belly-tendencies of his Bacchus. Though sprung "from a nocturnal root" emplanted in mother-earth, the "leaves and tendrils" of the "true" wine are "curled/ Among the silver hills of heaven" and "draw everlasting dew." By means of such alchemical distillation it becomes the "Wine of wine" and the "Form of forms" and in its final rarefied state is one with the pure Platonic Music of the Spheres: "Wine which Music is,—/Music and Wine are one...."

Nevertheless, in however modest and unostentatious a man-

---

*For a discussion of the transformative aspect of the anima and of the double nature of the feminine, cf. Erich Neumann, *The Great Mother: An Analysis of the Archetype*, trans. Ralph Mannheim (Princeton, N. J.: Princeton University Press, 1955), pp. 24–38, 64–83, 211–336.

ner, many of Emerson's poems move to that conjoining, metamorphic rhythm: "The lover watched his graceful maid" ("Each and All"); "And soft perfection of its plan—/ Willow and violet, maiden and man" ("May–Day"); "She [Nature] spawneth men as mallows fresh,/ Hero and maiden, flesh of her flesh" ("Nature II"); "Primal chimes of sun and shade,/ Of sound and echo, man and maid" ("Woodnotes II"); "Sex to sex, and even to odd" ("Ode Inscribed to W. H. Channing").* The following remarkable passage, which opens the second part of "Merlin," is Emerson's most extended and explicit celebration of the sexual life-force to which "Song of Myself" and many subsequent poems would give loud voice:

> The rhyme of the poet
> Modulates the king's affairs;
> Balance-loving Nature
> Made all things in pairs.
> To every foot its antipode;
> Each color with its counter glowed;
> To every tone beat answering tones,
> Higher or graver;
> Flavor gladly blends with flavor;
> Leaf answers leaf upon the bough;
> And match the paired cotyledons.
> Hands to hands, and feet to feet,
> In one body grooms and brides;
> Eldest rite, two married sides
> In every mortal meet.
> Light's far furnace shines,
> Smelting balls and bars,
> Forging double stars,
> Glittering twins and trines.
> The animals are sick with love,
> Lovesick with rhyme;
> Each with all propitious Time
> Into chorus wove.

The establishing of the poet's rhyme as the pairing which is the operational plan of "balance-loving Nature" sets up the style as well as the imagery of the passage. Emerson catalogues the senses:

*Cf. Swedenborg's vision of the sexual rhythm governing not only natural creation but man's relation to God, even in heaven (*Representative Men*, pp. 127–129).

sight ("color"), hearing ("tone beat"), taste and smell ("flavor"), and finally the most erotic sense, touch. The anatomical references ("Hands to hands, and feet to feet") identify the body not just as the ground for the individual's union with his sexual complement but also as the vessel for an androgynous consciousness within the individual, which deepens his capacity for union: "In one body grooms and brides;/ Eldest rite, two married sides/ In every mortal meet."* Under the pervasive lovesickness Emerson prolongs the anatomy chart into barely disguised genital imagery (the "furnace . . . smelting balls and bars") and perhaps even makes an outrageous pun when "Into chorus wove," read aloud, becomes "intercourse." If Emerson did not intend these last effects, as very probably he did not, this is a case of the poet's being carried so far along by inspiration that for once he spoke more wildly than he knew. In any case he recognized the fundamental importance of the sexual analogy and extended the sexual references into the subsequent verses, denigrating the barren virginity of "bachelors" and "an ungiven maid" in contrast with "equal couples mated" and "perfect-paired." The poem ends with the Fates as Great Mothers, playing out the rhythm of generation as they "build and unbuild our echoing clay."

It is true that this is an uncharacteristically full-bodied moment in Emerson. He could at times see in himself the disembodied remoteness that even his friends complained of; regretted to his journal that "the chief defect of my nature" was "the want of

---

*Cf. statements from the journals such as the following: "A highly endowed man with a good intellect & good conscience is a Man-woman & does not so much need the complement of Woman to his being, as another. Hence his relations to the sex are somewhat dislocated and unsatisfactory. He asks in Woman sometimes the Woman, sometimes the Man"; "the finest people marry the two sexes in their own person. Hermaphrodite is then the symbol of the finished soul. It was agreed that in every act should appear the married pair: the two elements should mix in every act." See *Journals and Miscellaneous Notebooks*, VIII ed. William H. Gilman and J. E. Parsons (Cambridge, Mass.: Harvard University Press, 1970), 175, 380. The journals, only now being published in full, confirm the fact that Emerson recognized very well that the metaphysical reality which "marries Matter and Mind" works humanly between the sexes and also in the marriage of the sexes in the individual's androgynous psyche. Both Freud and Jung would later postulate the bisexuality of the psyche, and Jung would study the fulfilled Self (which Emerson calls "the finished soul") symbolized as the Hermaphrodite, the Divine Syzygy, the alchemical *conjunctio oppositorum*, the mystical marriage.

animal spirits" and admitted in other journal entries: "I was born cold. My bodily habit is cold. I shiver in and out . . ."; "Even for those whom I really love I have not animal spirits." It is not difficult to see why he shrank from what seemed to him the vulgarity and coarseness of some of Whitman's poems, and why he had only harsh reproof for those would-be Dionysians who tried to induce vision with drugs, drink, and other sensual stimulants. Since "wine, mead, narcotics, coffee, tea, opium, the fumes of sandalwood and tobacco" are "*quasi*-mechanical substitutes for the true nectar," such "counterfeit excitement and fury" can end only in "dissipation and deterioration."[39]

Nonetheless, Emerson's advocacy of the Dionysian ideal could not have been more crucial for the course of American poetry. Emerson's informing presence made him, in fact, a chief target for twentieth-century poet-critics—Eliot, Allen Tate, Yvor Winters—who wanted to exorcise the deep, abiding influence of Romanticism. They disapproved of and dismissed Romanticism on moral and psychological as well as artistic grounds; they feared, in themselves as well as in others, that its individualism, its openness to the impulses of experience, its sourcing of inspiration in the emotions and the unconscious led to solipsism, madness, suicide. The sense of a Romantic conspiracy in arts and philosophy led them at times to extreme and rigorous denunciations. In 1967 Winters could make this reductive statement about his contemporary Williams, who had been a strong influence on his own early and now rejected poetry:

> William Carlos Williams (1883–1963), in his view of life and of poetry, was an uncompromising romantic. It is surprising, in the light of this fact, that he appears to have been a devoted husband, father and physician, eminently virtuous and practical in these capacities, and often naively shocked by the behavior of some of his Bohemian acquaintances who held the same ideas but acted upon them.

Emerson, like Williams, was particularly insidious because he too made Romanticism seem blandly wholesome, and it was not enough for Winters to note that neither "practice[s] what he preaches." He could say "Of Poe and Whitman, the less said the better" and take that assertion as fairly self-evident; Tate agreed that the disastrous influence of both sealed Hart Crane's doom.

But Winters' inverted acknowledgment of Emerson is expressed in his inveighing against Emerson "in defense of reason" with an urgent conviction that Emerson was his most dangerous adversary in America.[40]

Emerson may not have fully practiced what he preached, but his importance lies in the fact that he did state the principles and begin the experiments. He stands, nervous and self-conscious in the role, as our teetotaling Bacchus, our New England and ministerial Pan. Moreover, his experiments were only a departure, heralding Whitman's free verse, Pound's and Williams' innovations with speech rhythms and breath units, E. E. Cummings' refashioning of syntax and punctuation and typography, Charles Olson's "projective verse" and Denise Levertov's organic form, the long lines and cumulative periods of Robinson Jeffers, William Everson, and Allen Ginsberg. None of these poets, after Whitman, would share easily with Emerson the metaphysics which forms the basis for his poetics. But in almost all of them the metaphysical, even transcendental, impulse remains, however more intermittently, complexly, or obliquely in some instances: for example, in Pound's Platonism and in his indebtedness, especially in his notions of language and form, to Ernest Fenollosa, who was himself teaching in Japan the transcendental philosophy which he had imbibed at Harvard; in Jeffers' Calvinist pantheism; in Cummings' devotion to the spirit of his father, a Unitarian minister with a strongly Emersonian temperament; in Olson's profound interest in Jung's archetypal psychology and Alfred North Whitehead's process philosophy; in Levertov, through her father, a Jew steeped in Hasidic thought who became a Christian and an Anglican priest; in Ginsberg's Judaic, Oriental, and Blakean spirit; in Everson's fusion of Christian theology and Jungian psychology. As a result, most of these poets came to view the poet as a special seer, and all of them as a special perceiver. Their various explorations of ongoing form and emergent structure were grounded, in the organic yet—in one way or another—transcendent process of nature. Along with other poets akin in inclination they comprise a distinct, perhaps the distinctive, strain in the American poetic tradition. And Emerson is their source, more than some of them knew or wished to acknowledge and more than Emerson himself could have foreseen.

3

Though Emerson's verse did not adequately exemplify the dictum that "every poem must be made up of lines that are poems," though too many lines ring like rhyming aphorisms, there is a sufficient body of good and interesting poems and a large enough group of fine poems to rank Emerson beside Edgar Poe, his shadow, as the two most critically important American poets of the first half of the nineteenth century. Emerson's experiments and innovations—the simple diction and syntax, the rough rhythm, the direct tone which can rise to philosophical reflection while it incorporates homely detail, the occasional attempt at colloquial tang—all issue from the central premise of organic form. And what was happening to the language of his best poems would affect native poetic diction from that point on. Frost would later sum up Emerson's influence on his own sense of language as speech with Emerson's remark about Montaigne in *Representative Men*: "Cut these words, and they would bleed; they are vascular and alive."

The notion of organic form affected sound and measure as well as diction. At least ideally, each poetic experience requires its perfect and unique rhythm, "though the odds are immense against our finding it." Still, the conviction that "for every thought its proper melody or rhyme exists" affects the way in which the poet seeks and shapes the sound of the poem, and with the rare and transforming strokes of "genius" which come to poets, rhyme and meter sometimes move to express linguistically "the correspondence of parts in nature," just as rhythm corresponds to body-pulse and line-length to breath. Williams and such followers of his as Olson, Creeley, and Levertov might well have taken this statement of Emerson as their experimental point of departure: "Metre begins with the pulse-beat, and the length of lines in songs and poems is determined by the inhalation and exhalation of the lungs."* At the same time, Emerson did not automatically equate organic form with free or unmetered verse any more than Wordsworth or Coleridge or Levertov did. When he reflected that the English language over the centuries had naturally moved into certain measures and metrical patterns, he could only

*Or: "the earth-beat, sea-beat, heart-beat, which makes the tune to which the sun rolls and the globule of blood, and the sap of trees" (*Representative Men*, p. 141).

conclude that these meters were "organic, derived from the human pulse."* Therefore, meter and rhyme need not be inhibitive and impersonal if the poet's voice animates them; "there is under the seeming poverty of metres an infinite variety, as every artist knows," and as Frost among others would come to observe in good part by Emerson's example. Prosody, as such, whether strict or not-so-strict, is less important than the individual vitality which makes the language seem "vascular and alive." On the other hand, whether metered or irregular (like some of his own experiments), "every good poem that I know I recall by its rhythm."[41]

In much the same way, Emerson vociferously dismissed the jingle of rhyme invoked for its own sake or for an empty display of poetic virtuosity, but wrote mostly rhymed poems because organic rhyme could convey "the rhyme of things" in "balance-loving Nature." The coherence of rhyme and rhythm is the theme of "Merlin." After dismissing onomatopoetically the "jingling serenader's" thin "tinkle of piano strings," Emerson then strives to make the reader feel the bard's rude power. Through the rhyme and alliteration and sound effects, Emerson is using the individual line as a structuring device for the unfolding of the vision, stroke by stroke:

> The kingly bard
> Must smite the chords rudely and hard,
> As with hammer or with mace;
> That they may render back
> Artful thunder, which conveys
> Secrets of the solar track,
> Sparks of the supersolar blaze.
> Merlin's blows are strokes of fate,
> Chiming with the forest tone,
> When boughs buffet boughs in the wood;
> Chiming with the gasp and moan
> Of the ice-imprisoned flood;
> With the pulse of manly hearts;
> With the voice of orators;
> With the din of city arts;
> With the cannonade of wars;

*In *The Physiology of Verse* (1883) Oliver Wendell Holmes, who published a biography of Emerson two years later, drew on his medical knowledge to argue that prosody was a function of breath and pulse and specifically that the four-stress line (which Emerson found congenial) arose naturally because there are roughly four heartbeats to a human breath.

> With the marches of the brave;
> And prayers of might from martyrs' cave.

The alternating rhymes are bracketed by the couplets enclosing the passage, and the irregular four-stress pattern, held in tension by the rhymes, is flexible enough to allow "the kingly bard" to occupy an entire line. The hammering sounds of Merlin's chords find their source and end in the smooth sibilants of the couplet: "Secrets of the solar track,/ Sparks of the supersolar blaze." Emerson is trying to draw on the rhetorical resources of language—that is, all the resources of sound and rhythm and suggestion which exceed denotative statement—to cast the reader's experience into a dimension beyond rational argument, proof or disproof. If his language has so caught up the reader that he moves with the movement of the poem, then he will already know that Merlin's art conveys "Secrets of the solar track," and if the reader has reached that point, he will have no trouble recognizing that those secrets are "Sparks of the supersolar blaze." The next lines register Merlin's blows in a series of images; the first two images occupy phrasal units of two lines each, and once the reader has been rocked into rhythm with Merlin's blows Emerson drives his point home in an accelerating sequence of images with the longer last line "And prayers of might from martyrs' cave" rounding out the movement and bringing it to momentary rest.

With organic form in mind, let us glance back at some other lines from "Merlin" cited in the previous section of this chapter:

> Hands to hands, and feet to feet,
> In one body grooms and brides;
> Eldest rite, two married sides
> In every mortal meet.
> Light's far furnace shines,
> Smelting balls and bars,
> Forging double stars,
> Glittering twins and trines.
> The animals are sick with love,
> Lovesick with rhyme. . . .

Like Taylor before him and Frost after, Emerson found short rhyming lines well suited to the didactic and descriptive aims of discursive nature poetry. Here, besides the end-rhymes, the lines emphasize their meaning through repetition ("hands to hands, and feet to feet"), alliteration (married, mortal, meet; balls, bars, twins, trines), internal sound effects ("*far furnace*" surrounded by the assonance of "Light's" "shines"), contrast between lines ("one body," "two sides," "every mortal"), and effective inversion ("sick with love,/ Lovesick with rhyme"). The entire passage, filled with almost as many sound effects as a Poe poem, tries to exemplify—organically, in Emerson's mind—the rhyming of Nature.

More subtle is the use of the quatrain in "Brahma" to make seeming contrasts or alternatives cohere in a rounded and complete stanza. Here are the first two stanzas of the poem:

> If the red slayer think he slays,
>   Or if the slain think he is slain,
> They know not well the subtle ways
>   I keep, and pass, and turn again.
>
> Far or forgot to me is near;
>   Shadow and sunlight are the same;
> The vanished gods to me appear;
>   And one to me are shame and fame.

The deliberate balance of the first two lines expands into the second two lines, linked by enjambment. Lines 1 and 2 rock between two points of emphasis ("slayer," "slays"; "slain," "slain"); the third line is a single uninterrupted movement which spills over to the fourth; the four stresses of the last line move through a contrast ("keep," "pass") to a final phrase of two stresses ("turn again") which starts another spiral of Brahma. The second stanza opens with a complicated internal rhyme ("*far or forgot*") and ends with the simpler "shame and fame." These four lines reduce contraries to equals, the sound of "shame" at the end recalling the previous "Shadow." The words which receive the heaviest stress are "near," "same," and "one."

Although Emerson used blank verse less often than rhyme, some of his best pieces are loose iambic pentameter: among them, "Xenophanes," "The Day's Ration," "Blight," "Musketaquid," "Pan" (cited in full above), and "Philosopher." He cannot match Wordsworth at his supple best, but a passage like this from "Blight" is very good and very Wordsworthian indeed:

The Tenth Muse

If I knew
Only the herbs and simples of the wood,
Rue, cinquefoil, gill, vervain and agrimony,
Blue-vetch and trillium, hawkweed, sassafras,
Milkweeds and murky brakes, quaint pipes and sundew,
And rare and virtuous roots, which in these woods
Draw untold juices from the common earth,
Untold, unknown, and I could surely spell
Their fragrance, and their chemistry apply
By sweet affinities to human flesh,
Driving the foe and stablishing the friend,—
O, that were much, and I could be a part
Of the round day, related to the sun
And planted world, and full executor
Of their imperfect functions.

The lines suggest something of what it would be to become "a part of the round day." They absorb a catalogue of word objects into a swelling flow, so that what would otherwise be linear becomes constellated in circular movement. The continuity is maintained after the long list of things by the enjambment which swings almost every line into the next, and the circularity is symbolized in the poet's being "full executor" of the "round day," "the sun/ And planted world."

An excellent example of Emerson's ability to strike "infinite variety" through the blank verse pentameter is the first verse paragraph of "The Snow-storm":

Announced by all the trumpets of the sky,
Arrives the snow, and, driving o'er the fields,
Seems nowhere to alight: the whited air
Hides hills and woods, the river, and the heaven,
And veils the farm-house at the garden's end.
The sled and traveller stopped, the courier's feet
Delayed, all friends shut out, the housemates sit
Around the radiant fireplace, enclosed
In a tumultuous privacy of storm.

The first five lines comprise a single sentence describing the driving power of the storm. It begins by sounding the loud note with full, open vowels ("Announced by all") and exhausts itself with spent energy "at the garden's end." The gradual shift of stress and pace is accomplished by the repetition of several long vowels at the start of the sentence which taper off toward the conclusion: the long "i" in "sky," "arrives," "driving," "alight," "whited," "hides"; the long "o" of "snow," "O'er," "nowhere"; the assonance of "fields," "seems" and of "nowhere," "air," "veils." This long sequence of strong sounds interwoven through the first three lines emphasizes most of the words in an unbroken forward motion. In the fourth line "hills and woods" looks back to the previous words "whited" and "hides," but from this point to the conclusion of the sentence the sounds soften and lighten (with the lingering exceptions of "veils" and "house"); thus, with "hills and woods, the river, and the heaven,/ And veils the farm-house at the garden's end," the generally lighter sounds compact themselves ("farm," "garden"; "garden's end") to the single syllable "end." The fifth line brings the storm's wind and snow to the human habitation, and the second sentence of the verse paragraph contrasts the cessation of human activity with the storm's movement. The word "end" anticipates the stop-and-start pace of the next sentence. Abruptly the language breaks into short, discrete phrasal units, each chopping itself off with dental consonants: "The sled and traveller stopped, the courier's feet/ Delayed, all friends shut out." The courier feet halt suspended at the conclusion of the line as the housemates "sit" at the end of the next line and are "enclosed" at the end of the next. Between "sit" and "enclosed" is the family circle at the hearth, suggested by "around the radiant." The last line is a single rhythmic unit which includes the storm's ferocity and the human isolation in "a tumultuous privacy of storm." Within the pentameter structure Emerson has managed to give the lines such dramatic and organic shape that they become what Denise Levertov calls "a kind of extended onomatopoeia" for the experience.[42]

The rest of the poem explicates the "type" of the snowstorm, which has blown with bacchic abandon through the landscape tamed by man to his own productive purposes. The storm stands revealed as a "fierce artificer" who has reclaimed the natural world from man and reconstituted it through its own exuberant energy:

> Speeding, the myriad-handed, his wild work
> So fanciful, so savage, nought cares he
> For number or proportion.

Often, as in several passages quoted in previous sections of this chapter, Emerson made the wind symbolize the afflatus of the Over-soul through Nature, the "divine *aura* which breathes through forms," the Spiritus Sanctus which the poet inspires or breathes in (as Levertov observed above). Where the wind blowing through Coleridge's "Aeolian Harp" lulled the poet and the world into passive tranquillity, Emerson's wind whirls with Dionysian force, leaving

> astonished Art
> To mimic in slow structures, stone by stone
> Built in an age, the mad wind's night-work,
> The frolic architecture of the snow.

The power in Nature makes new forms of the known world, and Art can do no better with its more deliberative and self-conscious effort than to strive to translate into its own materials (paint, stone, words, and so on) the new creation hurled into being by the momentary blast of the night-wind. In fact, conscious deliberation alone—the rule of "number and proportion" disdained by the storm—cannot make such an imitation. For, as we have seen, only the artist "passive to the superincumbent spirit" can become a "bard of the Holy Ghost." So "the Power . . . abides in no man and in no woman, but for a moment speaks from this one, and for another moment from that one." Prophets and poets are only "pipes through which the breath of Pan [or of the snow-storm] doth blow/ A momentary music."[43] Only instruments; but they *are* the instruments through which the Music of the Spheres is heard.

"Hamatreya" strives for organic form by different means through variation of the density and length of the line. The first three lines describe the attachment of the Concord farmers to the land:

> Bulkeley, Hunt, Willard, Hosmer, Meriam, Flint,
> Possessed the land which rendered to their toil
> Hay, corn, roots, hemp, flax, apples, wool and wood.

The second line, a perfect iambic pentameter, links possessors and products, the names of the farmers as thick to the tongue and palpable to the hand as the crops they grow, so that men and things seem identified. From the farmers' viewpoint the list of names mirrored by the list of things exemplifies the physical contact between men and earth, but the ironic viewpoint which begins to emerge makes the proud possessors part of the land in a grisly sense which they do not comprehend. The next lines are strident with personal possessive pronouns: I, my, mine, me.

> I fancy these pure waters and the flags
> Know me, as does my dog: we sympathize;
> And I affirm, my actions smack of the soil.

Beneath the onomatopoetic effects, the increasing irony lies in the fact that though the farmers claim reciprocal sympathy with their possessions, they actually think themselves as superior as the master to his dog. The next verse paragraph demolishes the false pretensions, for those solid citizens are now very much of the land, six feet deep:

> Earth laughs in flowers, to see her boastful boys
> Earth-proud, proud of the earth which is not theirs;
> Who steer the plough, but cannot steer their feet
> Clear of the grave.

Earth has all along been the possessor, and men of any age are her immature children. The repetition of words ("earth," "proud," "steer," "not") and sounds ("flowers," "theirs"; "her," "earth"; "boastful boys"; "flowers," "proud," "plough"; "steer their feet clear") packs the lines with words like clods of earth. The third verse paragraph tightens the ironic tension:

> "This suits me for a pasture; that's my park;
> We must have clay, lime, gravel, granite-ledge,
> And misty lowland, where to go for peat."

Their thick, heavy words merely describe their burial plot:

> Ah! the hot owner sees not Death, who adds
> Him to his land, a lump of mould the more.

At this point a sudden shift in sound and meter marks a change in perspective. The lyric of the feminine Earth-Spirit has shorter lines chiming with sound effects to suggest, by contrast with the lumps of mould, the rhythms of the eternal feminine, who harmonizes life and death, Nature and Spirit:

> Mine and yours;
> Mine, not yours.
> Earth endures;
> Stars abide—
> Shine down in the old sea;
> Old are the shores;
> But where are old men?
> I who have seen much,
> Such have I never seen.

After hearing the Earth-Song, the chastened poet speaks for himself for the first time in a coda whose lines are reduced from the packed pentameters of the opening, yet have greater length and density than the airy, mostly two-beat lines of the Earth-Song:

> When I heard the Earth-Song,
> I was no longer brave;
> My avarice cooled
> Like lust in the chill of the grave.

The conflict between the ego and the life-process is concluded, if not resolved in the last two lines: first, tersely ("My avarice cooled"), then with the solemn finality in the last line. The association of "lust" with "avarice" in the previously "hot owner" specifies the sinister suggestions of rape in "possessed" and "rendered to their toil" at the beginning of the poem; these pioneer settlers force the land to yield to themselves and their progeny— till the land, virgin despite her rape and fertile despite her virginity, absorbs them, frail husks of masculine ego, back to her womb.

The imagery of Romantic poetry about Nature confirms the fact that man's relationship with Nature is fundamentally psychosexual and therefore has profound implications not just about his attitude toward the environment he lives in but more broadly about his attitude toward all the "dark," "feminine" aspects of his existence: matter, body, sexuality, passion, the unconscious. In his mythology Nature was to be at once "mother" and "virgin," fruitful yet inviolate, and so unthreatening. Men could revere Nature or at least pay her lip service exactly because she was set apart yet testified at a distance to his potency. However, once "she" became threatening, "she" had to be fought tooth for tooth and nail for nail; fought, subdued, and made to pay. Then it was man *against* Nature. The frontier experience and the frontier mystique which so inform the American character spell out that mortal combat. In psychosexual terms the pioneers—their manhood challenged by the seemingly superior power of Nature in all its sublime height and depth and horizonless immensity, the virgin-mother turned destroyer as luring as she was deadly— turned destroyers in turn: possessing, raping, razing, gauging their proof of manhood in patriarchal, contractual terms of dollars and cents.

But in the end "she" triumphed; such was the poet's vision. The combat was mortal because, in rejecting "her" and exploiting "her" for profit, men destroyed themselves; their avarice cooled with their lust in the chill of the womb-grave. The son of the Father-Spirit and the spiritual patriarch of America during its first burst of economic expansion, Emerson nonetheless sided with those who distrusted the logical, legalistic norms of the patriarchy; so he told his establishment audience in the Masonic Temple in his early "Transcendentalist" lecture. Like Pound a century later, he conceived the conflict in sharp polarities: the masculine world of economics and law against the feminine world of nature and metamorphic vision. Unlike such contemporaries as James Fenimore Cooper and Francis Parkman and later writers like Robert Frost, Ernest Hemingway, and William Faulkner— all men transfixed by the masculine mystique of the frontiersman so that unaggressive woodsmen such as Natty Bumppo, Ike Mac-Caslin, and Nick Adams are doomed to be psychologically and morally impotent—Emerson in his most unguarded moments knew that as a man his responsibility and opportunity led him not to contend with, but to live, with "her": that is, with nature, with the intuitive, the instinctual, the pre-verbal and supra-verbal. He knew the feminine Earth-Spirit, and in his masculine obeisance to her, Emerson assimilated her meaning deeply enough to be able to translate her inexpressible song. In the poem, Emerson sees life from her perspective and not from that of the vainglorious men; he sings not a masculine or patriarchal consciousness but a feminine or matriarchal consciousness. Thematically the poem anticipates passages in Pound's *Cantos,* most especially perhaps that marvelous moment in Canto 81 when the female spirit appears as eyes in Pound's tent in the prison camp at Pisa to open up to his eyes a vision of the green round of Nature in which assertive masculine ego has no proper or harmonious part:

> The ant's a centaur in his dragon world.
> Pull down thy vanity, it is not man
> Made courage, or made order, or made grace,
>   Pull down thy vanity, I say pull down.
> Learn of the green world what can be thy place
> In scaled invention or true artistry,
> Pull down thy vanity,
>   Paquin pull down!
> The green casque has outdone your elegance.

In the Emerson poems discussed so far in this section the poet has attempted, with considerable success, to use meter with greater variety, flexibility, and relevance to the experience presented, in order to demonstrate that meter can be employed organically. But most liberating for the prosody of the next generation of poets, which includes Emily Dickinson as well as Walt Whitman, were Emerson's experiments with what can only be called "free verse." Poems such as "Ode to Channing," "Ode to Beauty," "Give All to Love," Merlin," "Bacchus," "Threnody," and "Terminus" display variability in the number of syllables, the number of stresses, and the occurrence of end-rhyme. "Limits" is a free verse poem which has remained little known perhaps because the sentiment is untypical of Emerson; it is interesting for that reason as well as for its attempt to break the lines into more functional units:

> Who knows this or that?
> Hark in the wall to the rat:
> Since the world was, he has gnawed;
> Of his wisdom, of his fraud
> What dost thou know?
> In the wretched little beast
> Is life and heart,
> Child and parent,

Not without relation
To fruitful field and sun and moon.
What art thou? His wicked eye
Is cruel to thy cruelty.

The versification is seeking freedom from an expected pattern in order that each verse can suggest the movement of the imagination more convincingly as the meter-making argument makes the poem before our eyes. Ideally the reader would come to grasp the experience much as the poet did. Denise Levertov spoke of lines as indicating "the varying speed and gait of different strands of perception within an experience"; Charles Olson, discussing "projective verse," said that the breath-line gives us what "we are after": namely, "the PLAY of a mind."[44] If the individual breath-span and breath-unit correspond broadly to the play of the mind in speech, then Emerson's mind—in contrast, let us say, to Whitman's or Olson's—moves in a sequence of short, quite distinct units, summing up the situation fairly clearly and aphoristically throughout the process of articulation. Emerson's free verse is stiffer and less expansive than that of some of his successors, but again his practice points the way. Moreover, as we move through the quite irregular lines of a poem such as "Limits," juxtapositions, contrasts, and connections make for patterns of tension and relationship.

For example, if the fourth and fifth lines were written as one, there would be a great difference between the line "Of his wisdom, of his fraud what dost thou know?" (which feels more like Whitman) and the double lines which intensify the disparity and implicit connection between man and rat:

Of his wisdom, of his fraud
What dost thou know?

The next lines begin to make the analogy between them point by point: "the wretched little beast" is, whether vainglorious man recognizes it at first or not, an animate being ("life and heart"), immersed in the temporal life-process ("Child and parent") which is (by ironic understatement) "not without relation" to the universal scheme of nature ("fruitful field and sun and moon"). The hidden rat, gnawing away in the wall, is "wretched" and "wicked" and "cruel" because it mirrors to man, more than man knows, his own wretched cruelty adding to the attrition of time: "Since the world was, he has gnawed." Besides the limits of the mortal term, there are limits to human understanding ("Who knows this or that?"; "What dost thou know?") and to the human capacity for recognizing others and for self-recognition. The final lines—"What art thou? His wicked eye/ Is cruel to thy cruelty" —sum up man's double failure; he has not acknowledged the rat's place in the scheme of things and so has made it impossible to see how many qualities he and the rat share and how much alike their situations are.

Unlike "Limits," the following irregular lines from "Bacchus" are characteristically Emersonian. The incantatory cadences expand and contract as the poet rapt by the god drinks inspiration:

> We buy ashes for bread;
> We buy diluted wine;
> Give me of the true,–
> Whose ample leaves and tendrils curled
> Among the silver hills of heaven
> Draw everlasting dew;
> Wine of wine,
> Blood of the world,
> Form of forms, and mould of statures,
> That I intoxicated,
> And by a single draught assimilated,
> May float at pleasure through all natures;
> The bird-language rightly spell,
> And that which roses say so well.

The first two lines make unillusioned assessments of the fallen human state, but the passage soon spins off from the plea "Give me of the true" to an immediate response. After the three-line pulsation describing Bacchus' vine, the phrases pile up with accelerated intensity (the separate lines "Wine of wine,/ Blood of the world" caught up in the double "Form of forms, and mould of statures") until the elevated poet is dispersed throughout Nature in the drawn-out clause that fills the last five lines.

Emerson's poetry has often been underestimated, especially among those from Poe to Tuckerman to Tate and Winters who find the notion of the vatic poet presumptuous or fatuous. Even his admirers have to admit that many of his poems fall far short of the ideal he formulated, and so at times are tempted to apply to him the judgment which he passed on Wordsworth in a journal entry of 1838: "Wordsworth's merit is that he saw the truly great across the perverting influences of society & of English literature & though he lacks executive power yet his poetry is of the right kind."[45] Often we feel that Emerson's diction and imagery are conventional and undistinguished, inadequate to his conceptions, and that he is best in short poems or in parts of long poems— phrases, lines, passages—which crystallize an insight without the sententious reflections of the preacher-lecturer. Nevertheless, just as Emerson's recognition of Wordsworth's limitations did not lessen his admiration for Wordsworth and for many of his poems, we can find in Emerson's poetic work marvelous instances of poems in which thought and feeling, language and rhythm, com- bine in a form more or less organic to the experience. Moreover, so exhilarating and eye-opening were his words and conceptions, so original some of his experiments, so finely executed some of his poems, that it would in fact be difficult to overestimate his importance in his own time and his influence on the generations following in his wide wake.

4

In the intellectual life of America Emerson represented more than a development into a secular and nondenominational Puri- tanism, and his confrontation with Nature was, for all its connections with Edwards' typology, more than a neo-Platonic, neo-Germanic redaction of *Images or Shadows of Divine Things.* These generalizations are fair enough statements about Emerson's antecedents, but his adaptation and extension of the tradition dis- played an ambiguity about basic concepts which signaled a shift, perhaps a dislocation, in the American poetic consciousness.

Emerson did talk about types and tropes, and did make a distinction between them. Thus "the term 'genius' . . . implies imagination," and imagination sees in two ways: "symbols" and "figurative speech"—that is, types and tropes. Emerson echoed Coleridge's discrimination when he remarked that "the possi- bility of interpretation lies in the identity of the observer with the observed," but when the soul "plays with resemblances and types, for amusement," Fancy speaks, not Imagination. The difference is that "Fancy joins by accidental resemblance," while "Imagination uses an organic classification." To be explicit, Nature offers herself to the eye of the beholder not just as "picture-language" but as a panorama of "types."[46] In this roundabout way Emerson rediscovered his instinctive New England sense of types not by reading Edwards or the Puritans but by reading Swedenborg and Coleridge and the German Transcendentalists.

The circle became for Emerson the symbol of the relationship between the central identity and its circumambience finally concentered on the Platonic One. Many of the citations from Emerson in this discussion have invoked the circle image. From the viewpoint of the observer in "the centre of beings," "the eye is the first circle; the horizon which it forms is the second; and throughout nature this primary figure is repeated without end." So the activity of the "universal soul" in the "round day" moves in circles: "Throw a stone into the stream, and the circles that propagate themselves are the beautiful type of all influence [etymologically, flowing in]"—that is, "the type of Reason." Consequently, at the moment of identification between observer and observed "the currents of the Universal being circulate through me." Since "the visible creation is . . . the circumference of the invisible world," the "bard" has "a crystal soul,*/ Sphered and concentric with the whole."[47] The circle is the perfect figure because it is self-completing yet always in motion tracing out its inclusive sweep.

At times Emerson's discussion of the "radical [that is, from the root] correspondence" between man and Nature sounded exactly like Edwards. His response to the question, "Is there no intent of an analogy between man's life and the seasons?" differentiated between two kinds of analogy:

> Whilst we see that it [language] always stands ready to clothe what we would say [i.e., in tropes], we cannot avoid the question whether the characters are not significant of themselves [i.e., whether they are not types]. Have mountains, and waves, and skies, no significance but what we consciously give them as

*The phrase recalls (consciously or not) Coleridge's Neoplatonic image of natural forms as a perfect crystal irradiated with light.

emblems of our thoughts [as tropes]? The world is emblematic [i.e., typological]. Parts of speech are metaphors because the whole of nature is a metaphor of the human mind.

*   *   *

This relation between the mind and matter is not fancied by some poet, but stands in the will of God.[48]

However, the more closely Emerson's remarks are scrutinized and weighed, the more unclear does his sense of nature as a "metaphor" for the mind become, and so the more unstable and uncertain is his sense of types. To Emerson, Swedenborg's "theological bias . . . fatally narrowed his interpretation of nature," for he, like Edwards, "fastens each natural object to a theological notion." Unlike the poet, the mystic tries vainly and perversely to "nail a symbol to one sense" or interpretation, whereas "all symbols are fluxional," "all language is vehicular and transitive," and "the quality of the imagination is to flow, and not to freeze." For this reason Emerson renounced such mysticism as "the mistake of an accidental and individual symbol for an universal one." The perception of Beauty in which variety coalesces as unity, as Coleridge had said, is neither static nor complete; it is an insight into process. We cannot grasp the entire design and hold it in our heads; we can only become aware of the flow and of the interconnection, even coexistence, of all things in the flow, as Taoism had taught the Chinese for centuries. Therefore, the revelation comes not as a mechanical reduction of disparity to order but as a miraculous metamorphosis: "the moment of transition, as if the form were just ready to flow into other forms." Pound would bypass Emerson and go back to the *Tao* and to Ovid's *Metamorphoses* to recover a vision of process, but Ernest Fenollosa, a latter-day Transcendentalist teaching philosophy in Japan, is Pound's link with the American tradition. In Emerson he could have found a deep sense of the rhythms regulating natural process: "To this streaming or flowing belongs the beauty that all circular movement has; as the circulation of waters, the circulation of the blood, the periodical motion of planets, the annual wave of vegetation, the action and reaction of Nature."[49]

Therefore, while affirming the typology of Nature, Emerson

was—to turn his word against him—radically changing the notion of types. The inherent and established relationship between subject and object and between object and signification was being severely shaken without Emerson's being aware of how subversive his words were or how far the shock-waves would carry. As long as he could make man and Nature correspond through or in the Over-soul, the continuum would remain whole and unbroken; the currents of the Over-soul could circulate through subject and object, and the poet would be seeing types, however fluxional, in the natural flow. This conception of correspondence (poet—Nature—Over-soul) was the balancing point of Emerson's thought, and, as we can see now, a turning point in the development of the American imagination. For if the equilibrium should be upset or disregarded or displaced, then the interpretation of experience would start tilting and sliding in one direction or the other.

The balance could be upset in the direction of the Over-soul, with its omnipotence over the passive poet, to the extent that Nature, the material arena of phenomenological experience, seems to lose its integrity and shade off into the Over-soul. In that case everything—each of us and what we seem to be seeing and feeling and doing—dissolves into a swirling mist of insubstantial illusions. If matter has no objective substance, then individual identity becomes absorbed in the One. The objects which we think we know have no distinct existence; in the Divine Mind or as emanations of the Divine Mind they are a succession of varicolored symbols: a kaleidoscope of momentary impressions. Many passages in Emerson give credence to this strong idealistic tendency. The chapter on "Idealism" in *Nature* raises the "noble doubt" whether anything exists but mind. "Experience" warns that "there is an optical illusion about every person we meet"; since we can never test the evidence of the senses, we can only treat men and women "as if they were real; perhaps they are." The inclination to doubt the reality of matter makes even New Englanders like Emerson and Thoreau find Oriental religion in many ways more congenial to their turn of mind than Christianity, which holds the Incarnation as its central mystery. Emerson wrote poems about "Hamatreya," "Saadi," and "Brahma," but none about Jesus Christ. Later poets in the Emersonian line also turned to Hinduism, Buddhism, and Taoism to express the idealistic elevation of the Bacchic poet: Whitman wondering if this solid-seeming world was all "maya" or illusion, Ginsberg meditating in India and bathing in the Ganges, Kerouac celebrating *The Dharma Bums* and depicting experience as a "mind movie" projected by God in *The Scripture of the Golden Eternity*, Robert Duncan awakening to "an inner view of things."[50]

On the other hand, the equilibrium between poet-Nature-Over-soul could be upset in the other direction as well—shifted, that is, away from the Deity's total presence into the mind of the individual. Here, as before, though for the opposite reason, Nature would be invalidated; this time the object would be subjected to the eye of the observer's mind. No longer typological, nature would be reduced to providing flickering pictures which the beholder could piece and patch together into tropes according to his mood and skill. The poet imposes his mind on nature or uses nature as the mirror for his mind. In either case there can be no sure relationship between subject and object when the distinction between them has been lost. Even when discussing types, Emerson often professed his feeling that "the mind, penetrated by its sentiment or its thought, projects it outward on whatever it beholds," so that "the central identity enables any one symbol to express successively all the qualities and shades of real being." Or, in reverse perspective, nature symbolizes "the passage of the world into the soul of man"; by conforming "things to his thoughts," the poet uses nature "as exponent of his meaning" and "type" of his mind. In the next century Frost would ask of nature "what to make of a diminished thing"; and Stevens would substitute imaginative fiction for the truth of nature: "Poetry is the supreme fiction," so that the poet is "the single artificer of the world" he makes for himself in poetry.[51]

In Emerson's usage the terms "type" and "trope" were becoming so blurred that, while he employed them often, he sometimes used them interchangeably or used one where we might expect the other. When he wrote in the 1870's, "Nature itself is a vast trope, and all particular natures are tropes," it would not have occurred to him that he was exploding the typological axioms he had proclaimed in 1836: "Particular natural facts are symbols of particular spiritual facts. Nature is the symbol of spirit." To him the statements did not cancel one another; they said much the same thing. If it is true that "the Universe is the externization of the soul," it was often not clear whether Emerson was referring to his soul or to the Over-soul, or whether he would have wanted to make such distinctions.[52] At different times he could feel the tug in both directions: toward a phantasmagoria of brilliant shadows in the mind of God and then again toward his own determination of Nature. Both imbalances of correspondence undermined the authority and hence the typology of Nature. It could be argued that Edwards' very emphasis on the individual sense perception of types had already opened the way to this disruption. Perhaps so; in any case by Emerson's time the stable relation between perceiver and perceived in the act of perception had begun to pull apart.

Emerson's effort—some would say heroic, some would say vain—was to stabilize the seesawing balance by fixing the meeting between man and the Over-soul in Nature. In the course of his lifetime the metaphysical terms of reference were becoming increasingly uncertain and shaky, and unwittingly his own imprecision (e.g., about the distinction between types and tropes) helped to demolish them. For Emerson, Nature was the anchor against the assertion on the one hand that "all mean egotism vanishes" when the person becomes "part or parcel of God" and the assertion on the other hand that "nothing is at last sacred but the integrity of your own mind," that "no law can be sacred to me but that of my nature." Later poets concerned with process would continue to locate themselves in Nature amidst a deepening sense of dislocation. Thus Whitman in "Song of Myself": "I accept Reality and dare not question it,/ Materialism first and last imbuing"; thus Williams' insistence: "No ideas but in things"; thus Pound's rejection of both Platonist idealism and Baudelaire's decadent withdrawal into art: "Le Paradis n'est pas artificiel" (Canto 74); in fact Nature "coheres all right/ even if my notes do not cohere" (Canto 116). For Emerson, too, if the human and the divine could not meet and be stabilized and conjoined in Nature, the loss of equilibrium could not but spell disaster: the lapse into self-oblivion or into self-consciousness; in either case, a fall from "the infinitude of the private man." At times Emerson perceived the difficulty: "Gladly we would anchor, but the anchorage is quicksand"; but more characteristically Nature did seem to offer enough stability for man, apotheosized in the poet and awakened by him, to hold against mounting odds this teetering balance: in Olson's phrase, "topos/typos/tropos, 3 in 1." Then the sloughing of egotism and the inviolability of consciousness were, after all, not contradictory but equivalent. Self-reliance and self-transcendence could still cross into consonance: "I become a transparent eye-ball. I am nothing. I see all." In that same late canto, written about 1960, Pound, pondering man's place in nature, wrote: "to 'see again,'/ the verb is 'see,' not 'walk on.' "[53]

IV
EDGAR ALLAN POE:
The Hand of the Maker

At the time when Herman Melville was asking himself whether there was any metaphysical relation between man and nature, he was struck to the quick by Emerson's ideas and responses, although his friends and associates in the New York literary scene could muster nothing but big-city contempt for all things New England and most especially for Transcendental Concord. Melville tried vehemently to rest in an Emersonian belief in correspondences and so in types, and draw his life's conviction therefrom. On one level *Moby Dick* hinges, for Ishmael as well as for Captain Ahab, on the premise of correspondence—and turns to tragedy for Ahab and to disillusioned skepticism for Ishmael. The more Melville reflected on experience, the more he tested the premise, the less evidence he found for assurance. In *Pierre, or the Ambiguities* he voiced his saddened conclusion that there was no correspondence between man and nature: "Say what some poets will, Nature is not so much her own ever-sweet interpreter, as the mere supplier of that cunning alphabet, whereby selecting and combining as he pleases, each man reads his own peculiar lesson according to his own peculiar mind and mood."[1]

It was not Melville, however, with his yearnings toward Transcendentalism, but Edgar Allan Poe who most sharply and stingingly challenged Emerson's philosophical and aesthetic views, from the outset of Emerson's career and some years before Melville had even heard of Emerson. As the most important American poets and theoreticians of poetry in the first half of the nineteenth century, Emerson and Poe stood in bold and deliberate contradiction to one another on almost every point. Where Emerson celebrated the moral order inherent in Nature and where Emerson lived to become something of a venerated national institution, Poe epitomized the dark and dangerous outcast—*le poète maudit*, as Baudelaire would recognize. From the beginning he was more of an "*Isolato*," in Melville's phrase, than Melville himself. Without family, home, income, position—roots of any kind—he wandered feverishly from place to place, acting one role after another: precocious genius, soldier, wronged orphan, martyred poet, grubstreet journalist, southern gentleman, wild-eyed lover, would-be scientist, would-be philosopher, arbiter and scourge of public taste. These were all facets of his life and personality; what made them roles was the recognition underneath the braggadocio that the masks, however flamboyant, were inadequate substitutes for a stable identity. As an orphan he had no place in the Virginia aristocracy whose manners and dress he copied enviously, and he was not at home with the Allans who adopted him. As a Virginian, he stood outside the suspicious literary establishments of New York, Philadelphia, and Boston, and although he sided with the sophisticated New Yorkers against the philosophical New Englanders he found no place to rest anywhere North or South. Society, he came more and more to feel, condemned him to poverty, trapped him in hackwork, and would sooner rather than later drive him to madness and an early death. Poe was in part a self-dooming man, and he wore his bloodied heart on his sleeve as ostentatiously as he could. But if there was much heavy self-dramatization about Poe, his life was in fact filled with melodrama; and if he indulged in self-pity for the mistreatment of genius by the callow world, he unquestionably had ample grounds for complaint about how his compatriots and fate dealt with him.

What comforted (and confirmed) Poe in his fate, what at once explained and glorified his fate, was the sense of himself as a "genius"; that special power proclaimed from the jaws of ruin his triumph, or at least his vindication. If Emerson's "genius" stood at the organic center of things, Poe's "genius" stood apart from the world which turned his marked superiority into the brand of Cain, cutting him off from nature and his fellows. If Emerson's genius could join hands with Wordsworth's, Poe's sprang, muffled in a dark cape, from the forehead of the Byronic hero. Yet like Childe Harold or Manfred, who wanted at heart nothing so much as escape from the tyranny of ego into a Wordsworthian harmony with Nature, Poe could also feel that "it was our *sense of self* which debases, and which keeps us debased." Man's farthest reach is the unshackled moment when "the soul ... separates itself from its own idiosyncrasy, or individuality, and considers its own being, not as appertaining solely to itself, but as a portion of the universal Ens." However, in its very independence genius seems self-defeating, coiling back on itself like a devilish serpent, for release comes only "when the spirit seems to abandon, for a brief period, the body ... elevating itself above mortal affairs." Thus the ability to soar is itself the sign of difference which thereby sets the genius apart from nature and his fellows and condemns him to dwell alone in his *"sense of self."* The person who is gifted or rather accursed

> with an intellect *very* far superior to that of his race . . . would be conscious of his superiority; nor could he (if otherwise constituted as man is) help manifesting his consciousness. Thus he would make himself enemies at all points. And since his opinions and speculations would widely differ from those of *all* mankind— that he would be considered a madman, is evident. How horribly painful such a condition! Hell could invent no greater torture than that of being charged with abnormal weakness on account of being abnormally strong.[2]

Nonetheless, for all his attempts to cast the blame for his fate on his envious and scheming inferiors, Poe, like Byron, was too much the Calvinist, willy-nilly, not to regard the person who held himself above the limits of common humanity and the laws of common morality as Satanic—self-damned like Prometheus and Faustus. An obsessive motif in Poe's writings is the "imp of the perverse," which compels the guilty individual to precipitate his deserved punishment on himself. All the hints of demonism and diabolism underscore the conviction that the preternatural powers of genius incur damnation and indeed are their own hell, as Marlowe's Mephistophilis and Milton's Satan knew.

Even in terms of mortal life individuals who "soared above the plane of their race" could expect a shameful end "in prison, in Bedlam, or upon the gallows" at the hands of the churlish masses or of the vengeful gods. And even should he escape such public execution, his lifespan would be brief. Like the thunderbolt, he is consumed in his own incandescence; like the earthquake or other natural force which seems to exceed the frame of nature, his upheaval is destructive.

After the flash life is a flagging attempt to recapture that intensity:

> There are few men of that peculiar sensibility which is at the root of genius, who, in early youth, have not expended much of their mental energy in *living too fast*; and, in later years, comes the unconquerable desire to goad the imagination up to that point which it would have attained in an ordinary, normal, or well-regulated life. The earnest longing for artificial excitement,

which, unhappily, has characterized too many eminent men, may thus be regarded as a psychal want, or necessity,—an effort to regain the lost,—a struggle of the soul to assume the position which, under other circumstances, would have been its due.[3]

The statement comes from Poe's last years, during which he became increasingly haunted by foregone chances and inescapable disaster. He had no explanation, but the opportunity for action and response seemed canceled out by a sense, almost a memory, of some essential and initial harmony now beyond recall. "Alone," found after his death but written when he was about twenty, expresses this paralyzing sense of doom all the more effectively for its relative restraint and compression among Poe's poems:

> From childhood's hour I have not been
> As others were—I have not seen
> As others saw—I could not bring
> My passions from a common spring—
> From the same source I have not taken
> My sorrow—I could not awaken
> My heart to joy at the same tone—
> And all I lov'd—*I* loved alone.
> *Then*—in my childhood—in the dawn
> Of a most stormy life—was drawn
> From ev'ry depth of good and ill
> The mystery which binds me still—
> From the torrent, or the fountain—
> From the red cliff of the mountain—
> From the sun that 'round me roll'd
> In its autumn tint of gold—
> From the lightning in the sky
> As it passed me flying by—
> From the thunder, and the storm—
> And the cloud that took the form
> (When the rest of Heaven was blue)
> Of a demon in my view—

Emily Dickinson was to come to much the same conclusion: that loss and alienation are primary, incapacitating us for subsequent thought and action and for ordinary mortal satisfactions. The "demon" which beset the genius kept him at odds with flawed nature and inadequate human nature, and so lured him to his death rapt in the dream of an ideal harmony lost from the outset,

if it ever existed at all. "Dreams," written even before "Alone,"
concludes with these lines:

> I have been happy, tho' but in a dream.
> I have been happy—and I love the theme—
> Dreams! in their vivid coloring of life—
> As in that fleeting, shadowy, misty strife
> Of semblance with reality which brings
> To the delirious eye more lovely things
> Of Paradise and Love—and all our own!
> Than young Hope in his sunniest hour hath known.

The genius, then, did not look with Emerson's "transparent eye-
ball" into the heart of things but with a "delirious eye" at his private fantasies. And the more tantalizing the dreams of Paradise
were or seemed, the more confused became "semblance" and
"reality," until "semblance" unseated "reality." With "vision"
gone, everything faded into "A Dream within a Dream," written
in his last year:

> You are not wrong, who deem
> That my days have been a dream:
> Yet if hope has flown away
> In a night, or in a day,
> In a vision, or in none,
> Is it therefore the less *gone*?
> *All* that we see or seem
> Is but a dream within a dream.

The Romantics frequently symbolized the memory or dream-
image of the lost ideal in the glimmering figure of a beautiful
woman: either a spirit or a will-o-the-wisp lady so unearthly that
she was snatched away by an early death. Shelley's Alastor spent
his life pursuing the "veil'd maid" who came to him in a brief
dream; in Melville's *Mardi*, Taji sailed the Pacific in a lone quest
for the elusive Yilla; in his last hours Manfred glimpses his dead
Astarte again. With Poe the symbol took a more ghoulish turn,
but it is in the context of the lost lady-spirit or spiritual lady that
we must read Poe's famous statement (otherwise merely maudlin
necrophilia) that "the death . . . of a beautiful woman is, unquestionably, the most poetical topic in the world—and equally it is
beyond doubt that the lips best suited for such topic are those

of a bereaved lover."[4] The body, like all things mortal, is corrupt; and Beauty, like all things incorruptible, breaks free of temporal clay. Release comes in death when the spirit sloughs the body at last. Transfixed by the idea of "supernal Beauty," Poe wrote many melancholy rhapsodies for dead ladies: "Lenore," "The Sleeper," "Ulalume," "Annabel Lee"—all really names for the idea of the "One in Paradise." Where the early death of Emerson's wife Ellen only confirmed and deepened his transcendental affirmation of life, the death of Poe's frail girl-wife in 1847 only confirmed his high and tragic calling to the grave.

For no mundane object was worthy of or adequate to the powers of genius. Tennyson is "the noblest poet that every lived" because "no poet is so little of the earth, earthy." An engraving of Byron and Mary Chaworth, whom Byron had loved in his youth, provided the opportunity for Poe to describe the genius for whom the lady is merely the empty vehicle or receptacle for his own feelings and aspirations:

> It was a passion (if passion it can properly be termed) of the most thoroughly romantic, shadowy, and imaginative character. It was born of the hour, and of the youthful necessity to love, while it was nurtured by the waters and the hills, and the flowers and the stars. It had no peculiar regard to the person, or the character, or to the reciprocating affection of Mary Chaworth. . . . The result was not merely natural or merely probable, it was as inevitable as destiny itself. . . . Whatever of warmth, whatever of soul-passion, whatever of the truer nature and essentiality of romance was elicited during the youthful association is to be attributed altogether to the poet. If *she* felt at all, it was only while the magnetism of *his* actual presence compelled her to feel. If *she* responded at all, it was merely because the necromancy of *his* words of fire could not do otherwise than exhort a response. In absence, the bard easily bore with him all the fancies which were the basis of his flame—a flame which absence itself but served to keep in vigor. . . . She to him was the Egeria of his dreams—the Venus Aphrodite that sprang, in full and supernal loveliness, from the bright foam upon the Storm-tormented ocean of his thoughts.[5]

At what point does self-expression become self-indulgence and "soul-passion" become narcissism? Poe did not raise or even hint at the question here. In *The Confessions*, Jean-Jacques Rousseau spoke in much the same terms (but more frankly and perceptively) of his own psychological and emotional nature. But for Poe the gap between the poet's yearnings and life's possibilities was even greater than it was for Rousseau or Byron—was indeed an ever more precipitous threat to his sanity. Poe's inconsolable longing for the ideal beyond his reach pitched him past human relationships into a turbid and shadowy area in which there was nothing for him but to drown in the "fancies" of his "soul-passion." In the end the ideal could be conceived only in perverse and neurotic terms. The genius, it turned out, did not soar on bodiless wings into the empyrean, leaving his *"sense of self"* behind in the world of things; instead, his overreaching spun him down into the maelstrom of the psyche, terrified and fascinated at his descent into the underworld. Icarus and Narcissus were the two faces of genius. Poe's anima, imaged as the women in his poems and stories, was perverted into a death-force, luring him siren-like to drown in his own turbid depths.

Allen Tate saw so much of himself, both as a Southerner and as a modern man, prefigured in Poe that he called an essay on Poe "Our Cousin, Mr. Poe" and entitled that collection of essays *The Forlorn Demon.* For Tate, what makes Poe seem a close relative is the fact that Poe lived out the drama of the human personality divided against himself: the claims of body and spirit in conflict; intellect, emotion, and will unhinged from one another and operating independently, as though the rationalist philosophers since Descartes who had analyzed modern man into separate faculties had made it impossible for him to exist any longer as an organic entity. The result is not only that identity remains a void but that it is no longer possible to function within "the human scale." Alienated from himself and from his world, the individual is thrown back on his own emptiness; if contact, communication, and compassion, experienced most deeply in love, are not possible, then engagement with himself or anything outside himself will turn into aggressive conflict: feeding on one another or on one's self, vampirism or narcissism. Hence, in Tate's analysis, the symptomatic, almost prophetic quality of the psychological and spiritual world of Poe's poetry and fiction: "A nightmare of paranoia, schizophrenia, necrophilism, and vampirism . . . in which the natural affections are perverted by the will to destroy."[6]

The fragmented psyche in conflict with the body which it is

meant to animate, is, says Tate invoking a phrase from Jacques Maritain, "an angel inhabiting a machine." Calvinism, emptied of an active conviction of the Incarnation, leaves the body dead and the soul damned. The body is corruptible and so corrupting, and the soul, incapacitated by its own disintegration, strives in vain to be a pure spirit, like an angel or, more blasphemously, God. What's more, such an attempt at absolute existence is not only blasphemous; it is doomed to self-damnation. A living death, existence can only blunder somnambulistically to its conclusion.

Poem after poem witnesses to the doom of this existence at odds with itself. "Sonnet—Silence" begins with a reference to "a double life, which thus is made/ A type of that twin entity which springs/ From matter and light, evinced in solid and shade." Thus there is "a two-fold *Silence*–sea and shore–/ Body and soul." The first silence is that of the dead body and of the bereaved mourner for his absent loved one; the second, much more terrifying silence is that of "his shadow," unburied, disembodied, and wandering lost. The ambiguity of "his shadow" turns the lost love into the shade or spirit of the man himself, for the mortality which splits lover from beloved is only an external manifestation of the fundamental division within each person. Experience reveals types not of the One, as in Emerson, but of the Two. The stories and poems which enact the tragedy of love are all projections of a psychological conflict. The man and the woman are aspects of Poe's psyche, but where in Taylor and Emerson and Whitman they strive to combine in different ways and on different grounds into an androgynous wholeness, in Poe they always face the chasm of the grave.

"To One in Paradise" states the paradox of the "love"-poems most generally. The first stanza identifies the woman as the "all" for which the poet's soul pined, and then images that in Edenic terms: "A green isle in the sea, love,/ A fountain and a shrine,/ All wreathed with fairy fruits and flowers." The word "fairy" only confirms our sense that the landscape is ideal and artificial— and solipsistic: "And all the flowers were mine." Besides, the verbs are all in the past tense, and the inevitable death of the beloved, long since accomplished, has turned the psychological landscape into a scene of blight: a "thunder-blasted tree" and a "stricken eagle" unable to soar. The poet is left, torn between

Past and Future, retreating into "trances" and "dreams" of the "one in Paradise," but, unlike D. G. Rossetti's voluptuous "Blessed Damozel," Poe's lady is faceless and bodiless: an angel freed from the machine. Characteristically in these "love"-poems, the poet is the surviving mourner of his lost anima, but in a late poem, "For Annie," when Poe felt his own death upon him, the poet depicts himself lying in bed "so composedly" that "any beholder/ Might fancy me dead," and the memory of Annie is so overwhelming that she looms like Death herself. With him "bathing in many/ A dream" of Annie and finally "drowned in a bath/ Of the tresses of Annie," the poem finds its resolution: "And the fever called 'Living'/ Is conquered at last."

One of the most painful aspects of Poe's plight is his own awareness of how far below the sublime possibilities of genius his actual accomplishments fell. He could invoke the shades of Marlowe and Byron and Moore by making "Tamerlane" and "Al Aaraaf" the title poems of his first two volumes of verse; he could attest to the stirrings of genius within him; but in the 1845 "Preface" to his collected poems he surveyed his poetic work and dismissed "these trifles" with a weary arrogance as defensive as it is self-deprecating:

> I think nothing in this volume of much value to the public, or
> very creditable to myself. Events not to be controlled have
> prevented me from making, at any time, any serious effort in
> what, under happier circumstances, would have been the field of
> my choice. With me poetry has not been a purpose, but a
> passion; and the passions should be held in reverence; they must
> not—they cannot at will be excited, with an eye to the paltry
> compensations, or the more paltry commendations, of mankind.[7]

He often solaced himself and justified himself by parading as a genius before the clowns who called the tricks, but in the end he could not evade the damning recognition of his failure nor resist condemning the clowns for whom he paraded.

"Israfel" dramatizes Poe's double face: the poet he aspires to be and the poet he is. The genius Israfel hovers above the vicissitudes of earth in a realm—neither paradise nor earth—where thought and passion are absolute; in Olympian remove he sounds the full diapason of his moods so purely that his songs influence the movements of the spheres:

And they say (the starry choir
  And the other listening things)
That Israfeli's fire
Is owing to that lyre
  By which he sits and sings—
The trembling living wire
Of those unusual strings.

.   .   .   .

The ecstasies above
  With thy burning measures suit—
Thy grief, thy joy, thy hate, thy love,
  With the fervor of thy lute—
  Well may the stars be mute!

Against Israfel is set the earthbound singer:

Yes, Heaven is thine; but this
  Is a world of sweets and sours;
  Our flowers are merely—flowers,
And the shadow of thy perfect bliss
  Is the sunshine of ours.

If I could dwell
Where Israfel
  Hath dwelt, and he where I,
He might not sing so wildly well
  A mortal melody,
While a bolder note than this might swell
  From my lyre within the sky.

The poignancy of these lines lies in the unrealized potentiality; if in fact he is inferior to Israfel he might have been as great or greater.

The contrast between "Israfel" and Emerson's angel-poet "Uriel" is telling. For both Emerson and Poe man falls into the abysm of selfhood; but where Emerson found his way out by identifying the self with the "Aboriginal Self" of the Over-soul, Poe saw only the shattered and irrecoverable fragments. Unlike Israfel, Uriel actually falls from the heavens into nature and into isolation, but this "lapse" initiates "the procession of a soul in matter." The ending of "Uriel" is more equivocal than Emerson generally is, but the "procession" through Nature is begun. In

"Israfel," however, there is no chance of reconciliation or accommodation between the ideal of the poet and the paltry reality; the free spirit floats above the defilement of matter.

In the end the gentle Emerson delivered no more devastating indictment of Poe's verse than Poe heaped on himself in the rueful "Preface" to *The Raven and Other Poems,* and Emerson could have summed up the deficiencies of Poe's moral and philosophical outlook no more succinctly than Poe's own statement that for him "flowers are merely—flowers." Most of Poe's poems are (as he seemed to acknowledge) failing attempts to soar: overwrought technically as well as emotionally, straining by the wilful exercise of rhetoric for the escape or breakthrough which he could not, or could not because of his cultural situation, achieve.

As "Sonnet—Silence" indicated, Poe's soul, personified in the anima-figure of the woman, was not his visionary light but "his shadow," and his identification of the psyche with the shadow made Poe not only a shadow-figure for nineteenth-century America but also the archetypal shadow for the whole American consciousness. There were others to dissent from the progressive optimism of the American Romantic age, for which inventors like Robert Fulton and David McKay were the technological geniuses and Emerson the chief philosopher and poet. There were writers other than Poe to question the Emersonian Transcendentalism they felt as a powerful force: Hawthorne, F. G. Tuckerman, Melville, Emily Dickinson. Dickinson's sharing with Poe a taste for macabre, necrophiliac sentimentality, as shown in some of her love poems and in the indulgence of both for the popular women versifiers of the period, illustrates a similar turn that the Calvinist sensibility took in New England and Virginia in the mid-nineteenth century. But because of the extreme state of emotion which his fiction and poetry expressed and because of the desperate life which culminated in an early death, Poe was for his contemporaries and for more recent writers the most notable instance in America of the *poète maudit,* the poet as shadow.

When Whitman reread Poe in 1880, it seemed to him that Poe contrasted with figures like Burns, Byron, Schiller, and George Sand. These other writers, he felt, were geniuses because they pressed on toward the never-attained ideals of virtue and heroism, but Poe was some more perverse kind of genius:

Almost without the first sign of moral principle, or of the
concrete or its heroisms, or the simpler affections of the heart,
Poe's verses illustrate an intense faculty for technical and abstract
beauty, with the rhyming art to excess, an incorrigible propensity
toward nocturnal themes, a demoniac undertone behind every
page—and, by final judgment, probably belong among the
electric lights of imaginative literature, brilliant and dazzling, but
with no heat.[8]

This judgment was conditioned, as Whitman admitted, by his
own prescription for the poet, yet even Whitman had to acknowledge that although "non-complying with these requirements,
Poe's genius has yet conquer'd a special recognition for itself and
I too have come to fully admit it, and appreciate it and him."
Whitman even paid public homage to Poe. One of the significant
literary footnotes of the period is the fact that the ailing and
paralytic Whitman went out of his way to attend the ceremonial
dedication of a plaque to Poe at his Baltimore grave—the only
major literary figure who came to the ceremonies.

By acknowledging Poe, Whitman was recognizing just how
symptomatic, as well as sympathetic, a figure he was. In his
outcast state he was so representative of the time and place that
Whitman could not deny the "indescribable magnetism about the
poet's life and reminiscences, as well as the poems." Since poets
were the "calibres" of their age, Poe's brief career flared up as an
alarming danger signal to the man who wanted only healthy
and democratic songs. Poe has always had a wide and steady
audience across a wider spectrum of social and educational levels
than most American poets have attracted. Whitman might well
ask what Poe's popularity and notoriety (much greater than his
own at the time and since) disclosed about the psychological and
moral state of America.

The lush and the weird that have taken such extraordinary possession of Nineteeth century verse-lovers—what mean they? The
inevitable tendency of poetic culture to morbidity, abnormal
beauty—the sickliness of all technical thought or refinement in
itself—the abnegation of the perennial and democratic concretes
at first hand, the body, the earth and sea, sex and the like—and
the substitution of something for them at second or third hand
—what bearing have they on current pathological study?

Since Poe's decadent self-absorption called into question all the premises of Whitman's moral and aesthetic life, who was the more accurate calibre of the age? Perhaps the face beneath the robust and smiling American mask was twisted and neurotic.[9]

Obviously Whitman saw in Poe's face (or mask) his own antagonistic anti-self. Certain passages in *Leaves of Grass* give us glimpses of a morbid and tormented Whitman, and "Edgar Poe's Significance" in *Specimen Days* explicitly makes the connection between the two men. Whitman tells of a dream in which "no great fullrigg'd ship, nor majestic steamer" but a "superb little schooner" was "flying uncontroll'd with torn sails and broken spars through the wild sleet and winds and waves of the night." The lone human aboard was "a slender, slight, beautiful figure, a dim man, apparently enjoying all the terror, the murk, and the dislocation of which he was the centre and the victim." In this recollection long after the dream, Whitman remarked that the figure "might stand for Edgar Poe, his spirit, his fortunes, and his poems—themselves all lurid dreams."[10] But Whitman was revealing something more, or at any rate different, from his words. Since he was not dreaming of Poe at the time, the man on the lashed and driven ship could only be an image of the dreamer himself. Hindsight allowed him to call the figure Poe, but the figure was not Poe. Poe came to Whitman's mind because he had acted out Whitman's secret nightmare of his own possibilities to their perilous end.

When T. S. Eliot came to designate the "landmarks" of American literature, the names he chose were not New Englanders like Emerson or Hawthorne or Dickinson but the oddly matched trio of Poe, Whitman, and Twain, because each in his own way exemplified "strong local flavor combined with unconscious universality." His remarks about Poe are particularly interesting. In contrast to those of Whitman and Twain, Poe's settings were not identifiably American but imaginary—places in some psychic region, even when they were designated as Paris or Venice. Yet, Eliot argues, Poe's very ignorance of Europe served him well as an American artist; it allowed him to imagine "Europe" as a fantastic version, or rather inversion, of contemporary America. His dream-scapes were nightmares of his own life and circumstances:

> Perhaps all that one can say about Poe is that his was a type of imagination that created its own dream world; that anyone's dream world is conditioned by the world in which he lives; and that the real world behind Poe's fancy was the world of the Baltimore and Richmond and Philadelphia that he knew.[11]

Like Whitman, Eliot was seeing Poe's work as the shadow-image of the society he knew all too well, bent as it was on bourgeois, capitalist success; it traced out the weird pattern woven in the underside of the tapestry scene.

An important part of Poe's shadow quality is his Southern roots. The Civil War only acted out the tragic fact that for many reasons the Southerner and the Northerner are one another's fratricidal shadows. But the direction of history, epitomized in the outcome of the Civil War, has cast the Yankee in the dominant role and the Southerner as the Cain-brother, linked with Negro slavery, and therefore repressed and victimized as a vindication of the white Northerner's rectitude. But such psychological and sociological projection is not exorcism, and the Southern imagination, forced to confront and admit its own shadow, has found its strength in that encounter and has haunted the Northerner with its dark vision of itself—and himself. In the dialectic of the American consciousness it has been the function of Southern writings to body forth the most violent impulses and most sinister motives of the American mind and let them work out their destructive wills—in the fiction of Twain, in Faulkner's saga of Yoknapatawpha County, in the plays of Tennessee Williams, in the Gothic tales of Eudora Welty, Carson McCullers, and Flannery O'Connor, just as much as in the poems and stories of Poe. Tate made that recognition explicit for his generation of Southern writers, and the nominal rejection of Romanticism by him and John Crowe Ransom, like that by Yvor Winters, stems from the realization in Poe and in a contemporary like Hart Crane that the Romantic imagination can turn reckless and propel the genius into lunacy, isolation, death, and suicide. But the proclivities which Poe personified were real, even to those who saw them as dangerous. Narcissism and vampirism are recurrent themes in Tate's work, and Ransom's poems, like many of Tate's, dramatize the isolation of the divided personality and the theme of death, especially the death of a beautiful woman. In part we are our shadows, or at least cannot ever exorcise them completely, however much part of our minds may wish to deny it; and that fact, reinforced by the ineffectuality of the denial, helps to account for the magnetism of Poe's personality and the perennial popularity of his writings: a magnetism and popularity that cannot be fully accounted for on intrinsic aesthetic merits alone.

2

At the same time, Poe's personality is associated with—and was even more forcefully during his own time associated with—a distinctive set of literary qualities and manners as well as a distinctive set of critical standards and procedures. As a twentieth-century Virginian, Ellen Glasgow saw "the Southern essence in his genius":

> Poe is, to a large extent, a distillation of the Southern. The formalism of his tone, the classical element in his poetry, and in many of his stories, the drift toward rhetoric, the aloof and elusive intensity,—all these qualities are Southern. And in his more serious faults of overwriting, sentimental exaggeration, and lapses, now and then, into a pompous or florid style, he belongs to his epoch and even more to his South.[12]

Even where the impact of his style was not felt, the importance of his critical position has been deeply registered. Eliot, for example, had little good to say for Poe's style but saw himself in a line descending from him; for Poe's personality and imaginative vision issued in critical assumptions and a theory of poetry which had stimulated and shaped symbolist poetry since the mid-nineteenth century on the Continent, in England, and in America.

As is always true, Poe's theory arose from the immediate literary situation in which he was struggling to write. Lack of money and position forced him into journalism, and he cranked out articles and reviews for the money which would allow him, he hoped, to write the poetry that was his most serious commitment. The achievement of these scattered pieces, taken together, is therefore all the more astonishing. For Edmund Wilson they add up to "the most remarkable body of criticism ever produced in the United States." Unaffected by Poe's style or themes, Wil-

liam Carlos Williams saw Poe's opposition to the literary establishment as a "single gesture . . . to sweep all worthless chaff
aside," a necessary and therapeutic "gesture to BE CLEAN," "to
clear the GROUND" for original and *"local* literature." In most
obvious ways Williams is closer to the Emersonian tradition of
organic poetry than to Poe's formalism, and he would have dis-
agreed with many of Poe's particular judgments and opinions.
Despite all that, Williams argued that on Poe "is FOUNDED A
LITERATURE," because his criticism "gives the sense for the
first time in America, that literature is *serious.*"[13]

A perusal of Poe's reviews shows that they were on the
whole amazingly just and perceptive: substantiated by argument,
exemplified by specific example, and as often as not enthusiastic.
Nevertheless, his contemporaries feared him with good reason,
because his words could be corrosive. For instance, on one occasion he surveyed the literary scene and pronounced that
"among all the *pioneers* of American literature, whether prose or
poetical, there is *not one* whose productions have not been over-
rated by his countrymen." By "becoming boisterous and arrogant
in the pride of a too speedily assumed literary freedom," we "often
find ourselves involved in the gross paradox of liking a stupid
book the better, because, sure enough, its stupidity is American."
His judgments cut through the crust of received opinion. He implied that Emerson was just "aping" Carlyle; he declared that
Bryant's verse, "even in its happiest manifestation, is not of the
highest order"; he scrapped with Longfellow, Lowell, and most of
the influential literati North and South.

Nevertheless, beneath the now unimportant details of his
squabbles burned the belief, or the desire to believe, that *"we are
a poetical people"*: "Because we were not all Homers in the beginning, it has been somewhat too rashly taken for granted that
we shall be all Jeremy Benthams to the end. But this is the purest
insanity."[14] And if Poe's concern for American writing made him
attack some of the literary lions, it could also make him lenient
at times in encouraging some of the literary lambs. Because Poe
loathed a "hyperpatriotic" adulation of American arts on the one
hand and a cowed subservience to foreign models on the other,
his criticism had in turn to scourge, evaluate, educate, and en-

courage. Even his disgust with America, like Ezra Pound's a century later, was a twisted hope for genuine culture. For Poe, again as for Pound, only canons of taste and judgment which transcended a cheap contemporary nationalism could train Americans to recognize artistic excellence and discipline them to attain it: "As if any true literature *could be* 'national'—as if the world at large were not the only proper stage for the literary *histrio*."[15] Though Poe never had the chance to travel abroad (except for a time in England with the Allans as a teenaged boy), he belongs in that native line of cosmopolitans from Washington Irving and Cooper to Pound to Tate, which includes as well such nontraveling internationalists as Wallace Stevens and Yvor Winters. Although Poe was in fact more provincial than he realized, or at any rate would admit, he excoriated the greater provinciality of his America in a determined, if sometimes condescending, effort to initiate a milieu in which the arts could take hold in America.

Time and again Poe turned his exacting attention to the basic constitutive element of the poem: language. Literature was, no matter what Emerson or Bronson Alcott might intone, words composed into sentences and rhythms and rhymes, and the critic's primary task was to analyze the means and effects of language. Since flowers were merely flowers, words were no more than words. "An Orphicist—or a SEER—or whatever else he may choose to call himself, while the rest of the world calls him an ass," would have us believe that his idea is "so vast—so novel— that ordinary words, in ordinary collocations, will be insufficient for its comfortable evolution." Then, Poe reasons, the seer's only honorable option is silence "until some Mesmeric mode of intercommunication shall be invented, whereby the antipodal brains of the SEER and of the man of Common Sense shall be brought into the necessary *rapport*." If the befogged Transcendentalists had no respect for the instrument they wielded, he took proud satisfaction in being the writer "who has spent more time in analyzing the construction of our language than any living grammarian, critic, or essayist."[16]

Consequently his reviews fasten on the linguistic materials and techniques of writings: diction, syntax, rhetoric, scansion, versification, texture, punctuation; they are a poet's meticulous comments on the practice of the craft. Often he reviewed a volume poem by poem; here, for example, are his observations on "To a Waterfowl" from a long discussion of Bryant's *Poems*:

> The *Waterfowl* is very beautiful, but still not entitled to the admiration which it has occasionally elicited. There is a fidelity and force in the picture of the fowl as brought before the eye of the mind, and a fine sense of *effect* in throwing its figure on the background of the "crimson sky," amid "falling dew," "while glow the heavens with the last steps of day." But the merits which possibly have had the most weight in the public estimation of the poem, are the melody and strength of versification (which is indeed excellent) and more particularly its *completeness*.[17]

This general remark is then substantiated by examining particular phrases and lines. Poe's consideration of textual details can be so exhaustive that at one point he takes several pages to demonstrate how a seemingly extra syllable in a given line actually operates to calculated purpose, and for evidence he presents analogous lines for comparison and contrast of their metrical effect. Poe's reviews often anticipated what I. A. Richards would call "practical criticism," and Poe was in point of fact our first textual critic a century before John Crowe Ransom named the New Criticism and Cleanth Brooks, Yvor Winters, and R. P. Blackmur turned their exacting attention to the poem as object to be analyzed and explicated. Whatever gaffs Poe made in overestimating some authors and underestimating others, he brought to American criticism for the first time the rigorous standards and systematic method of a pseudoscience.

Indeed, all Poe's writings—fiction and verse as well as criticism—are characterized by the effort to master materials by method and to reduce method to system; it was the mind's attempt to triumph over its muddled situation. Poe went so far as to argue that "man's chief idiosyncrasy being reason," the unselfconscious simplicity of the savage—whom sentimental folly would dub "noble"—was the "*un*natural state" of man; cultivated civilization marked man's rational advance over barbarism.[18] Some of Poe's most interesting essays were written during his last years as a final effort at asserting design out of disintegration. "The Rationale of Verse" tried to discard outmoded notions of versification falsely adapted from classical models in favor of a system of scansion based on musical time as the closest to mathematical precision. The idea is less convincing than the determination with which Poe constructs his argument from examples. His most ostentatiously programmatic essay, "The Philosophy of Composition" (1846), explicates "The Raven" in order to show how the composition "proceeded, step by step, to its completion with the precision and rigid consequence of a mathematical problem."[19] Whether or not Poe actually wrote the poem with as much conscious planning as he would have us believe—and that seems difficult to accept—conscious planning was, he insists, the governing purpose and theoretical goal. "The Poetic Principle," a lecture published posthumously in 1850, is a last summing-up, rehearsing his fundamental ideas about poetry with copious illustrations of effective poetic language.

For language, if handled with the trained skill of a scientist or technician, can be made to impose order—or a semblance of order—on the tumult of experience and draw from it the beauty of design. Words specified things, and because naming lent shape and color to shadows, it made clarity (and if you will, sanity) possible:

> It is certain that the mere act of inditing, tends, in a great degree, to the localization of thought. Whenever, on account of its vagueness, I am dissatisfied with a conception of the brain, I resort forthwith to the pen, for the purpose of obtaining, through its aid, the necessary form, consequence and precision.

The pen provides "the necessary form, consequence and precision." Nothing could have seemed to Poe more destructive of the poetic principle than the nonsense about "organic form" which Emerson and the Transcendentalists were noising about: he dismissed it as that false "species of poetry" in which "some natural phenomenon is observed, and the poet taxes his ingenuity to find a parallel in the moral world. In general, we may assume, that the more successful he is in maintaining the parallel, the farther he departs from the true province of the Muse."[20]

The poem is generated, as Wallace Stevens would also come to conclude sadly, from the realization that the phenomena of experience are a jumble of unrelated impressions, not types of a divine order. Indeed, method and form are necessary precisely in order to remake images of experience into tropes and figures of speech and fix them in a relationship found in and founded on the artifices of language. The poem—its images, words, and verbal structure—does not fill the gap between object and idea, nature and spirit; but it offers a positive substitute: an achieved *objet d'art*, a tapestry of tropes, in which images, extracted from nature and arranged purposefully, are invested with infinite suggestions and "*indefinite* sensations, to which end music is an *essential*." The analogy between music and poetry proceeds from the possibility of combining mathematical structure with intangible nuance: "Music, when combined with a pleasurable idea, is poetry; music without the idea is simply music; the idea without the music is prose from its very definitiveness." The sublime possibilities of music and verse lie in the conviction that their "*indefinite* sensations" are echoes of, perhaps intimations of, at least gestures toward, a "supernal Beauty." (Stevens would later write "Notes toward a Supreme Fiction.") "Supernal Beauty" remains disembodied, beyond even the artist's grasp, and yet it is the only theme commensurate with the powers of the artist.[21]

Only in the artifact can the artist realize or recognize in an object outside himself any reflection of his finest aspirations. Since the inaccessibility of the supreme poetic idea demonstrates the failure of nature, the poet can only speak in tropes, not types. Consequently he must rely on his disillusioned genius or, on a lower level, his craft, to project what is not there or intimate what remains out of sight. In other words, he is constrained to make a fictional world since he cannot remake this one, so that his creation supplies what actual things lack: "form, consequence and precision." As the looseness and openness of organic form proceed from a notion of natural and metaphysical order, so in Poe this emphasis on structure and technique, as is true of many other formalists as well, derives from a sense of chaos: fallen nature, original sin, metaphysical uncertainty. In other words, form follows from flux in resistance to it: a positive statement against nihilism, like the wave in Frost's "West-Running Brook" rising against the stream's downward flow. Stevens' baroque ornamentation and musical effects, like Poe's, are a countermeasure to "the malady of the quotidian." Two later Stevens collections are called *Ideas of Order* and *Parts of a World*. And even for poets who choose a chaster, plainer style, form has a similar function. Frost described a finished poem as "a momentary stay against confusion"; J. V. Cunningham described the disciplined discriminations of his verse in the title *The Exclusions of a Rhyme*; Edgar Bowers called his first collection *The Form of Loss*.[22] Cunningham and Bowers would insist that theirs is an unillusioned look at the world, no fictional substitute; but it remains true for them, as for Yvor Winters, with whom they studied, that verbal constructions provide the necessary terms and forms for skeptical, stoical statements about the world as it is.

By contrast, Poe and Stevens often turn their powers of perception—decadently, Winters, Cunningham, and Bowers, even Frost, would say—to consciously dreaming another world, the dream itself often obsessed by the corruption of the flesh, the torments of the spirit, and the hopelessness of the Ideal. However, by planned arrangement and careful execution and a happy chance of mood, Poe and Stevens believe, the poet may at times succeed where nature has failed. Such an assumption is the basis of Poe's "Philosophy of Composition":

> Nothing is more clear than that every plot [or poem], worth the name, must be elaborated to its *dénouement* before anything be attempted with the pen. It is only with the *dénouement* constantly in view that we can give a plot its indispensable air of consequence, or causation, by making the incidents, and especially the tone at all points, tend to the development of the intention.

In other words, the work of art is a self-fulfilling world, sealed off from nature's carelessness and completing its assumptions, intentions, and expectations. "Having chosen a novel, first, and secondly a vivid effect," the writer sifts through the means at his disposal to concoct "such combinations of event, or tone, as shall best aid [him] in the construction of the effect," until the composition attains "its ultimate point of completion," in which "consequence" and "tone" sustain one another. The skilled artist could only reject those who would subvert the disciplines of the art by airily claiming spontaneous inspiration. For Poe such "Emersonizing in prose, Wordsworth-izing in poetry" falsifies the artistic process and denies the artist the respect he has earned and merited. "The Philosophy of Composition" is a withering attack on what Poe takes to be the fakery of any conception of art as "ecstatic intuition":

> Most writers—poets in especial—prefer having it understood
> that they compose by a species of fine frenzy—an ecstatic
> intuition—and would positively shudder at letting the public take
> a peep behind the scenes, at the elaborate and vacillating crudities
> of thought—at the true purposes seized only at the last moment—
> at the innumerable glimpses of idea that arrived not at the
> maturity of full view—at the fully matured fancies discarded
> in despair as unmanageable—at the cautious selections and
> rejections—at the painful erasures and interpolations—in a word,
> at the wheels and pinions—the tackle for scene-shifting—the
> step-ladders and demon-traps —the cock's feathers, the red paint
> and the black patches, which, in ninety-nine cases out of the
> hundred, constitute the properties of the literary *histrio*.[23]

Poe is not arguing here that the poetic impulse is mechanical and technical; only that poetic practice is. Poetry begins in the aspiration toward Beauty—not the beauty of some limited object but ideal Beauty itself. That aspiration is "an immortal instinct," "a thirst unquenchable," "the desire of the moth for the star":

> Inspired by an ecstatic prescience of the glories beyond the grave,
> we struggle, by multiform combinations among the things and
> thoughts of Time, to attain a portion of that Loveliness whose
> very elements, perhaps, appertain to eternity alone.

In other words, the poet is inspired to undertake, within and against his limits, the work of contrivance. The poem is pure (or rather impure) artifice, but the choice and execution of proper means can achieve an effect. The poem can excite and elevate the soul with a pleasure (quite naturally mixed with pain) by gesturing toward a Beauty more ethereally complete than mortality can contain. Brooding on Poe, Baudelaire would come to find the origin of our sense "correspondences" between nature and heaven in "this immortal instinct of the beautiful":[24]

> It is at the same time by poetry and *through* poetry, by and
> *through* music that the soul glimpses the splendors beyond the
> tomb; and when an exquisite poem brings us to the verge of

tears, those tears are not the proof of excessive pleasure; they are rather evidence of an aroused melancholy, of a condition of nerves, of a nature which has been exiled amid the imperfect and which would like to take possession immediately, on this very earth, of a revealed paradise.

Consequently, all the wits and labors of the poet are bent toward the impossible task of sharpening the "vague and therefore . . . spiritual *effect*" to "definitiveness" of verbal expression. Since "supernal Beauty" is "not a quality, as is supposed [by the Transcendentalists], but an effect," "originality . . . is by no means a matter, as some suppose, of impulse or intuition," and for that reason "it is an obvious rule of Art that effects should be made to spring from direct causes—that objects should be attained through means best adapted for their attainment." The artist's singular effort is to create—cause—"unity of impression" through the handling of materials which either resist his touch or crumble beneath it. Craftsmanship, then, is essential for two reasons: to give form to the formless and to contrive intimations of the unrealized Ideal.[25] Poetry manipulates its limited means to press against its limits; it proceeds scientifically to contrive an elegy for—and a substitute for—ecstasy. Thus the poem is not only its own means but also its own meaning, self-validating. The subject of art is itself, as Stevens too would argue, like his jar constellating the surrounding wilderness of Tennessee simply by its presence there.

3

The basic mistake which the Transcendentalists made was reliance on philosophic truth and metaphysical absolutes. For Poe it is the heresy of metaphysics which destroyed Wordsworth's talent and "the heresy of *The Didactic*" which "turns into prose (and that of the very flattest kind) the so-called poetry of the so-called transcendentalists."[26] Poetry is not Truth but Beauty, and Beauty and Truth (no matter what Plato, Wordsworth or Emerson, Keats or Emily Dickinson might say) are distinct qualities. What made Poe so violent in his denunciation of Emerson and his disciples was his own agonized need for metaphysical certitude and personal stability, but since "metaphysics is at present a chaos" he had to seek design elsewhere—in aesthetics instead of metaphysics:

> I would define, in brief, the Poetry of words as *The Rhythmical Creation of Beauty*. Its sole arbiter is Taste. With the Intellect or with the Conscience, it has only collateral relations. Unless incidentally, it has no concern whatever with Duty or with Truth.

Not that aesthetics was metaphysics *manqué*; it had its own peculiar and autotelic quality—the integrity not of Poetry in the abstract but of "the Poetry of words," i.e., the poem on the page which is only itself:

> There neither exists nor *can* exist any work more thoroughly dignified—more supremely noble than this very poem—this poem *per se*—this poem which is a poem and nothing more—this poem written solely for the poem's sake.[27]

Against the belief of Emerson and Whitman that mere skill with language indicated only "poetical talent" and not poetic genius, Poe insisted that if genius yearned for more than words, it had only its vague aspirations and the materials of his art; his genius came down to his talent with words, which could at least give form to his aspirations in tropes and rhythms. Coleridge had dissociated the insights of the Imagination from the language of Fancy, but Poe's rejoinder denied the distinction by reducing both to Fancy: "The Fancy as nearly creates as the imagination, and neither at all. Novel conceptions are merely unusual combinations." Where Emerson wanted to see through the "transparent eyeball" into Nature, Poe would prefer to avert his gaze: "We can . . . double the true beauty of an actual landscape by half closing our eyes as we look at it." Nature was never for Poe the source of inspiration; in fact, genius "flashes from the unopened eye."[28] Only with eyes closed or half-closed or averted could the artist reconstruct the raw materials within the limits of his medium into the finished product:

> In the hands of the *true* artist the theme, or "work," is but a mass of clay, of which anything (within the compass of the mass and quality of clay) may be fashioned at will and according to the skill of the workman. The clay is, in fact, the slave of the artist. It belongs to him. His genius, to be sure, is manifested very distinctively in *the choice* of the clay.[29]

The hand of the craftsman, not the eye of the seer. If nature is flux and metaphysics chaos, then the artist could master his materials either by articulating the disorder or reconstituting its elements into a new order. Most of the poems and stories move from a relatively stable situation or a recollected impression of wholeness toward disintegration, catastrophe, madness. The elaborate patterning of the poems and the elaborate plotting of the fiction allow at least a description of "The Descent into the Maelstrom," as one story is called; the centripetal pressures of form contain artificially the dispersive and entropic energies which are the law of nature and of the psyche.

Moreover the individual could also pit his powers of mind and imagination against the confusion by engaging it more directly; herein lie the satisfactions of the mystery or detective story and the fictional fantasy. In the mystery story Poe could show the masterminding detective applying his powers of induction and deduction in order to explain the disorder and reduce the confusion to motive; he could not prevent or undo the crime but after the fact he could hold the unraveled mystery in his head. In the fictional fantasy Poe could dream awake a reconstructed world. "The Domain of Arnheim" is Poe's response to Edward Taylor's divine garden and, more pointedly, to Emerson's *Nature*. It contrasts the natural landscape with the fancied landscape and pronounces the superiority of artifice over nature: "No such combination of scenery exists in nature as the painter of genius may produce. No such paradises are to be found as have glowed on the canvass of Claude."* The proportions of Nature are marred by "many excesses and defects" which offend the "artistical eye," but against the irrevocable loss of Eden the landscape gardener can create the artist's vision in three dimensions, by mapping out "a nature which is not God, nor an emanation from

---

*Claude Lorrain (1600–1682), the French painter whose idyllic landscapes exerted a powerful influence over both the neoclassical and Romantic imagination, among poets as well as visual artists. Poe's idealized landscapes—e.g., the one cited earlier from "To One in Paradise"—often recall Claude. Jeffrey A. Hess has argued in persuasive detail that Poe modeled "The Domain of Arnheim" on American landscape: not just on accounts of the Hudson Valley and the paintings of the Hudson River School, as well as Poe's own excursions in that region, but expressly on Thomas Cole's great series of panels, *The Voyage of Life*, and on Cole's printed notes about the paintings; see Jeffrey A Hess, "Sources and Aesthetics of Poe's Landscape Fiction," *American Quarterly*, 22: 2 (Summer 1970), 176–189, esp. 180–184.

God, but which still is nature in the sense of the handiwork of the angels that hover between man and God."[30] As with Israfel, the genius is an angel, more than mere mortal and reaching toward godhead, but capable of a creation more perfect and therefore in a sense more absolute than God's.

In *Eureka: A Prose Poem,* written in the last year of his life, Poe pushed the prerogatives of genius to the extreme by making a direct analogy with Deity. Poe was enough of an eighteenth-century man still (in part because he was an antebellum Southerner) to think of God as the master mathematician and physicist. In *Eureka* the universe, otherwise depicted in Poe's work as a maelstrom, is imagined from the supreme detachment of the God-scientist as a cyclic pattern of movement. Poe's "sublime" theme is nothing less than the cosmological workings of the universe: "*its Essence, its Origin, its Creation, its Present Condition and its Destiny.*" To the scoffer who would remark that such an undertaking would require that "*we should have to be God ourselves!*" Poe had a Promethean rejoinder: "With a phrase so startling as this yet ringing in my ears, I nevertheless venture to demand if this our present ignorance of the Deity is an ignorance to which the soul is *everlastingly* condemned." And with that he set about deifying himself by explaining God's creation as He had not explained it.[31]

Eureka must be read as Poe's final, most heroic and most desperate effort to grasp the flux of time and space as system. He called the book a prose poem because he wanted to transcend the distinction he felt between logic and intuition, identify eighteenth-century reason with Transcendental Reason, and concentrate the whole psyche, integrated at last, to his high purpose. Dedicating the book to Alexander Von Humboldt, part of whose *Kosmos* had recently been published, Poe insisted that it be read "as an Art-Product alone:—let us say as a Romance." If the poet were the scientist, and vice versa, perhaps the synchronicity of reason and imagination might yield not just data and fantasy but a vision of the universe both intuitive and demonstrable, both transcendent and precise. Baudelaire would describe the genius in precisely such synthesizing terms: "For a long time I have said that the poet is *supremely* intelligent, that he is *intelligence* par excellence—and that *imagination* is the most *scientific* of the faculties, because it alone understands *universal analogy*, or what a mystic religion calls *correspondence*."[32]

Emerson and Poe saw the same fundamental question, even if they diverged in responding to it. Emerson spoke of reconciling "the one and the two," and Poe set out in *Eureka* to reduce "the *extent* and *diversity*" of the universe to "the sublimity of its *oneness*." Poe's approach was neither metaphysical nor humanist nor ethical, for he could accept no philosophical explanation; instead, *Eureka* has the diagrammatic clarity of an abstract intellectual problem worked out by a wild and frenzied imagination with the lucidity of lunacy. But if *Eureka* reads like nonsense or madness, it is serious nonsense and compelling madness, for it is trying to deny the absurdity of chaos by concocting an absurdly logical plan. Poe's last fantasy unriddles the perfect plot of the astronomical detective story; therein the artist reveals himself once and for all as master scientist, and the scientist as master-dreamer. To his own satisfaction the angel has blueprinted the machine and patented it in his own name.

The outline of *Eureka* is simple enough. God first posited Himself into a single solid particle of matter, an All-Atom, which at the moment of its creation exploded into the myriad particles that comprise the planets, satellites, and galaxies. The physical laws of matter work out the conflict of contradictory forces: the dispersive force which propels atoms farther and farther apart, out and out into the infinite void; and the gravitational attraction of atoms for one another. According to Poe's theory, the material universe has expanded as far as it can go; now that gravity has overcome the energy of dispersion, atoms, planets, and stars are moving back together with accelerating speed toward their original center. Explosion has become implosion, or, as Poe puts it, "My general proposition, then, is this:—*In the Original Unity of the First Thing lies the Secondary Cause of All Things, with the Germ of their Inevitable Annihilation*." For Matter is only "*Spirit individualized*," and the reversion to Unity would dissolve Matter, particularized in the operations of the time-space machinery, back into Spirit. In that final moment when all things, hurtling through space, smash back into the original atom, the atom would again become God: "All will return to Nothingness in returning to Unity," and "God would remain all in all." Then perhaps "the Heart Divine" will dilate and contract in further pulsations of Matter, diffusing and concentrating again and again. From this distance, exceeding geological aeons, the convulsions of material objects, even of human beings, turn into "the perfect plot" of God, and the poet's comprehension of that plot transforms what would be apocalyptic catastrophe into apocalyptic revelation.[33]

Eureka declares the triumph of Spirit over corruptible Matter and the triumph of the poet's mind over the vast riddle of its existence. The poet's apotheosis becomes explicit in the last paragraphs: "And now—this Heart Divine—what is it? *It is our own.*" The genius is God. In fact, since God "passes his Eternity in perpetual variation of Concentrated Self and almost infinite Self-Diffusion," all creatures are in essence "infinite individualizations of Himself." This is the reason why "no thinking being lives who, at some luminous point of his life of thought, has not felt himself lost amid the surges of futile effort at understanding, or believing, that anything exists *greater than his own soul.*" Most especially the genius comes to realize not just "a proper identity" but in that "an identity with God." Consequently where it had previously seemed that genius could only elevate nature into art, as in "The Domain of Arnheim," now it turns out—or so Poe was trying frantically to convince himself here at the end—that the mental and imaginative thrust of genius toward design brings him at last to perceive the divine energy which propels all nature according to its appointed and ordained eschatology. The fantasy-argument which began as cosmic Materialism or Pantheism—God transmogrifying Himself into material creation—reveals itself as a weird Idealism—creatures dying into Spirit, history dying into vision. Poe ends up matching Emerson in giving his version of typology; "phaenomena," he says (even using Edwards' phrasing), are but "spiritual shadows." Here are the final words of *Eureka*:

> Think that the sense of individual identity will be gradually merged in the general consciousness—that Man, for example, ceasing imperceptibly to feel himself Man, will at length attain that awfully triumphant epoch when he shall recognize his existence as that of Jehovah. In the meantime bear in mind that all is Life—Life—Life within Life—the less within the greater, and all within the *Spirit Divine*.

But having achieved that point of elevation, how could one live "in the meantime"? Helen Whitman, who knew Poe well in the years after Virginia's death, said that after *Eureka* there was nothing left for him to do but die. Poe made the same declaration in a letter to Virginia's mother, and in fact he did not live out the following year.[34]

4

However, since Poe's life was lived for the most part as the genius of a merely mechanical universe, his poems register on this lower level the conflict between dispersion and gravity which regulated his cosmology. To begin with, the peculiar mingling of clarity and haze which characterizes most of Poe's fiction and verse is the result, among other factors, of the particular interaction of intuition and logic which constituted for him the process of literary expression. The finest and most "spiritual" moments, he said, were those ideas and intimations which came often in the limbo between sleep and waking and which always emerged "*so shadowy as to escape our consciousness, elude our reason, or defy our capacity for expression*"; and at that exact point arose the necessity for conscious and rational concentration toward expression. Orphicists like Emerson might claim that language was inevitably inadequate to the idea, but for Poe inchoate intuition would dissipate itself without language. If he could hold the fancies that hover between dream and vision long enough to transfer them "*into the realm of memory*," he could "survey them with the eye of analysis" and fix them as words. At such times of exalted creative realization his "faith in the *power of words*" was "entire."[35]

When we read Poe's lines, the words and images often seem too disembodied or too detached from the ostensible subject or point of reference. Many of the poems cited in this chapter illustrate the point. Even in so famous and admired a piece as "To Helen" the language spins out on the rhymes a diffuse succession of free-floating associations; these associations are meant to avoid descriptive detail and instead surround Helen's beauty— the subject announced in the opening words—with an opaque atmosphere, but they threaten to befog the subject with dense irrelevancies.

143

Helen, thy beauty is to me
  Like those Nicéan barks of yore,
That gently, o'er a perfumed sea,
  The weary, way-worn wanderer bore
To his own native shore.

On desperate seas long wont to roam,
  Thy hyacinth hair, thy classic face,
Thy Naiad airs have brought me home
  To the glory that was Greece
And the grandeur that was Rome.

Lo! in yon brilliant window-niche
  How statue-like I see thee stand,
The agate lamp within thy hand!
  Ah, Psyche, from the regions which
Are Holy-Land!

The phrases and figures seem intended for tonal and atmospheric coloration or alliterative and onomatopoetic effect—in short for their abstract suggestive quality rather than strict or consistent contextual pertinence.

However, what has been taken as mere carelessness or imprecision or indulgence by many critics (including Eliot) must be seen as the deliberate attempt to make language catch these shadows shimmering just beyond the conscious mind. The paradox in Poe's literary theory lies in the conviction that only the passive and dreaming mind (we might say the unconscious) can give passage to these phantom shades, but only the craftsman's cunning can keep them from vanishing into the light of day. The *"power of words,"* therefore, is evocative and symbolic; they seek to "embody even the evanescence of fancies." Once again, there appear more affinities between Poe and Emerson than they, and many critics after them, have wanted to admit. But the differences between their sense of language and form can be summarized in the fact that while Emerson's symbols are natural, Poe's are artificial and literary, contrived for their incantatory effect in the work itself.

Poe could not have been nearly so deliberate about his incantation as he wanted to claim, any more than Emerson was as ecstatically spontaneous as he wanted to claim. Each man was taking a strong theoretical position, in part out of deliberate opposition to the other's attitude. Poe's memorable poems—for all their murky diction and imagery, the Gothic baggage and ornamentation, the blurring of edges and connections—do have a kind of "logic," or at least sequence, but in large part because of the qualities listed above the "logic" strikes us as surreal and not rational. The hallucinatory effect indicates that Poe's best work is a projection from the unconscious in a way that "The Philosophy of Composition" refuses to acknowledge. But like much surrealist work (for example, Salvador Dali's or Giorgio di Chirico's paintings) and unlike automatic writing or spontaneous composition, Poe's best poems and stories are those in which he ordered his hallucinations to form. The achieved effect has the inexplicable but credible movement of dream or nightmare.

Much more exclusively than is true for the other poets discussed in this book, Poe's psyche is his muse—so suffocatingly that a major theme is being buried alive in one's grave (or the grave of one's self) and the characteristic effect of his stories and poems is a gasping claustrophobia. In his recent study of Poe, David Halliburton has pointed to the theme of containment: "Poe's created world is a series of containers, each of which is itself contained in a container, and so on, through an expanding series to the universe itself."[36] But where such a system of ontological boxes establishes for Edward Taylor the providential scheme of the universe, Poe's Calvinist sense of damnation makes him see the box as the death-trap: the coffin, crypt, pit, where the corpse is walled in. *Eureka*, as we have seen, is Poe's climactic effort to pitch himself beyond a deterministic existence verging toward nothingness. In response to the sense of being boxed in, man must create his own containers; in art as in life, forms, conventions, decorums are necessary precisely because they enclose the void or the death-throes that lapse into the void.

We have already mentioned the configuration of poems (there are stories as well) explicitly about Poe's psyche personified as the beloved woman, despite her various names a single image of his doom: his anima expiring young or buried alive, leaving him a talking dead man. They are poems of crisis, even hysteria, but the crisis is detached from the continuity of living, as though it hung suspended and encapsulated in the poet's mind. The form, with its rhyme and meter and sound effects, seals the poem into an echo chamber resonating the only live voice, the poet's. Neat structure and obscure reference—the combination characterizes his best work.

A number of poems develop a geographical conceit, often contrasting landscape with the architecture of a building or a city. The poems read like the map of a maze or the arranged irrationality of a surrealist scene. For example, "The City in the Sea":

Lo! Death has reared himself a throne
In a strange city lying alone
Far down within the dim West,
Where the good and the bad and the worst and the best
Have gone to their eternal rest.
There shrines and palaces and towers
(Time-eaten towers that tremble not!)
Resemble nothing that is ours.
Around, by lifting winds forgot,
Resignedly beneath the sky
The melancholy waters lie.
No rays from the holy heaven come down
On the long night-time of that town;
But light from out the lurid sea
Streams up the turret silently—
Gleams up the pinnacles far and free—
Up domes—up spires—up kingly halls—
Up fanes—up Babylon-like walls—
Up shadowy long-forgotten bowers
Of sculptured ivy and stone flowers—
Up many and many a marvellous shrine
Whose wreathéd friezes intertwine
The viol, the violet, and the vine.

Resignedly beneath the sky
The melancholy waters lie.
So blend the turrets and shadows there
That all seem pendulous in air,
While from a proud tower in the town
Death looks gigantically down.

There open fanes and gaping graves
Yawn level with the luminous waves;
But not the riches there that lie
In each idol's diamond eye—
Not the gaily-jewelled dead

Tempt the waters from their bed;
For no ripples curl, alas!
Along that wilderness of glass—
No swellings tell that winds may be
Upon some far-off happier sea—
No heavings hint that winds have been
On seas less hideously serene.

But lo, a stir is in the air!
The wave—there is a movement there!
As if the towers had thrust aside,
In slightly sinking, the dull tide—
As if their tops had feebly given
A void within the filmy Heaven.
The waves have now a redder glow—
The hours are breathing faint and low—
And when, amid no earthly moans,
Down, down that town shall settle hence,
Hell, rising from a thousand thrones,
Shall do it reverence.

The poem has a linear "plot" of sorts, in which suspended movement gives way to action, but what sustains the poem is the hyp-
notic spell of sound and imagery. It is difficult to discern exactly
what and where this place is, what it represents, what the visual
images depict, why particular details are noted, or even what is
happening. All we can say is that the tyranny of Death grips the
Atlantis-like city "down within the dim West" (at the ends of the
earth, an American ultima Thule? at the boundaries of Time or
of one's lifetime? in the farthest recesses of the psyche?) and that
the city is disturbed at last from its death-in-life, life-in-death
suspension, not to be roused into life but to subside once and for
all into the infernal abyss beneath the sea.

"The Haunted Palace" is more obviously plotted:

In the greenest of our valleys
    By good angels tenanted,
Once a fair and stately palace—
    Radiant palace—reared its head.
In the Monarch Thought's dominion,
    It stood there!
Never seraph spread a pinion
    Over fabric half so fair!

Banners yellow, glorious, golden,
   On its roof did float and flow—
(This—all this—was in the olden
   Time long ago)
And every gentle air that dallied,
   In that sweet day,
Along the ramparts plumed and pallid,
   A wingéd odor went away.

Wanderers in that happy valley,
   Through two luminous windows, saw
Spirits moving musically,
   To a lute's well-tunéd law,
Round about a throne where, sitting,
   Porphyrogene,
In state his glory well befitting,
   The ruler of the realm was seen.

And all with pearl and ruby glowing
   Was the fair palace door,
Through which came flowing, flowing, flowing,
   And sparkling evermore,
A troop of Echoes, whose sweet duty
   Was but to sing,
In voices of surpassing beauty,
   The wit and wisdom of their king.

But evil things, in robes of sorrow,
   Assailed the monarch's high estate.
(Ah, let us mourn!—for never morrow
   Shall dawn upon him, desolate!)
And round about his home the glory
   That blushed and bloomed,
Is but a dim-remembered story
   Of the old-time entombed.

And travellers, now, within that valley,
   Through the encrimsoned windows see
Vast forms that move fantastically
   To a discordant melody,
While, like a ghastly rapid river,
   Through the pale door
A hideous throng rush out forever,
   And laugh—but smile no more.

The palace, explicitly the seat of "Monarch Thought's dominion," symbolizes the psyche; the "story" represents the derangement of the psyche. Still, the "haunting" effect of the poem lies not in its allegory but in the witchery of sound and imagistic detail. Whether the symbols of "The Haunted Palace" and "The City in the Sea" are translated from the poet's dreams or invented for his purpose, their reference and relevance derive not from nature (as Emerson's symbols would) or from any verifiable frame of reference but from their place in the poem as a recreation of a state of mind.

Poe had no immediate disciples in America, except perhaps Sidney Lanier, who was significantly a fellow Southerner. Though Lanier liked to minimize his indebtedness to the more famous and notorious Poe, they both exhibited an overwrought and fevered sensibility which manifested itself in elaborately rhymed verse; in fact, Lanier's *Science of English Verse* draws on his musical knowledge to develop Poe's analogy between meters and the length and tonality of musical notes. Nevertheless, although Poe generated few immediate disciples and successors, as Emerson did, he remained a powerful presence, because, as the shadow-figure of the American nineteenth century, he continued to be read widely and avidly. Moreover, he had a transformative influence abroad. French *symboliste* poets like Baudelaire, Rimbaud, Mallarmé, and Valéry saw his poems and stories—and the theory behind them—as extraordinarily original departures which anticipated and spurred on their own experiments with the values and aims of language. Poe had defined the poem in aesthetic terms as an almost musical structure of symbols, in which the selection and combination of elements register, in and of the pattern itself, subtle and indefinable effects. Looking back over the century-long Symbolist movement in "From Poe to Valéry," Eliot summarized its source and final development:

> Here we have, brought to their culmination by Valéry, two notions which can be traced back to Poe. There is first the doctrine, elicited from Poe by Baudelaire, which I have already quoted: 'A poem should have nothing in view but itself'; second the notion that the composition of a poem should be as conscious and deliberate as possible, that the poet should observe himself in the act of composition.[37]

Poe's theory, therefore, came to exert a profound, if indirect, influence on many English and American poets of the twentieth century through the intermediary influence of the French Symbolists, and many of them have come to recognize Poe as a precursor—"our Cousin, Mr. Poe," as Allen Tate called him. In the long run the lone figure of Poe cast a long shadow which has fallen at various angles on such different poets as Eliot, Stevens, Tate, Hart Crane, Robert Lowell, and Richard Wilbur—all formalists of one kind or another.

5

Just before the middle of the last century, when there was a literary awakening so astonishing that it came to be called the "American Renaissance," Emerson and Poe enunciated two extreme and diametrically opposed conceptions of the poet based on contradictory assumptions about the relation between the poet and his experience and the poem he writes from his experience. It is emblematic of the yeasty divisions of that exploratory period that both poets acknowledged the precept and example of Coleridge in stating their opposite theories. Emerson drew on Coleridge's Transcendental metaphysics, on his notions of the Imagination and organic form, and on his religious and moral reflections. Poe regretted Coleridge's philosophical penchant and instead revered him as a pioneer in "psychological science" and as a practical literary critic very much concerned with the details of poetic technique. Poe snorted that the publication of the *Biographia Literaria* in America would not only introduce "a work of great scope and power" but also "do away with the generally received impression here entertained of the *mysticism* of the writer." Far from being the expansive Transcendentalist, Coleridge was to Poe another angel caught in the machine: "a 'myriad-minded man,' and ah, how little understood, and how pitifully vilified!" Superior to the public and yet tragically dependent on it, "he not only sacrificed all present prospects of wealth and advancement, but in his inmost soul stood aloof from temporary reputation." His genius is attested to by the fact that his "great mental power," though "conscious of its greatness," was nonetheless capable of "submitting to the indignities of the world."[38]

Since Poe would have liked to believe all this of himself as well, it is clear that he is seeing Coleridge in the same Byronic mirror in which he saw himself reflected.

From the outset, therefore, American Romanticism was Janus-faced, and Emerson and Poe were each other's anti-self or shadow: Emerson's ruddy vigor persisting into the sage's venerable old age, Poe's brilliance burning itself out at mid-career in a dark, violent, but expected death. Their different conceptions of the poet proceeded from their different personalities and situations. For Emerson the poet was ideally a Dionysian god, voicing instinctively the organic order of things under the spell of the divine frenzy; for Poe he was ideally an Apollonian god extending his masterful hand over the confusion of things in the shaping act of language. The development of modern American poetry has been a complicated extension of the dialectical interaction between these two polar positions.

V
WALT WHITMAN:
The Self as Circumference

Regularly, but perhaps most notably in "The American Scholar," Emerson felt compelled to call upon Americans to shrug off the literary tyranny of Europe, and especially of England, as they had shrugged off political tyranny decades before, so that native artists and writers could emerge in full power and invest us with the moral energy which the political opportunity required. Toward the end of the essay on "The Poet" Emerson spoke of the advent of the bard in tones which mingle anticipation with disappointment: impatience that he had not yet come, assurance that his arrival must be at hand.

> I look in vain for the poet whom I describe. We do not with sufficient plainness or sufficient profoundness address ourselves to life, nor dare we chaunt our own times and social circumstance. If we filled the day with bravery, we should not shrink from celebrating it. Time and nature yield us many gifts, but not yet the timely man, the new religion, the reconciler, whom all things await.

Emerson prophesied that the "timely man" would proclaim the "new religion" in the celebratory chants of "our own times and social circumstances" and thus reconcile the waiting masses to a sense of American identity and destiny. The "tyrannous eye" of the genius would see in "the barbarism and materialism of the time" "incomparable materials" for the "new religion" of American democracy, which would take its place in the history of Western man after the paganism of the ancients, the Catholicism of the Middle Ages, and the Protestantism of the modern era. At the prospect Emerson spontaneously incanted a catalogue of some of the "incomparable materials" America offers its poetic titan:

> Banks and tariffs, the newspaper and caucus, Methodism and Unitarianism, are flat and dull to dull people, but rest on the same foundations of wonder as the town of Troy and the temple of Delphi, and are as swiftly passing away. Our logrolling, our stumps and their politics, our fisheries, our Negroes and Indians, our boats and our repudiations, the wrath of rogues and the pusillanimity of honest men, the northern trade, the southern planting, the western clearing, Oregon and Texas, are yet unsung. Yet America is a poem in our eyes; its ample geography dazzles the imagination, and it will not wait long for metres.

Although admittedly Emerson could not as yet find in America the realization of this "idea of the poet," he certainly would never find him anywhere in the long annals of European literary history. The new epic would be sung by a native bard, for "when we adhere to the ideal of the poet, we have our difficulties even with Milton and Homer. Milton is too literary, and Homer too literal and historical." Still the disconcerting fear was that "we have yet had no genius in America."[1] The Tenth Muse had still to spring up in the New World.

"The Poet" was published in 1844, and within a few years this prophetic call reached a Brooklyn printer and journalist named Walter Whitman, who found that Emerson's words served to crystallize all his own developing dispositions. Whitman may have heard Emerson lecture in New York as early as 1842, and was certainly reading Emerson by the late forties—with particular intensity during the early fifties when he was writing his first poems. There were other, more "foreign" influences; for example, Roger Asselineau summarizes the case to be made for Thomas Carlyle and George Sand.[2] But Bronson Alcott reported Whitman's attitude in 1856: "Walt thinks the best thing it [America] has done is the growing of Emerson, the only man there is in it—unless it be himself." And in 1860, even after Whitman had differed with Emerson about the sexual element in his poetry, he told his friend J. T. Trowbridge about stumbling on Emerson's writings and becoming enthralled by them; he summed it up with: "I was simmering, simmering, simmering; Emerson brought me to a boil."[3]

What boiled up was a steaming batch of poems, including the one that came to be called "Song of Myself," the collection published in 1855 at his own expense in a book of his own design under the title *Leaves of Grass*. The same year also saw the publication of *The Song of Hiawatha*, and the contrast between the books dramatizes the difference between the poetry of the Tenth Muse and poetry still in the service of the Muses of the Old World.* Longfellow was self-consciously drawing a native legend

---

*In "The Song of the Exposition," commissioned for the National Industrial Exhibition in New York in 1871, Whitman described at length the migration of the Muse from the Old World to the New. Interrupting his long incantation at one point, he gives a wonderfully witty picture of the Muse in technological America:

for an American epic, but the Scandinavian meter in which he incongruously cast the poem betrayed his Europeanized sophistication. Instinctively, Whitman's "chants" launched an American epic more barbarous and autochthonous. The long prose Preface to *Leaves of Grass* whose rhythms and rhythmic structure lead right into the verse, was Whitman's manifesto, and almost point for point he cast himself in the role which Emerson had proclaimed.

Compare the following declarations with Emerson's previously quoted sentiments. The second paragraph picks up Emerson's tone and sounds it more loudly: "The Americans of all nations at any time upon the earth have probably the fullest poetical nature. The United States themselves are essentially the greatest poem." Emerson had said that "America is a poem in our eyes" and identified "its ample geography" as the open field of the imagination. What did this mean? Whitman could give no analytical description, but he could expatiate on what it felt like: "The American poets are to enclose old and new for America is the race of races. Of them the bard is to be commensurate with a people. To him the other continents arrive as contributions . . . he gives them reception for their sake and his own sake. His spirit responds to his country's spirit . . . he incarnates its geography and natural life and rivers and lakes." Not the poet pondering as the theme of his "sacred Art" God's Incarnation in matter and history and man's counter-effort to be joined to God in this divine marriage, as Edward Taylor conceived the function of his private poetry; but the poet himself as national incarnation. In short, a bard identified by and with a polyglot mixture of peoples and a various landmass continental in immensity. The assertion is immediately substantiated in the first of Whitman's catalogues, which echoes and expands upon Emerson's more manageable list for two pages:

> The blue breadth over the inland sea of Virginia and Maryland
> and the sea off Massachusetts and Maine and over Manhattan bay
> and over Champlain and Erie and over Ontario and Huron and
> Michigan and Superior, and over the seas off California and

---

By the thud of machinery and shrill steam-whistle undismayed,
Bluff'd not a bit by drain-pipe, gasometers, artificial fertilizers,
Smiling and pleas'd with palpable intent to stay,
She's here, install'd amid the kitchen ware!

Oregon . . . the tribes of red aborigines . . . the free commerce—
the fisheries and whaling and gold-digging—the endless
gestation of new states—the convening of Congress every
December, the members duly coming up from all climates and
the uttermost parts . . . the factories and mercantile life and
labor saving machinery—the Yankee swap—the New-York
firemen and the target excursion—the southern plantation life—
the character of the northeast and of the northwest and
southwest—slavery.

What was the character of the bard? He is to be a democratic
hero: the center and "equalizer" of his people, their representative and "common referee." He is to be their priest, his teachings
their scriptures, his songs the new rites. He is to be the medium
through which energies and objects move to come to focus and
form: "the channel of thoughts and things" and "the free channel of himself." Preeminently—the secret of it all—"he is a seer"
and his power is his eye. References to sight and insight run
through the description: "What eyesight does to the rest he does
to the rest. Who knows the curious mystery of eyesight?" Moreover, by extension the articulation of the vision is also a mystery
and a law unto itself, at once organic and spiritual:

> The poetic quality is not marshalled in rhyme or uniformity or
> abstract addresses to things nor in melancholy complaints or good
> precepts, but is the life of these and much else and is in the
> soul. . . . The rhyme and uniformity of perfect poems show the
> free growth of metrical forms and bud from them as unerringly
> and loosely as lilacs or roses or a bush, and take shapes as
> compact as the shapes of chestnuts and oranges and melons and
> pears, and shed the perfume impalpable to form.

Hence Whitman's "free verse"—undisciplined by convention or
tradition, liberated from the formal dress of rhyme and stanza
and meter. After all, Emerson had said—whatever impression his
poems might give—that the poet and his poems should grow in
the sun like corn and melons.[4]

Whitman could not resolve the philosophical question of
whether the seer, looking out and looking in, reached the motive
power of Nature, or "complete in himself," wrought his vision on
Nature; in other words, no more than Emerson could he say
whether the mystery of eyesight, in essence, spelled out Incarna-

tion or Idealism. During the connective experience intellectual quibbles about subject and object did not arise, and afterward they were unanswerable. But with Emerson he affirmed the world despite the intuition from time to time that it was all an illusion, and concerning the social function of the bard, his reciprocity with his people, Whitman was clear: "Of all nations the United States with veins full of poetical stuff most need poets and will doubtless have the greatest and use them the greatest"; for "the proof of a poet is that his country absorbs him as affectionately as he has absorbed it."[5] Even when he did not rally the audience he had anticipated, even when he had to learn with some bitterness to bank on assimilation by his country in the future rather than in the present, Whitman never lost the conviction that in time the nation would tally him as he had tallied the nation.

Meanwhile, in the first ecstasy of discovery, he offered the twelve poems of the 1855 edition as evidence that in being himself he was the poet Emerson had called for and had not been able to be. The book was anonymous yet uniquely personal. No name on the title page, cover, or spine; no titles to the poems except that most were called "Leaves of Grass." The author could be identified only by the fine print of the copyright until he named himself well into the first poem. Nonetheless, his presence was pervasive, not only throughout the text but in his design of type, page, and binding. Opposite the authorless title page was the picture of the poet himself: the seer made visible and almost tangible in face and physique, his name to follow from his presence.

The reception of the first edition could not match his expectations. Nonetheless, given the innovations of the poetry and the extravagance of the Preface, it received surprisingly mixed reviews and, by Whitman's testimony, sold its thousand copies. Some discerning reviewers felt and liked what was new in his poetry from the outset, but he could not but be stung by the chorus of jeers and expressions of shocked disgust. In fact, three of the most understanding and adulatory reviews Whitman wrote himself and planted anonymously in friendly periodicals.

In the honored tradition of fledgling poets who wished to announce their arrival to the literary establishment, Whitman sent copies of his book to most of the recognized literati of the time.

Whittier reportedly cast his copy into the fireplace to obliterate its wickedness on the spot. Thomas Wentworth Higginson was to intone some years later that the disgrace was not that Whitman had written the book but that he had not burned it himself afterward. But among the complimentary copies one had been sent, appropriately, to the oracle himself, and soon from Concord came Emerson's astonishing salutation: "I greet you at the beginning of a great career," since "the wonderful gift of *Leaves of Grass*" represented "the most extraordinary piece of wit and wisdom that America has yet contributed." The letter rang with phrases that echoed the disciple's highest hopes: "great power," "free and brave thought," "incomparable things said incomparably well, as they must be," "courage of treatment," "large perception," "solid sense." So overwhelming was Whitman's appearance that Emerson "felt much like striking my tasks and visiting New York to pay my respects." Cosmopolites like Charles Eliot Norton might sniff at "Emerson's enthusiasm" for this "one of the roughs": "It is no wonder that he [Emerson] likes him, for Walt Whitman has read *The Dial, Nature,* and combines the characteristics of a Concord philosopher with those of a New York fireman." Emerson himself described the poems as "a combination of the *Baghavat-Gita* and the *New York Herald*." In other words, a lowbrow transcendentalist, a guru of the people. Still, the patrician Emerson was so sure that he had heard the answer to his summons, in however vulgar tones, that he felt emboldened to recommend the book, not without some fidgety caveats, to his testy friend Carlyle (without knowing about Carlyle's influence on Whitman or the latter's reviews of *Sartor Resartus, Heroes and Hero-Worship* and *Past and Present*); *Leaves* was, Emerson told Carlyle, "a nondescript monster which yet had terrible eyes and buffalo strength, and was indisputably American."[6]

Whitman was as bowled over by Emerson's instantaneous recognition of *Leaves of Grass* as Emerson was by the book. Emerson's response was, beyond question, a decisive factor in Whitman's career: the confirmation of the prophet by the patriarchal sage. Whitman was boiling over into new poems, many of them long. Within a year he published an edition of *Leaves* enlarged from twelve to thirty-two poems. The spine of the 1856 edition now displayed his name with Emerson's words, "I greet you at the beginning of a great career"; the full text of Emerson's letter was printed as an Appendix with a rhapsodic reply from the poet returning the compliment to Emerson as the "Master," "dear Master," "dear Friend and Master" who had pioneered the "new moral American continent":

> Those shores you found. I say you have led The States there—
> have led Me there. I say that none has ever done, or ever can do,
> a greater deed for The States, than your deed. Others may line
> out the lines, build cities, work mines, break up farms; it is yours
> to have been the original true Captain who put to sea, intuitive,
> positive, rendering the first report, to be told less by any report,
> and more by the mariners of a thousand bays, in each tack of
> their arriving and departing, many years after you.[7]

Instinctively, Whitman cast Emerson in the archetypal role of hero-explorer, like Columbus, who would become his own self-image in "Passage to India," "Prayer of Columbus," and "A Thought of Columbus," Whitman's last poem.

However, as Whitman should have anticipated, this maneuver occasioned the first difficulty between the poets. Before reprinting the letter, Whitman had shrewdly neglected to ask of Emerson the permission he might have refused, and Emerson was chagrined at Whitman's bumptiousness in using his avowed "Master" as his unwitting publicist. After this gaucherie the enthusiasm was to cool on both sides. Emerson expressed strong disapproval of the blatant sexuality of some of the poems, especially the "Children of Adam" section added in 1860, and for all his talk about organic form Emerson worried about the long catalogues and the lack of form and meter in *Leaves of Grass*. On Whitman's part the disciple began, predictably, to resent the master (Thoreau had to face the same problem), and as Whitman became in time the center of a circle of awed disciples, he preferred to minimize his indebtedness to Emerson. Moreover, he had specific complaints: Emerson had argued for censoring "Children of Adam"; he had, quite inexplicably, not included a single selection from Whitman in an anthology of American poets he edited in 1872; and visitors to Concord would bring back rumors that Emerson was disappointed in Whitman's development. Consequently, toward the end of his life Whitman wrote out in *Specimen Days and Collect* criticisms he had often made in conversation; Emerson's "cold and bloodless intellectuality" and his "singularly dandified theory of manners" would encourage "a well-wash'd and grammatical, but bloodless and helpless, race" of Americans. In one late letter, and earlier through his friend John Burroughs, he even denied that he had read Emerson before starting *Leaves of Grass*.[8]

The root of the difficulty lay not alone in the difference in background, education, and social class between the two men but in their fundamental temperaments; and the differences were implicit even in the 1855 "Preface" and the 1856 "Letter." In the "Preface" Whitman instinctively saw the poet sexually as the "one complete lover" whose "very flesh shall be a great poem." In the "Letter" he asks of America the usual nervous question of literary nationalists, "Where [are] the born throngs of poets, literats, orators, you promised?"; but his response is cast almost in terms of phallic measurement: "There is no great author; every one has demeaned himself to some etiquette or some impotence. There is no manhood or life-power in poems; there are shoats and geldings more like." Against the prevailing impotence Whitman swaggeringly offered himself to America as mate and sire: "Submit to the most robust bard till he remedy your barrenness. Then you will not need to adopt the heirs of others; you will have true heirs, begotten of yourself, blooded upon your own blood." What's more, the triumph of amativeness between the sexes and of manly friendship would constitute the political union within which individuals would coexist collectively. Finally, not only was Whitman more explicitly sexual and political than Emerson; in the face of Emerson's virtuous rectitude Whitman espoused what seemed like tolerance pushed to the point of indifference: "The greatest poet does not moralize or make applications of morals"; "Men and women and the earth and all upon it are simply to be taken as they are."[9] Whitman found in Emerson's Transcendentalism a philosophical basis for personal vision; his mother's Quaker attitude was unconscious and inarticulate, and he needed the authority and intellectual tradition which Emerson's words provided. At the same time, he came from a large, unstable, uneducated urban family, and in the end his lower-class and metropolitan origins made the difference in Whitman's social and ethical instincts.

Nevertheless, the differences between the poets all correctly noted, the connection between them is more profound and real, and it is to their credit that, despite differences that would perhaps have divided others irrevocably, they respected each other to the end. Emerson received and entertained Whitman, and he responded immediately to Whitman's occasional appeals for help with a publisher. On his part Whitman continued generally to call Emerson the pioneer and trail-blazer, and his account in *Specimen Days* of a visit with Emerson shortly before his death speaks of the master with hushed reverence. This abiding respect on both sides is fitting. After all, if Whitman had gone his own way, he had only followed Emerson's injunction; "His final influence," Whitman said, "is to make his students cease to worship anything—almost cease to believe in anything, outside of themselves." And, after all, Emerson's first instinct was right in hailing Whitman as his heir. That line of transmission, more than Emerson could guess at the time and more than he liked when he guessed it, made Whitman the first fully Dionysian poet in America. Whitman knew it all the time; he kept pictures of Hercules, Bacchus, and a satyr on the walls of his bedroom as emblems and reminders. He embodied the image so successfully that Alcott spoke admiringly of him as "broad-shouldered, rouge-fleshed, Bacchus-browed, bearded like a satyr, and rank."[10]

2

The poem which filled most of the 1855 edition was a sprawling piece without an individual title (all the poems in that initial groundbreaking were only individual leaves of common grass) which was called "Poem of Walt Whitman, an American" in 1856 and thereafter merely "Walt Whitman" until the "authoritative" arrangement of 1881 gave it the title by which it is known: "Song of Myself." It is Whitman's finest and fullest poem and one of the radical works of American literature—more radical than "Crossing Brooklyn Ferry," "Out of the Cradle Endlessly Rocking" and "When Lilacs Last in the Dooryard Bloom'd," not just because it is earlier but because it is a more extended and adventurous exploration of the premises and techniques which make Whitman's poetry revolutionary. Without exaggeration "Song of Myself" can be read as the embryo and epitome of *Leaves of Grass*.

Many Whitman critics, failing to recognize the structural development and accumulating coherence of "Song of Myself" (Pound was to meet the same incomprehension with *The Cantos*), have talked about the poem as an interesting but finally inchoate mélange distinguished by brilliant pieces and passages.*

The revolutionary element in Whitman's poetry, as in William Blake's, is less political than psychological. In many ways Whitman's politics, strictly speaking, were more conservative than Thoreau's or even Emerson's; his mystical conception of the American republic rested on a conviction that the Constitution and the "scriptures" of the Founding Fathers were revealed truth of the new religion: the unchanging guide and gauge, outside of time and America's historical evolution. His notion of America and Americans derived from prophecy rather than politics; his approach was spiritual and psychological, not legislative or socioeconomic, especially when compared, for example, to the gritty way in which Ezra Pound would feel compelled to extend his prophecy into an explicit politics and economics.

From the first lines of "Song of Myself" Whitman left no doubt that he was laying claims to prophecy, and he would later leave no doubt about what he meant by prophecy:

> The word prophecy is much misused; it seems narrow'd to prediction merely. That is not the main sense of the Hebrew word translated "prophet"; it means one whose mind bubbles up and pours forth as a fountain, from inner, divine spontaneities reveal-

---

*Before presenting my own reading of "Song of Myself" as a poetic totality whose experiments foreshadow in many ways some of the boldest efforts in open-form poetry in the twentieth century (I think of *The Cantos*, Williams' *Paterson*, Olson's *Maximus Poems*, Robert Duncan's *Passages*), let me cite some earlier critics who have offered extended—and different—readings of the poem as a whole: Malcolm Cowley, "Introduction" to *Leaves of Grass: The First (1855) Edition* (New York: Viking Press, 1959), pp. x–xxxvii; James E. Miller, Jr., *A Critical Guide to Leaves of Grass* (Chicago: University of Chicago Press, 1957), pp. 6–35; Richard Chase, *Walt Whitman Reconsidered* (New York: William Sloane Associates, 1955), pp. 58–98; Roy Harvey Pearce, *The Continuity of American Poetry* (Princeton: Princeton University Press, 1961), pp. 69–82; Edwin Haviland Miller, *Walt Whitman's Poetry: A Psychological Journey* (New York: New York University Press, 1968), pp. 85–114; E. Fred Carlisle, *The Uncertain Self: Whitman's Drama of Identity* (East Lansing: Michigan State University, 1973), pp. 177–204.

ing God. Prediction is a very minor part of prophecy. The great matter is to reveal and outpour the God-like suggestions pressing for birth in the soul.[11]

Etymologically the word means to "speak for." The prophet speaks for God by singing himself; and even if that does not make man a god (at the end of *Nature* Emerson had said "A man is a god in ruins"), even if God is a transcendent Being, still He can "speak" only through the prophet's human tongue.

No wonder, then, that Whitman states from the outset that his words draw upon and conduct energies and lines of force that move above and below the fallible human ego, clinging as it does to the categories of reason and logic. Moreover, Whitman was far in advance of his time in anticipating later psychiatric discoveries that irrational impulses could not be sorted out into subrational and superrational. Whitman already saw that the id and the superego, to use Freud's labels, were not necessarily locked in conflict; if we did not fear and degrade the libido, if we did not elevate the superego into a stern moralist and intimidating judge, then we could see that the id and superego which create different kinds of problems for the ego are related, perhaps indistinguishable as manifestations of the Life-mystery which the individual ego must learn to acknowledge and assimilate and express. So in its diction, imagery, and associational method Whitman's language is serving an exploratory function, releasing the nameless and striving to name it. And since naming is not just a later reflex of knowledge but the coming-to-know, his poems are no residual analogues of an unanalytical and unanalyzable process; they are the process itself through which irrational forces break— from above, from below: who knows?—into the bright space of ego-consciousness, there to form the individual's gradual comprehension of his nature and capacities.

One of the difficulties of Whitman studies so far has been that such poetry does not lend itself to the investigation of literary criticism, narrowly conceived, and especially not to the pseudo-scientific methods of textual explication, which isolates the words on the page as a code to be broken and finds its most suitable material in the tensions and verbal conundrums of, say, seventeenth-century verse and much twentieth-century verse. Whitman himself, who knew the challenge that he represented, once remarked that because he had never addressed a single word to the intellect in all his writings, his poetry had to be tested on the pulse and nerve-ends and ear. It is not that his poems are above discussion, but that the vocabulary and methods of the "new critics" and their successors are largely irrelevant to the mode of communication in Whitman. As a result, critics have tended either to content themselves with digestible bits—lines and passages and short poems that are recognizably imagist or symbolist in tendency—or to pass over the poems in consideration of Whitman's attitudes and ideas. Either way, the peculiar structure and dynamics of Whitman's kind of poetry have been discreetly ignored. What critics need to do now is to ingest what is happening in Whitman's poetry in order to find ways of describing it, or—perhaps the same thing—to find ways of describing what is happening in Whitman's poetry as a way of understanding it. In short, a different vocabulary and methodology.

Just as organic form assumes process, so the Whitman poem exists temporally in a distinctive way. Traditionally, of course, poetry has been described as a temporal art different from spatial arts like painting or sculpture. But we have come to see that time and space exist only correlatively, so that we now have to reflect on the complex ways in which different artistic modes exist temporally and spatially at once. Thus, poems which derive from a strict formal structure are striving for something like the comprehensible totality and simultaneity of a painting, something like the polished surface of an object that occupies space. Keats's Grecian urn and Wallace Stevens' jar placed in the disordered wilderness of Tennessee, not to mention the poems about them, are designed to achieve this sort of unmoving finality. The techniques of such poems are meant to define dimensions and design, to line out and compose, through selection and discrimination, a delimited and integrated area. In this sense, then, a typical poem of Taylor, Poe, or Dickinson, of Eliot, Allen Tate, or Yvor Winters, is more "spatial" than Whitman's process-poetry. What such "spatiality" means for a temporal art like poetry is that the poem moves, as it is read, from beginning to end and thereby traces out, for all the contrasts and complications involved, a line of development clear and unbroken enough so that the completed poem closes on itself to be grasped as a self-contained and self-containing entity, like a jar or urn. Of course, "spatiality" and "temporality" are not absolute or mutually exclusive terms. Thus the spatial simultaneity of a painting or statue becomes temporal when we "read" it temporally detail by detail, area by area, and all poems have spatial structure of some sort if the elements coalesce into a coherent whole. Whitman's poems have structure and even proportion, but the distinction between Whitman and the other poets mentioned derives, as has already been suggested, from different materials and a different imaginative—that is to say, psychological—engagement with those materials. As a result, the relationship of part to part—and the assumptions behind these modes of relationship—finds a different way of existing in time and space. Whitman's poetry fills the page and characteristically spills over page after page, but it needs all that space to evolve temporally toward its meaning in a way that a poem by Poe or Dickinson need not and cannot. It is not merely a matter of length; the difference in length proceeds from the different ways in which the poems develop.

It was clear to Whitman that divinity, whether a personal God or a Life-force, expresses itself, finds its temporal-spatial form in man, not in terms of his ego but in terms of his passions and his spirit. The creature whom the philosophers dubbed a rational animal, Whitman saw as a spiritual animal, the rational ego providing the individual point of connection between the seeming dualism of sexuality and soul. The function of ego-consciousness is precisely to comprehend what "bubbles up" from the unknown and to absorb it into a fuller awareness of Self and Cosmos. Freud's "id" and "superego" are what Jung preferred to call "instinct" and "spirit," aspects of man's unconscious potentiality twinned in the psyche in direct correspondence to the pairing of psyche and soma to comprise a single person. As the "inner, divine spontaneities" of instinct and spirit become consciously acknowledged through the agency of the ego, the individual discovers that his ego concenters a Self more capacious and mysterious than he could ever have dreamed at the start. So the Whitman poem moves forward in irregular but progressive spurts or cycles, adding and adjusting and changing, finding its way, having to find its way and its form as elements from the unconscious find expression or correspondences in consciousness or in the external world, moving the reader along through this erratic growth, finding completion and dispersal in the reader's own recognition and Self-recognition. If such a description suggests male orgasm and female pregnancy, that is, as we shall see, exactly to the point.

Certain developments in modern literature have paralleled revelations in psychology to make Whitman more accessible to us. In the 1950s the Beat poets invoked Whitman and the Projectivists, clustered loosely around Charles Olson at Black Mountain College, invoked Pound and Williams, as well as Whitman, as antecedents in rejecting the rational criteria of the New Criticism and returning to a poetry of organic process. Through their cumulative influence, poets and students of poetry could recover from Whitman—and, for that matter, from Emerson—what had been misjudged or ignored through the influence of formalist poet-critics like Eliot, Ransom, Tate, and Winters. As open-form poets of the intervening generations, Pound and Williams had felt compelled to resist Whitman at the start because he was so strong a father-figure and because they associated him with Romantic optimism and Transcendental metaphysics; consequently their acknowledgement of Whitman had to come late, after they had achieved their own more self-conscious and intellectualized brand of organicism. By the fifties, however, Allen Ginsberg endorsed Whitman openly, and Olson's connection, though less direct, was no less real. Olson thought that he was reacting against egotism like Whitman's, as Keats had reacted against Wordsworth's "egotistical sublime," and his reaction helps to characterize the difference between Olson's poetry, with its muted but pervasive "I," and Whitman's with its blatantly omnipresent "I." But when in "Projective Verse" Olson derives the rhythm and structure of the poem somatically from breath and pulse and speaks of the poem as an "open field" corresponding to the world the poet occupies, when he describes the spatial "kinetics" of "composition by field" as a transmission of energy from "where the poet got it" through the poem-field to the reader, and when Williams quotes most of Olson's essay in his *Autobiography* as the poetics he had himself been trying to formulate all his life, the line of influence, if not acknowledged descent, becomes clear, and it is a connection between poetic generations which Robert Duncan, if not his friend Olson, has freely recognized.[12]

From the perspective outlined above, the entire volume of *Leaves of Grass*, composed over a forty-year span, can be seen as an ongoing poem which wanted to be renewed and fulfilled year after year in its readers. In "Song of Myself" Whitman announced that he hoped "to cease not till death," and he more than lived out that hope: there were pieces to be added posthumously even after the "Deathbed" edition published during his last months. He had noticed in a charming old-age piece called "After the Supper and Talk" that he was indeed remaining "garrulous to the very last."

As the first projection of the final evolution, the 1855 text of "Song of Myself" was a single outpouring, undivided into separate chants, reaching from page to page in a great tidal surge, the phrases often paced more openly by dots instead of commas. The numbering of the fifty-two sections (adopted in the 1867 edition after an arrangement in stanzas in 1860 and maintained thereafter) does interrupt to a certain extent the continuous sweep of the first version, and some critics, notably Malcolm Cowley, have bemoaned such fragmentation and later emendations as evidences of a decline in visionary power as Whitman became a more conscious artist. On the other hand, despite the sometimes arbitrary nature of the divisions, the spacing affords breathing room in a long and challenging poem which is making demands on the reader that no previous poem had made. Whatever is lost in continuity may be compensated for by the chance to engage the poem spatially as well as temporally and thus enter the structure as it unfolds through a series of overlapping psychic pulsations.

The first section of "Song of Myself" establishes the speaker, his subject, and his relation to the reader. It begins: "I celebrate myself, and sing myself." The 1855 text had read only: "I celebrate myself"; the second phrase contributes little to the thought of the line, but it makes explicit the epic intentions in a regular iambic pentameter: the line associated since Milton with the epic in English. The implied contrast with Vergil's "Arma virumque cano" established the connection with and distinction from all previous epics. The 1855 "Preface" had declared: "The expression of the American poet is to be transcendent and new. It is to be indirect and not direct or descriptive or epic."[13] At any rate, not Homer's or Vergil's kind of epic, not a mythic-historical narrative of arms and the legendary hero. The modern epic would take as its theme the drama of identity and would have to be "indirect" to tap the unconscious sources of identity. The poet, as representative man, would live out that drama publicly in the indirections of his poetry and thereby mythicize himself. In that way the drama of personal identity would become the "epic of Democracy"; the subject would know himself in a peopled and occupied world. Beginning with the 1871 edition, *Leaves* is introduced by a series of "Inscriptions," and the first of these, "One's Self I Sing," gives a precis of "Song of Myself" and of the entire book by linking the "simple separate person" to the democratic "En-Masse." The second "Inscription" sounds the epic note again. To the traditional question *"Know'st thou not there is but one theme for ever-enduring bards?"* the poet responds unhesitatingly: *"I . . . also sing war, and a longer and greater one than any"*: the life-long struggle for selfhood in a populous republic. As the bard-psalmist-prophet of the New World he sings not the legendary past but the mythic present and future; "To a Historian," another "Inscription," ends: "Chanter of Personality, outlining what is yet to be,/ I project the history of the future." As epic hero, he displays as symbolic talisman not the swordblade of Aeneas but "a spear of summer grass."

Whitman returns to these basic assumptions again and again in his prose. The "prophetic vision" of the "orbic bard" must be "autochthonous"—sprung from the native earth—so that his speech will articulate for the people their "autochthons," their "national, original archetypes," concentered in the "orbic bard" himself.[14] So, in lines added to the first section of "Song of Myself" Whitman roots himself autochthonously: "My tongue, every atom of my blood, form'd from this soil, this air,/ Born here of parents born here from parents the same, and their parents the same"—a procession like a biblical genealogy, from the earth and back to it. But since as archetype "I" subsume each and all, the second line addresses the reader with peremptory directness, drawing him into the process of the poem before his disarmed ego can construct defenses:

Walt Whitman

> I celebrate myself, and sing myself,
> And what I assume you shall assume,
> For every atom belonging to me as good belongs to you.

The pun on "assume" links the beginning and the end of the process; "assume" refers both to initial axiomatic attitudes and to the realizations arrived at and assimilated en route.

The singer displays from the start a characteristic bisexuality. It is not just that, as "One's Self I Sing" declares, he must make room for "the Female equally with the Male." Political and social equality follows from psychological integration, and the sexual basis for Whitman's politics is there to begin with. We recognize him as bard and trust his invitation because he begins by admitting and expressing within himself qualities and dispositions usually polarized as feminine or masculine. So, languidly receptive as the female earth on which his body "loafes" and from which he seems barely to have emerged, he contemplates the phallic grass blade as the emblem and evidence of spiritual potentiality: "I loafe and invite my soul,/ I lean and loafe at my ease observing a spear of summer grass." The lines themselves are relaxed and repetitive, and another poet, seeking concise definition, might seek to tighten them up. But Whitman wants room for the unconscious to emerge not only in the measured words of the poem but through the spaces between the phrases. Such revelations will exceed the articulated systems of the rational mind without contradicting or contending with them:

> Creeds and schools in abeyance,
> Retiring back a while sufficed at what they are,
>   but never forgotten,
> I harbor for good or bad, I permit to speak at every
>   hazard,
> Nature without check with original energy.

The word "original" again conjoins beginning and end, as it did in Emerson's phrase, "an original relation to the universe"; the double meaning specifies both the source and the individual who is its unique mediating point. Thus Section 1 immediately adumbrates the substance of the poem: what Whitman later spoke of as his new "attitude towards God, towards the objective universe, and still more (by reflection, confession, assumption, &c.) the quite changed attitude of the ego, the one chanting or talking towards himself and his fellow-humanity."[15]

Critics, like Malcolm Cowley, who argue that Whitman's revisions signify increasing poetic care at the expense of visionary spontaneity, might cite the first section of "Song of Myself" as a case in point. The 1855 text contained only the first five lines, minus the second half of the first line, as noted above. It has been argued that the additions merely make didactic what is already implicit and interrupt the natural eruptive energy of the experience. But the greater explicitness is not necessarily a mark of decline but of enrichment and realization—especially since the more "spontaneous" passages are allowed to stand. In fact, the drawing out of the implications of the initial revelation enacts the comprehension and absorption of the materials from the unconscious into consciousness, and that act of incorporation is, in essence, the dynamic of Whitman's poetry.

Section 2 dramatizes just such a breakthrough of unfathomed resources from the psychic deeps. It is made possible by the poet's rejection of the comfortable enticements of "houses and rooms"— little man-made boxes for supposedly civilized living, equivalent to the intellectual pigeonholes of the "creeds and school" held "in abeyance" in Section 1. The echoing rhyme of the first clause, "Houses and rooms are full of perfumes," sounds the hollow artificiality of what he is resisting. Unlike Edward Taylor, Whitman will not rest within walls and yearn for distillation into Godhead; unlike Emily Dickinson, he cannot live in a private chamber and distill "the Attar from the Rose." The essence is not in the "essence" but in the open air:

> The atmosphere is not a perfume, it has no taste
> of the distillation, it is odorless,
> It is for my mouth forever, I am in love with it,
> I will go to the bank by the wood and become
> undisguised and naked,
> I am mad for it to be in contact with me.

In "Bacchus" Emerson had declared that under the influence (inflowing) of the divine wine "seeming-solid walls of use/ Open

and flow." But, like Taylor, Emerson was still talking about distilled and ethereal liquors. Whitman speaks for an immediate
sensual drunkenness and "madness." The first line above is
languidly repetitious, but it establishes a rhythm within which
the parallel clauses begin to modulate from negation to increasingly erotic affirmation. With the contact between the poet's
mouth and the "atmosphere" (a word that means literally "vapor-
sphere" and connotes its encircling pervasiveness) he is propelled
into seeking total immersion, and the accelerating intensity of
rapt speech catches up the reader, included as "you" in Section
1, into the frenzy.

In Whitman, Hebrew prophecy and the Quaker "inner light"
are made consonant with the passionate lunacy of the Dionysian.
Psychologists since Freud have talked about "polymorphous perversity." The label is unfortunate because of the connotations of
"perversity" (and indicates the negative Freudian attitude in the
matter); but the concept describes the quality of Whitman's imagination, grounding itself in elemental erotic contact. The passage
into adulthood involves—and by strict Freudian principles should
involve—a strong concentration of sexuality in the genitals. Erik
Erikson, following Freud, posits "the 'primacy' of genitality over
pregenitality." However, whatever focusing and intensification
the assumption of genital sexuality brings, it also entails the
sacrifice of a more diffuse but total eroticism which makes the
child's entire body tinglingly alive and responsive to stimuli. And
so in *Life Against Death* Norman O. Brown, himself a Freudian,
elaborates Freud's notion of polymorphous perversity into a positive factor: "Infantile sexuality is the pursuit of pleasure obtained
through the activity of any and all organs of the human body."
Moreover, Brown extends his advocacy of polymorphous perversity on the basis of what he reads as an ambivalence in Freud
concerning the primacy of genitality. "In Freud's theory of infantile sexuality there is first of all a critique of the genital function
and an implied rejection of genital intercourse—'free love' and
the orgasm—as a solution to the sexual problem," though most
Freudians have ignored or contradicted this direction in Freud's
analysis. Thus, "if infantile sexuality, judged by the standards of
normal adult sexuality, is perverse, by the same token normal
adult sexuality, judged by the standard of infantile sexuality, is

an unnatural restriction of the erotic potentialities of the human body."[16] Consequently, citing Freud, Brown argues for a recovery of the child's polymorphous (many-formed, many-forming) perversity, which, far from being a neurotic regression, offers an escape from the anxieties and prescriptions of genital sexuality into a freer, fuller development of our sexual nature. Freud's discussion of the difference between a clitoral and vaginal orgasm poses a related question in terms of the woman's sexual orientation, but for a man the shift would mean a turn from a concentration on phallic experience to a more distributed and inclusive—and "feminine"—eroticism.

Whitman anticipated Freud and Brown. In Section 3 of "Song of Myself": "Welcome is every organ and attribute of me, and of any man hearty and clean,/ Not an inch nor a particle of an inch is vile, and none shall be less familiar than the rest." In Section 24:

> I believe in the flesh and the appetites,
> Seeing, hearing, feeling, are miracles, and each
>   part and tag of me is a miracle.
>
> Divine am I inside and out, and I make holy whatever
>   I touch or am touch'd from. . . .

In Section 27: "I have instant conductors all over me whether I pass or stop," and this section was expanded into a poem included in the posthumous additions to *Leaves of Grass*:

> To be at all—what is better than that?
> I think if there were nothing more developed, the
>   clam in its callous shell in the sand were
>   august enough.
> I am not in any callous shell;
> I am cased with supple conductors, all over,
> They take every object by the hand, and lead it
>   within me;
> They are thousands, each one with his entry to
>   himself;
> They are always watching with their little eyes,
>   from my head to my feet;
> One no more than a point lets in and out of me such
>   bliss and magnitude,

Walt Whitman

> I think I could lift the girder of the house away
>   if it lay between me and whatever I wanted.

Whitman is unequivocally refusing the restraints of civilized conduct in order to return to a more primitive revelling of the body in its surroundings. So in Section 2 the mouth's first exposure to the atmosphere proceeds, with quick instinctiveness, to the undisguised nakedness of the entire person.

This contact touches off the first catalogue of the poem. Images and perceptions rush in free association from the unconscious, and the poet sees and feels as would never be possible with intellectual control. William Blake would say that Whitman was not merely seeing with his eyes as physical organs gathering sensory data but seeing through his eyes into the mystery of being; Emerson would say that his inward and outward senses were working in consonance; Jung might say that he is seeing with a double set of eyes, the full four-fold act of vision, like Blake's *Four Zoas*. The sequence of elements in the catalogue reveals much about the operation of Whitman's imagination:

> The smoke of my own breath,
> Echoes, ripples, buzz'd whispers, love-root,
>   silk-thread, crotch and vine,
> My respiration and inspiration, the beating of my
>   heart, the passing of blood and air through
>   my lungs,
> The sniff of green leaves and dry leaves, and of the
>   shore and dark-color'd sea-rocks, and of hay
>   in the barn,
> The sound of the belch'd words of my voice loos'd to
>   the eddies of the wind,
> A few light kisses, a few embraces, a reaching
>   around of arms,
> The play of shine and shade on the trees as the
>   supple boughs wag,
> The delight alone or in the rush of the streets, or
>   along the fields and hill-sides,
> The feeling of health, the full-noon trill, the
>   song of me rising from bed and meeting the sun.

The activating image stands alone with a line to itself: the poet's own breath inspired from the atmosphere and expired visibly. Inhalation and exhalation are the compensatory rhythms of the single immersion. Immediately that image summons a series of other manifestations of the activated atmosphere, as spirit-breath runs through material forms: sound-waves, ripples of wind on water, voices whispering secrets. The erotic possibilities of "buzz'd whispers" arouse intimations of a sexuality pervading natural objects as well as the human body: "love-root, silk-thread, crotch and vine." So the second line of the catalogue tumbles from the first in a proliferation of associated images, each leading to the next. The subsequent lines then alternate images of the human body with natural images: in the third line, breath-rhythm, blood-beat; in the fourth, the complementary variety of scene and cycle; in the fifth, the eruption of the poet's voice into the wind, which awakens in the sixth line increasingly erotic details: "A few light kisses, a few embraces, a reaching around of arms"; in the seventh, the phallicism and fertility of the "supple boughs" on burgeoning spring trees. The leap of associations pieces out its own unexpected and irregular pattern, and the effect of the pattern is to make us sense with the poet all things seething with sexual vitality: the individual, the social community, the natural landscape, "alone or in the rush of the streets, or along the fields and hill-sides." In this divine passion the poet comes to "possess the origin of all poems" and "the meaning of poems," which he instantly presses upon each of "you" for realization.

Section 3 makes explicit what the catalogue has conveyed—namely, that the mystery of being and the origin of poems is sex, coming to climax in each instant, "now . . . now . . . now," as the second cluster of lines insists. The rhythm of the following lines develops through balance and contrast to final conjunction:

> Urge and urge and urge,
> Always the procreant urge of the world.
> Out of the dimness opposite equals advance, always
>   substance and increase, always sex,
> Always a knit of identity, always distinction,
>   always a breed of life.

Here Whitman resolves the dualism bisecting nature (as Emerson put the dilemma) not through an impersonal Over-soul but through an incarnational force ceaselessly breeding life in bodies. For Emerson, sex is only one of the evidences of Nature's "Compensation"—and not strongly stressed either. For Whitman it is the inclusive fact; sex is body-energy, the androgynous spirit-breath: distinct and opposite equals not just compelling men and women into a breed of life but also knitting the individual man's or woman's psyche into a personal identity. In his old age Whitman summed up the difference between Emerson and himself concisely: "L. of G.'s word is *the body, including all,* including intellect and soul; E.'s word is mind (or intellect or soul)."[17] The distinction is crucial; at the beginning of *Nature* Emerson had included the body in the "not-me" of Nature, the material envelope within which the soul, or real "me," operated.

To the end Whitman maintained against objections more hostile and insinuating than those Emerson voiced to him in 1860, that sex was essential to the meaning and movement of his poems. "A Woman Waits for Me," added in 1856, leaves no doubt about what "Song of Myself" was saying:

> Sex contains all, bodies, souls,
> Meanings, proofs, purities, delicacies, results,
>   promulgations,
> Songs, commands, health, pride, the maternal
>   mystery, the seminal milk,
> All hopes, benefactions, bestowals, all the passions,
>   loves, beauties, delights of the earth,
> All the governments, judges, gods, follow'd persons
>   of the earth,
> These are contain'd in sex as parts of itself and
>   justifications of itself.

"A Backward Glance O'er Travel'd Roads," the preface to *November Boughs* in 1888, forbade the excision of offensive poems or lines because sexual energy, as the source and "enclosing basis" of the book, "so gives breath of life to my whole scheme that the bulk of the pieces might as well have been left unwritten were those lines omitted. . . . the work must stand or fall with them, as the human body and soul must remain as an entirety." The sexuality which is organic to man and nature is thereby essential to "the whole construction, organism, and intentions of *Leaves of Grass.*"[18] It is true that the sexual element became less insistent as Whitman grew older, especially after the strokes which crippled him in the mid-1870s—not, after all, a surprising fact; but it is also true that to the end he could write poems like "The Dalliance of the Eagles" and "Unseen Buds," awestruck still by the sexual mystery and sounding it in terms as vigorous as those of "Song of Myself."

The poet's identification with this "electrical" mystery in Section 3 reveals him to himself as a stud, "stout as a horse." The last lines of the section tell of his experience of the sexual mystery with a "hugging and loving bedfellow" who departs leaving signs of their shared plenitude: "baskets cover'd with white towels swelling the house with their plenty." The 1855 text read: "As God comes a loving bedfellow and sleeps at my side all night. . . ." The substitution of a human lover makes the experience more credible and immediate and less open to charges of blasphemy at the same time that it subdues the mystical element until it can be fully expressed in Section 5. Moreover, the unspecified sex of the bedfellow leaves ambiguous here the homosexual feelings which surface time and again in Whitman's work. But the substitution of "bulging" for "swelling" in describing the bedfellow's pregnant baskets, linked with the substitution of "swelling" for "bulging" in describing the young men's naked bellies in Section 11, may provide an unconscious connection between these two "homosexual" passages. However, for the time being at least, that vexed question is passed over to clear the way for the major mystical experience dramatized in Section 5. That experience is prefigured in the meeting described here, and the fulfillment of that meeting is the image of pregnancy: the baskets left behind "swelling . . . with their plenty." Is it the poet quickened into life by the other person? Or is it a type of God's abundance which exceeds human distinctions? In either case the encounter results in a sense of completion which is felt explicitly as androgynous.

Before Whitman can proceed to the self-realization of Section 5, however, he holds us off still a little while longer in order to make a necessary distinction between levels of psychological experience and corresponding levels of identity. Dramatically, Section 4 interrupts the development which is building toward Section 5, but the deliberate and self-conscious distinction made here provides something of an intellectual framework for the mysterious event that is about to be described. In his experience of himself there is an "I" and there is a "Me myself." "I" is engaged, as detailed in the first eight lines of the section, in a round of activities and obligations, but beyond stands the "Me myself":

> Apart from the pulling and hauling stands what I am,
> Stands amused, complacent, compassionating, idle,
> unitary,
> Looks down, is erect, or bends an arm on an impalpable
> certain rest,
> Looking with side-curving head curious what will come
> next,
> Both in and out of the game and watching and wondering
> at it.

In his book on *The Psychology of Consciousness* Robert Ornstein describes a double awareness much like Whitman's:

> In Yoga, a form of self-observation is called "the Witness." Here the attempt is to observe oneself as if one were another person. One tries to notice exactly what one is doing—to invest ordinary activity with attention. The Witness does not judge action nor does it initiate action. The Witness simply observes.

The result, Dr. Ornstein points out, is that the individual can "develop a present-centered consciousness, [and] 'open up' awareness of daily activities *while* engaged in them."[19]

The contrast between active engagement and passive observation is only part of the point. More exactly, it is the double sense of ego and Self which Whitman later spoke of, in "Backward Glance," as "the quite changed attitude of the ego . . . towards himself." These words anticipate quite precisely the distinction Jung would make between ego and Self: the ego being the center of consciousness acting out the persona of its public, social role; the Self being a more remote and mysterious identity, "in and out of the game," which includes all the potentialities and possibilities waiting latent in the unconscious to be brought into active play and realization as the Self. The Self, then, involves one in the transmutation of what one might be in the fullness of one's powers into what one is or is closer to being; the Self is the inclusive entity: the end of the process, the initiating power, and the sustaining energy along the way. The envelope of external material circumstances is the area in which the ego operates and constructs a persona in order to operate.

But the center and balance of all this activity is—or ought to be—a transcendent Self, if the individual is not to harden into his ego's persona or dissolve into the rush of activities, as Whitman foresees in Section 4. Not only is the potential Self given form as it moves into consciousness, but simultaneously it enlarges that consciousness and stabilizes the ego which is its operating center. Nor is the psyche, engaged in this process, abstracted from matter; in fact, it is indistinguishable from the body. So in the lines quoted above Whitman describes the "Me myself" not as spirit or concept but as the face and posture of the man who peered out at the reader from the frontispiece of the book. One of the questions which "Song of Myself" will be living out is the relation of the ego, which must risk contact, and the Self, which must hold itself "apart from the pulling and hauling." This early stage of the poem, however, can only intimate the problem and indeed can only intimate the "Me myself" whose definition will be arrived at more fully through the poem and whose presence is first felt through the overpowering revelation of identity presented in Section 5. But it is important to note that Whitman refuses Emerson's intellectualization and spiritualizing and grounds the revelation in the body, just as D. H. Lawrence would reject both Freud's and Jung's theories of the unconscious psyche to seat the soul in the solar plexus and later in the genitals.

Section 5 loops back to the speaker's invitation to "you my soul" to "lean and loafe" at the opening of the poem, as the resumption of alliterations, especially "l" alliterations, suggests: "Loafe with me on the grass, loose the stop from your throat, . . . Only the lull I like, the hum of your valvèd voice." In Section 1 "you" and "my soul" were distinct; "you" was the reader, and the soul was mentioned without being addressed. The phrase "you my soul" here implicates the reader in the action and extends it beyond the merely private and personal. The intervening sections have prepared for one of the supreme passages in Whitman, as the soul fleshes itself into personality and the body awakens to the soul:

> I mind how once we lay such a transparent summer
>   morning,

How you settled your head athwart my hips and gently
        turn'd over upon me,
And parted the shirt from my bosom-bone, and plunged
        your tongue to my bare-stript heart,
And reach'd till you felt my beard, and reach'd till
        you held my feet.

The sustained explicitness of the passage has led Cowley and other critics to speculate that Whitman is describing an actual orgasmic encounter, and they cite the 1855 version, "I mind how we lay in June" as evidence of a specific incident which constitutes the genesis not just of this poem but of Whitman's poetic inspiration. However, the lines themselves attest much more strongly to a psychological penetration no less transformative for being internal.

The experience is the enactment of the "knit of identity": the union of body and spirit into a personal existence in which soul is a sexual force and body is possessed by spirit and in which sexual distinctions disappear. The image is not of a bearded body and a female soul, as in some of Blake's drawings, but of a bearded body in the woman's position, gripped by a spiritual power that matches the body it mates. It is this mating which allows the ego to break through to its first intimation of the Me myself and allows the Me myself its first intimation of what will reach full expression only in the last sections of the poem.

In the description the lulling rhythms and sounds give way to the stress of strong verbs: "settled . . . turn'd over . . . parted . . . plunged . . . reach'd . . . reach'd." And the "knit of identity" immediately turns out, diffusing him through all creation:

Swiftly arose and spread around me the peace and
        knowledge that pass all the argument of the
        earth,
And I know that the hand of God is the promise of
        my own,
And I know that the spirit of God is the brother of
        my own,
And that all the men ever born are also my brothers,
        and the women my sisters and lovers,
And that a kelson of the creation is love,
And limitless are leaves stiff or drooping in the
        fields,

And brown ants in the little wells beneath them,
And mossy scabs of the worm fence, heap'd stones,
    elder, mullein and poke-weed.

Thinking of Whitman, Robert Duncan sees "in the ecstasy of the orgasm a return into present feeling, into consciousness, of the origins, the return to a life . . . going back beyond the boundaries of the individual, beyond the boundaries of species, to the Primal Scene of Creation—the Sea of the Universe in which suns pour forth, live and die."[20] The first line of Whitman's incantation paraphrases both St. Paul and the Upanishads;* then a series of paratactic clauses joined together by "and" expresses identification with God, with all men and women, and with nature's teeming sexuality. The infinite expansiveness of the first lines of the passage comes to be substantiated in the humble particulars of the present place, anticipating the extended meditation on the grass, at once common and universal, in the next section.

Section 5 has enacted a conversion-experience, simultaneously sexual and religious, simultaneously personal and cosmic, which effects the changed attitude toward God, Self, and world which Whitman noted as the radical element in his experiment. He experienced an intimation of his identity so profound that the mystery of Self was revealed as a manifestation of the secret of Nature and the divinity of Life itself. Self is inseparable from God; or, to invoke the Indian mysticism in which Whitman came later to discover a vision corresponding to his own, the *atman* (the individual soul) and the *Brahman* (the World Soul) are one: the *atman* manifesting the *Brahman* and the *Brahman* manifesting itself in the *atman*. As a historian of religions, Mircea Eliade has described the epiphany of spirit in and through the body as it has been experienced and rendered in different cultures; and the interesting point relevant to Whitman is the frequent identification of spiritual energy with sexuality, of the divine light-seed with the *semen virile*. As a psychologist, Erich Neumann has described the primitive awareness of a body-self which is the first phase in the development of identity from the unconscious into consciousness: "Long before a consciousness centered in the ego takes

*Eliot would link Eastern and Western mysticism in *The Waste Land* through a linked allusion to St. Augustine and Buddha, as well as through the "Shantih," which links St. Paul and the Upanishads as Whitman did.

cognizance of the self as the center of psychological reality, the self appears as a body-self, i.e., as a totality directing the body and all its functions." The final phase of the realized Self "is centered in consciousness, ego, and will," but the process begins with the simultaneous exploration of external nature and one's own nature, starting with the body. Norman Brown noted that "children, at the stage of early infancy which Freud thinks critical, are unable to distinguish between their souls and their bodies; in Freudian terminology, they are their own ideal." The sense of the body-self at the beginning of the process of coming to conscious-ness is a development from the child's obliviousness; but it is still closely associated with the unconscious and with the material-maternal order of experience. So, for a man, this body-self exists as "a feminine self" to be integrated into his final masculine iden-tity. Whitman intuited the body-self, as evidenced by passages like Section 5 or by his speaking of *"the body, including all,* in-cluding the intellect and soul."[21]

In Section 6 the child-self born of (or recovered from) the "knit of identity" asks, with a wise innocence that Blake and Wordsworth and Emerson would have recognized, *"What is the grass?"* and the adult "sayer" in Whitman must find the words to construe the child's visionary question. Emerson had remarked in "The Poet" that the mystic mistakenly reads a symbol as having a fixed, intrinsic significance (what the Puritans used to call "types"), whereas the poet knows that all symbols are "flux-ional," as much in process as Nature itself. So a symbol conveys different things to different perceivers and different things to the same perceiver at different times, and all interpretations are valid. In the first section of the poem Whitman had singled out the blade of grass as his special sign, and now, questioned by his newborn Self, he is able to see the grass as the recapitulation of the whole cycle of life, death and rebirth; it is the symbol of the individual ("the flag of my disposition"), of Deity ("the handkerchief of the Lord"), of reproduction ("the produced babe of the vegetation"), of the new social order of American democracy ("a uniform hieroglyphic"), of death ("the beautiful uncut hair of graves"), and finally of the new forms into which death transmogrifies life.

The fact that death occupies more time and attention than any other aspect of the cycle indicates the sticking point: the individual must come to see death not as terminus but as transition. Mythology recapitulates the stories through which every culture, no matter of what geographical region or what historical period, has come to recognize that life does not spell death; each has its myth of death and rebirth. "Song of Myself" projects the archetypes of the New World, and so in Sections 6 and 7, and indeed in the entire poem, the thrust is not merely to resign the individual to his death but to accommodate death into a process that survives the individual. The answer here is an American-democratic form of metempsychosis and reincarnation; the individual dies into other lives and other forms of life. Section 7 picks up the last line of 6 and extends a lucky death into an immortality of ongoing life; as the perceiver and so the epitome of such a continuity the poet is necessarily androgynous: both "the mate and companion of people," "for me mine male and female."

The bard's insight gives him a centralizing role in the process of dissolution and reincarnation, exemplified at length in the catalogues of the poem. Thereby the catalogues reveal themselves as a form of magic, confirming the fact that nothing exists in itself, that all things define themselves in terms of all other things. The catalogues project a field of relations, a network of identifications that strengthen the individual by extending him into the ongoing process of existence which will finally absorb him. If "Song of Myself" makes Whitman the center of the myth, the catalogues define him in rings of circumferences. Consequently it is no mere fancy to conceive the catalogues as taking on something of the function of primitive magic in substantiating the interaction between the individual and the world of objects. In primitive societies, where individuals live in both an instinctive affinity with and fears of their natural environment, it is altogether common for a person to combat the alienation by relying upon the affinity; he feels his spirit objectified in a special tree or rock and that totem-object yields him its strength and thus paradoxically yields to him power over it. Whitman is operating so deeply from the primitive unconscious that the catalogues act as a kind of verbal totemism on a sweepingly democratic scale. He possesses things by naming them simultaneously; he extends himself into them and draws them into definition and relationship in himself; he absorbs their strength, yet at the same time subdues and transforms them through the magic of his words. Thereby Whitman becomes the shaman of an increasingly urban tribe that has to cope not just with the natural round of life and death but with the peculiarly bewildering facts of its historical destiny: the size and diversity of its people and its "territory," the size and complexity of its social and economic system—all indicative of divisions that sundered the nation into Civil War and threatened the poet's dream of a utopian "America." Whitman's care for the victims of both sides of the Civil War in military hospitals became only a practical application of the mystical and visionary role of American medicine man.

Consequently, after the introductory sections, precipitating in the sudden and transformative experience of Self in Section 5, the next phase of the poem—Sections 8 through 17—consists of a massive and uninterrupted procession of catalogues. The astonishing solidification of the center issues in an equally astonishing dispersal of circumference: the centrifugal force a function and measure of the centripetal. Whitman begins by rocking the reader slowly into the rhythm of the catalogues. Section 8 opens with three two-line groups, each sketching a vignette:

> The little one sleeps in its cradle,
> I lift the gauze and look a long time, and silently
>   brush away flies with my hand.
>
> The youngster and the red-faced girl turn aside up
>   the bushy hill,
> I peeringly view them from the top.
>
> The suicide sprawls on the bloody floor of the
>   bedroom,
> I witness the corpse with its dabbled hair, I note
>   where the pistol has fallen.

The cycle, again, of birth, sex, and death, with the "I" of the poet taking each incident into himself as responsive perceiver. The captivating detail—the netting on the cradle and the gesture of brushing away flies, the girl's blush both modest and passionate, the bloodied hair and the position of the pistol—validates the poet's identification with the scene. The suicide jars somewhat with the previous acceptance of life and death as natural stages;

but Whitman here is either unmindful of the inconsistency, or he quite rightly chooses to pass over it as inappropriate to his present purpose. In any case, with the method of the catalogues demonstrated by these three cyclic vignettes, Whitman launches into a conglomeration of images and incidents, constellated only in the last line of the section by reference to the perceiving center: "I mind them or the show or resonance of them—I come and I depart." Thereafter, the next eight sections consist of an unbroken sequence of glimpses in a loose configuration around the personal references that punctuate the flow here and there.

The catalogues free the poet from any single limiting definition into a succession of identities—the Self "fluxional" as any other symbol or myth. But the number and rapidity of the acts of identification impose their own intrinsic limitations: a fact that Whitman does not recognize or acknowledge here. Each fleeting glimpse precludes a deep or lasting contact. Identification is not synonymous with identity; in fact, the poet must withhold himself as he gives himself. The verbs in Section 8 themselves suggest the detached observer ("both in and out of the game") rather than the empathetic participant: "look," "peeringly view . . . from the top," "witness," "note," "mind them or the show or resonance of them," "come and . . . depart." "Who needs be afraid of the merge?" he had asked in the 1855 version of Section 7. The subsequent cancellation of the line indicates that the matter was not so easily settled affirmatively. How to maintain a center and a circumference? When does expansiveness lose touch with personal identity? Can he insist that his definition is lack of definition? These difficult questions press to the surface later in the poem and are already latent in the verbs used in Section 8. At this point, however, because of the powerful centering of energies in Section 5, Whitman can successfully radiate a dizzying swirl of circumferential identifications.

The briefly sketched images in Section 8 are followed by somewhat more developed episodes in Section 9 through 14, dissolving into the climactic kaleidoscope of impressions in Sections 15 and 16. The catalogues, then, comprise the second large movement of "Song of Myself," substantiating and enlarging upon the revelation that comes in the introductory sections. The bodyself, inspirited by God, is now incorporated into nature and society. So Section 16 concludes with the observation that "I resist anything better than my own diversity"; Emerson had said in "Self-Reliance" that "a foolish consistency is the hobgoblin of little minds," but he was again thinking of intellectual attitudes, whereas Whitman meant something more fundamental. Section 17 rounds the movement out by recapitulating the elements that compose the material matrix of all things: "the grass that grows wherever the land is and the water is," "the common air that bathes the globe."

The reality into which the body-self is projected is, as we have noted, not just nature as it came from God's hand but urban society. As shaman for a far-flung tribe, whose western frontier would soon be closed, he has to cast his spell over the modern metropolis as well as the small town and rural settlement. Emerson had foreseen that the American bard would have to render the heretofore unpoetic fact of the crowded, mechanized city available to any vision that would speak to men after the Industrial Revolution. Whitman took up Emerson's challenge and in "Give Me the Splendid Silent Sun," for example, he supplemented the traditional plea of the nature poet when, after creating a pastoral landscape, he broke out with:

> Keep your splendid silent sun,
> Keep your woods, O nature, and the quiet places by
>   the woods . . .
> Give me faces and streets—give me those phantoms
>   incessant along the trottoirs!

Nothing is really taken back or rejected; what is added is a cityscape of teeming crowds and humming energies. And from the first, the catalogues of "Song of Myself" exemplify the conviction that "not Nature alone is great . . . [but] the work of man too is equally great"[22]—and equally a circumferential part of the body-self.

Up to this point "Song of Myself" has presented the auto-apotheosis of the bacchic poet-prophet fleshing his personal identity in his natural and democratic environment. The third movement (if movement can be used to describe pulsations that lap and overlap like waves on a beach) speculates more reflectively about the moral attitude and character of the poet-prophet who is now a potent fact. The question of Sections 18 through 24 is posed in Section 20: "Who goes there? . . . What is a man anyhow? what am I? what are you?" Whitman sees his moral attitude and moral character as distinguishable but complementary matters. If he is to take all things into himself, if he is to extend his circumference around all things, then he must be equally open and responsive to contradictions: the wicked with the good, the weak with the strong, the diseased with the robust, the criminal with the hero. He must refuse to judge or condemn or even discriminate. It is this indifference that made Whitman seem a moral barbarian to someone like George Santayana as well as to critics of his own time, his boastful "yawp" consonant with the ape's grunt. Nothing could be further from Emerson's ethical idealism than these lines from Section 22:

> I am not the poet of goodness only, I do not decline
>   to be the poet of wickedness also.

> What blurt is this about virtue and about vice?
> Evil propels me and reform of evil propels me, I
>   stand indifferent,
> My gait is no fault-finder's or rejector's gait,
> I moisten the roots of all that has grown.

These sections reiterate the refusal to exclude: "It is for the wicked just the same as the righteous, I make appointments with all" (Section 19); "In all people I see myself, none more and not one a barley-corn less,/ And the good or bad I say of myself I say of them" (Section 20). Such amoral tolerance, the poet says, enables him to accept Time and Reality absolutely, so much so that the only absolute seems the totality of flux: "I accept Reality and dare not question it,/ Materialism first and last imbuing" (Section 23).

The metaphysics of the total acceptance of Reality led to "Chanting the Square Deific," first published in 1865. Whitman redrew the Christian Trinity into a Square, in order to include Satan in the Godhead as the force of the dark, violent, and destructive aspects of Reality. The "Square Deific" consists of the powerful and judging Father, the compassionate and loving Son, the rebellious and scheming Satan, and the all-pervasive breath of the Santa Spirita. Four-fold configurations, as Jung and others have observed, frequently signify completeness in dreams as well as in myth and ritual. So a four-fold Deific of Reality matches the square emblematic of psychological wholeness. Characteristically the fourth "side" of such a square in myth or dreams is associated with the powers of earth and darkness, sometimes in the image of Satan and sometimes in the image of woman. Even in the Christian Trinity the Son became flesh and joined the divine and human in one person; and, although outside the Trinity, Satan and Mary are constellated immediately around the Trinity, both doctrinally and iconographically. As Anti-Christ, Satan is the inescapable shadow who must be reckoned with and overcome by the Son and his legions under the archangel Michael. And Mary, the mother of the God-man and the representative embodiment of all human generations, enjoys so special and intimate a relation to the Trinity that she is regularly shown with the Trinity and in some medieval depictions even incorporates into herself the three Persons of the Godhead. Whitman's configuration brackets the Good Son and the Rebel between the Father and the Santa Spirita, a feminine conception of the Sanctus Spiritus.

However, "Chanting the Square Deific" ends with the poet's own identification with the masculine-feminine Santa Spirita, the life-breath of all things. And the Santa Spirita is androgynous: not just "lighter than light," the pure masculine archetype, but "beyond the light"—that is, beyond the dualities of sex, of heaven and hell, of "Savior and Satan." This "essence of forms, life of the real identities" is "permanent and positive," and "I," identified with the Santa Spirita, becomes "the general soul," "finishing" the square in Myself and "breathing my breath also through these songs." This means that, however indifferent the poet must be in his moral attitude and judgment, he must in his own character be so "permanent and positive," so healthy and affirmative (not diseased and neurotic like Poe), that the final effect of his identification with all things will be life-enhancing. Willy-nilly his embrace resolves contradiction into affirmation. Section 22, which contains the amoral lines cited above, concludes with this uplifting statement: "What behaved well in the past or behaves well to-day is not such a wonder,/ The wonder is always and always how there can be a mean man or an infidel." As inclusive

"I" he had said in the previous section: "The pleasures of heaven are with me and the pains of hell are with me"; but as shaman and prophet he immediately adds: "The first I graft and increase upon myself, the latter I translate into a new tongue." Good grows through his prophetic power, and evil is elevated into a new dimension, drawn more and more into good. Worrying years later in the "Preface" to the Centennial Edition of 1876 about the charge that his poetry condoned immorality, Whitman would declare that his poetry prepared for morality because, like Nature itself, it was moral in its overall "purport and last intelligence," though there is "nothing of the moral in the works, or laws, or shows of Nature." Or again in 1889: "Nature evidently achieves specimens only—plants the seeds of suggestions—is not so intolerant of what is call'd evil—relies on *law* and *character* more than on special cases or partialities; and in my little scope I have follow'd or tried to follow the lesson."[23]

All the translation, transformation, and transfiguration of "what is called evil" climaxes in Section 24 when the "forbidden" and "indecent" "voices of sexes and lusts" become "clarified and transfigur'd" in the poet as "the current and index" of the divine "afflatus." Just as the Spirit is not merely masculine but feminine, so sexuality is revealed as an activity not just of earth, dark and female, but of the masculine, transfiguring light. "Clarify" means to "make light," and in the ecstasy of His Transfiguration Christ's Godhood shone through the features and limbs of His body. So the third major movement of "Song of Myself" ends with "Walt Whitman, a Kosmos, of Manhattan the son," named for the first time with an individual-universal identity, reveling in his body-self, as Blake before him and D. H. Lawrence after him also celebrated the divinity of the "mystical body," or what Blake called "the human form divine."* Whitman was deeply moved by Swin-

*In a chapter of *Life Against Death* entitled "The Resurrection of the Body" Norman O. Brown takes that notion not merely as an eschatological goal, as orthodox theology does, but as a transfiguring possibility here and now. Following out the psychological and spiritual implications, Brown contrasts the mystical tradition which denies matter and yearns for release into spirit—he calls it "Apollonian or sublimation mysticism"—with a "Dionysian or body mysticism, which stays with life . . . and seeks to transform and perfect" the body. Brown suggests three sources or analogues: "The Christian (Pauline) notion of the 'spiritual' body, the Jewish (cabalistic) notion of Adam's perfect body before the Fall, and the alchemical notion of the subtle body" (p. 310).

burne's essay linking him with Blake, and in "Poetry of the Present" Lawrence was to point to Whitman as the only poet before him who dared to derive his poetry from the instinctual energies of the sexual life-force. In one of the masterful passages of the poem Section 24 expands the first catalogue of Section 2 and envisions the poet's body so much a part of nature and humanity that anatomy is described as landscape and landscape as anatomy—all "translucent mould":

> If I worship one thing more than another it shall be
> the spread of my own body, or any part of it,
> Translucent mould of me it shall be you!
> Shaded ledges and rests it shall be you!
> Firm masculine colter it shall be you!
> Whatever goes to the tilth of me it shall be you!
> You my rich blood! your milky stream pale strippings
> of my life!

> . . . .

> You sweaty brooks and dews it shall be you!
> Winds whose soft-tickling genitals rub against me it
> shall be you!
> Broad muscular fields, branches of live oak, loving
> lounger of my winding paths, it shall be you!
> Hands I have taken, faces I have kiss'd, mortal I
> have ever touch'd, it shall be you.

Again "I" am male and female, colter and tilth, plowshare and plowed field, stretching in all directions.

The danger in such self-worship is that it may become its own trap. Narcissus loved himself so exclusively that he could see nothing outside of himself except in terms of gratification, could finally not see beyond himself. The following groups of lines frame the catalogue quoted just above:

> Divine am I inside and out, and I make holy whatever
> I touch or am touch'd from,
> The scent of these arm-pits aroma finer than prayer,
> This head more than churches, bibles, and all the
> creeds.

> . . . .

I dote on myself, there is that lot of me and all so
    luscious,
Each moment and whatever happens thrills me with
    joy. . . .

Richard Chase found such boasts absurdly exaggerated and taste-less; he argued that since they cannot be meant seriously, they must be a measure of the comic realism which Whitman employed to deflate his own wild fantasies. Chase chose to cast Whitman as a comic realist, kinned with Mark Twain, because Chase did not want to consider what Whitman obviously means us to take as the revolutionary and prophetic message of his poetry: namely, his extravagant claims for the body-self. Whitman is aware of the charge (and the problem) of narcissism. In Section 42, for example, he will say: "I know perfectly well my own egotism . . . And would fetch you whoever you are flush with myself." His escape from Narcissus' drowning self-embrace is to hug the peo-ple and objects around him. His deepest realizations of identity, he insists, knit him more deeply to the world, and thus his prophetic role not only serves the world as hortatory inspiration; it also serves to direct his egotism outward.

Norman Brown summed up the dilemma precisely: "The aim of Eros is union with objects outside the self; and at the same time Eros is fundamentally narcissistic, self-loving. How can a fundamentally narcissistic orientation lead to union with objects in the world?" The narcissism of Eros derives from infantile sex-uality when the child discovers his own body and plays with it, and polymorphous perversity such as Whitman's is an extension of that autoerotic fascination. Brown quotes Freud directly:

> Love originates in the capacity of the ego to satisfy some of its instincts autoerotically through the obtaining of organ-pleasure. It is primarily narcissistic, is then transferred to those objects which have been incorporated in the ego, now much extended, and expresses the motor striving of the ego after these objects as sources of pleasure.

Brown concluded: "Thus the human libido is essentially narcissis-tic, but it seeks a world to love as it loves itself." This reasserts the dilemma without solving it, and the inability to solve it Brown saw as a major cause of Freud's increasing pessimism. In reaction

Brown called for "an extension and development of the Freudian doctrine of narcissism."[24] One such extension is Erich Neumann's argument that "narcissism is a necessary transitional phase during the consolidation of the ego," as it locates itself as an entity separate from the enveloping maternal presence and as a consciousness formed from the original unconscious state. This psychological centralization is accompanied by "love of one's own body, its adornment and sacralization," so that "a generalized body feeling" of its unity is "the first expression of individuality." "The danger inherent in this line of development is exaggerated self-importance," which is inverted insecurity, and an unstable or threatening relationship with the mother could accentuate the negative response and turn differentiation into alienated withdrawal. However, a nourishing acceptance by the mother and her support during this awkward period—as Whitman surely had from his own mother during his prolonged adolescence through the stressful years of discovery into his serene maturity and old age—would sustain the ego to define identity not only in relation to the inhabited world but through the agency of the psychic resources which Whitman associated with the "Me myself." Thus, according to Neumann, while "the isolation of an ego, whose relation to the 'you' has been disturbed, is manifested not only in the loss of relationship to the 'you' within, the unconscious, but also to the 'you outside,' its fellow man," the ego's ability to admit its dependence on the Self opens the way to developing "the psychic totality" of the "Me myself" in relation to the "you." The resulting consciousness is so different from the analytical discriminations of ego-consciousness that Neumann called it "matriarchal" to indicate its rootedness in the "feminine" ground of nature, intuition and the unconscious. "Matriarchal consciousness" wrote Neumann, ". . . is dominant in the psychology of woman and of the creative man," who incorporates his feminine nature into his total personality.[25]

It is not as easy to embrace the world as Whitman sometimes seemed to suggest, but he had found a way out of the trap through his perception of levels of psychic identity, much as Jung would respond to Freud by distinguishing between ego and Self. The ego initially experiences itself as a separate, encapsulated entity among myriad others. As a result, the presence of others becomes the pressure of others, becomes conflict with others; and the supreme Other presents the most fearsome threat. The thrust of Eros to break out of the entrenched ego is countered by a compulsion to protect ego-integrity. So in Section 4 Whitman had already come to see the ego surrounded by "trippers and askers," embroiled in contacts that seemed more like contests. But perception at a deeper psychic level—what Whitman called "the Me myself"—allowed him to engage in contact without being threatened by it, "both in and out of the game." Self-awareness disclosed the psychic resources and life-energies which the individual shared with all other things, so that he could pass beyond the initial conflicts between the "me" and the "not-me" into a participation with others in the continuity of existence.

Not that an awareness of "the Me myself" obviated the difficulties once and for all. Such transcendence was difficult to maintain, especially against the external threats which collapsed Whitman back into the defensive ego, riddled with fears and frustrations. The middle sections of "Song of Myself" present a disturbing instance of Whitman's psychic vulnerability. In Section 24 "Walt Whitman, a kosmos," reveling in the radiant interpenetration of his body and its circumambience, turns out exultantly: "To behold the daybreak!" Just as the immediately preceding catalogue in Section 24 looks back to the catalogue in Section 2 and expands it, so this consequent confrontation with the sunrise recapitulates the moment which concludes the catalogue in Section 2: "the song of me rising from bed and meeting the sun." But here almost immediately a gulf opens up between him and the world which he had just felt that he tallied. The dawn-world tingles with sexual energy as his body does; or is it more potent than he? Suddenly "something I cannot see puts up libidinous prongs,/ Seas of bright juice suffuse heaven." The still unseen sun's power has shattered the organic wholeness of the poet's Self-awareness and left his ego exposed and at bay. The menace implicit in the lines quoted above closes in immediately after:

> The earth by the sky staid with, the daily close of
>   their junction,
> The heav'd challenge from the east that moment over
>   my head,
> The mocking taunt, See whether you shall be master!

Section 25 is the poet's effort to meet the challenge. He has no doubts about the deadliness of the rivalry: "how quick the sun-rise would kill me,/ If I could not now and always send the sun-rise out of me." But it is precisely the "now and always" which is in doubt. He falls back on the boast that his soul is as "dazzling and tremendous as the sun," that the poet's power over language adequately matches, though on different terms, the sun's light: "My voice goes after what my eyes cannot reach"; "Speech is the twin of my vision." But his vulnerability forces the honest question: *"Walt you contain enough, why don't you let it out then?"* In response to which he withdraws his boast: "you conceive too much of articulation." With that admission he can only submit to the inarticulate power of the sunrise, abandoning words for wordless "prophetical screams" like the cries of birds and animals and, finally, for silence itself. The word-power which was "the twin of my vision" now comes down to "the hush of my lips" and some cagey maneuvering: "My final merit I refuse you, I refuse putting from me what I really am,/ Encompass worlds, but never try to encompass me"; "Writing and talk do not prove me." Whitman is not in rout; he offers the look on his passive face as "the plenum of proof" for his claims. But the section marks an unmistakable retraction and redeployment, so that in Section 26 the poet soothes his smarting ego by yielding to sounds, disembodied yet thereby perhaps the most suggestive of sense-impressions.

As usual in Whitman, submission inaugurates a gathering of forces, and by the end of Section 26 he is so quickly refreshed and strengthened by the sound-impressions of the catalogue that he risks his polymorphous perversity to touch, the most arousing sense. Bristling with "instant conductors all over me," "I merely stir, press, feel with my fingers, and am happy,/ To touch my person to someone else's is about as much as I can stand" (Section 27).

In the next section the ensuing orgasm is so intense in the responses which it summons and the surrender which it demands that resistance to passion becomes an element in its fierceness, even violence. Freud argued that genital sexuality was a manifestation of the death-instinct as much as the erotic impulse and saw in genital sexuality the conflict between Eros and Thanatos. Death is life's climax as well as life's antagonist; because our intensest moments portend death, extinction is what we most desire and dread. Section 28 must be cited in full because the tangle of emotions represents the major obstacle to the progress of the poem and to the resolution of Whitman's sexual anxieties:

Is this then a touch? quivering me to a new identity,
Flames and ether making a rush for my veins,
Treacherous tip of me reaching and crowding to help them,
My flesh and blood playing out lightning to strike what is
        hardly different from myself,
On all sides prurient provokers stiffening my limbs,
Straining the udder of my heart for its withheld drip,
Behaving licentious toward me, taking no denial,
Depriving me of my best as for a purpose,
Unbuttoning my clothes, holding me by the bare waist,
Deluding my confusion with the calm of the sunlight
        and pasture-fields,
Immodestly sliding the fellow-senses away,
They bribed to swap off with touch and go and graze
        at the edges of me,
No consideration, no regard for my draining strength
        or my anger,
Fetching the rest of the herd around to enjoy them a while,
Then all uniting to stand on a headland and worry me.

The sentries desert every other part of me,
They have left me helpless to a red marauder,
They all come to the headland to witness and assist against me.
I am given up by traitors,
I talk wildly, I have lost my wits, I and nobody
        else am the greatest traitor,
I went myself first to the headland, my own hands
        carried me there.

You villain touch! what are you doing? my breath is
        tight in its throat,
Unclench your floodgates, you are too much for me.

The constriction of the senses to touch and, even more, of polymorphous stimulation to a genital climax is diffused in tender subsidence throughout the landscape in Section 29 ("Rich showering rain, and recompense richer after"; "Landscapes projected masculine, full-sized and golden") and diffused further in Section 30 into "omnific" relationships with "all things." These passages bear powerful testimony to Whitman's erotic nature; and, just as sexuality draws together "opposite equals" in loving contest, so Whitman's experience combines within the individual as well active and passive responses, violence and victimization, maddening desire and maddening fear—in short, the double drive to possess and be possessed. In the imagery of the passage phallic aggressor and raped woman merge. However, his polymorphousness is so basic to his nature that it carries him through the tormenting ecstasy of orgasm back to a more dispersed and generalized eroticism beyond the stresses and counterstresses of genital sexuality.

But the passage is more complicated than even the recognition of all these tensions would indicate. Throughout 28 and early in 29 there are suggestions of unusual and particular anxiety, fear, even shame and guilt, which raise inescapable questions concerning Whitman's sexuality in the middle of a poem proclaiming his newfound sexual self. Nor is this crisis surprising or inappropriate. Whitman's psyche is the ground of that poem's drama. It provides the matrix within which the ego, racked with anxieties, struggles to break out of its ambivalences and failures into a recognition of Self. That struggle is, as Whitman had said, the subject matter of the modern American epic. To see it as a struggle, and a struggle most of us recognize, not only rescues Whitman from being dismissed as a loud-mouthed, simpleminded braggart, as some critics would wish to do, but it also means that whatever is earned through the struggle is an achieved fact, more convincing and acceptable because the reader, too, has arrived there through the action of the poem. The issue is whether a recognition of Whitman's sexual ambivalences can be reconciled with the vaunting claims he made for himself as prophet of the sexual life-force, claims which were in part correctives and solutions for his difficulties. Once again, the key lies in the connection and distinction which we have heard Whitman make between the personal and the archetypal, the ego and the Self.

There is ample evidence of sexual anxiety in Whitman's poetry as well as in his biography. Section 11, in the midst of the ebullient catalogues which make up the second major movement of "Song of Myself," is only one instance. It is the most fully developed episode in that long list of episodes and images precisely because, whether or not Whitman was fully conscious of the fact, it dramatizes a deep-rooted snarl of psychic difficulties. The episode tells of the twenty-eight young men, swimming and romping in healthy nakedness, and the Victorian lady, enclosed in her "fine house" behind "the blinds of the window," dallying in her imagination with the young men in the surf. We do not have to remember Whitman's rejection of "houses and rooms . . . full of perfumes" in Section 2 to see the lady's fevered fantasy as the result of the sexual inhibition and repression that social mores enforce. But what the reader comes to feel, more keenly perhaps than Whitman would wish, is the fact that the passage displays how divided Whitman himself is; he identifies as much with the lone lady as with the robust young men she lusts for:

> An unseen hand also pass'd over their bodies,
> It descended tremblingly from their temples and ribs.
>
> The young men float on their backs, their white
>   bellies bulge to the sun, they do not ask
>   who seizes fast to them,
> They do not know who puffs and declines with
>   pendant and bending arch,
> They do not think whom they souse with spray.

The division, as we see, is not just between participation and observation, but, more troublesomely, between actual contact and self-titillation. The understanding of both sides is rendered through the bisexuality, and so the homosexuality, of the poet's perspective.

The story of the twenty-eight swimmers points ahead to Sections 28 through 30. There are suggestions of self-gratification in the orgiastic passage already quoted. In fact, it is impossible to distinguish the assault of external stimuli from masturbatory stimulation at the poet's own hand, but both conditions, intermingled, signify the dislocation which separates Narcissus from the world. The conflict and tension are ended through the dispersal of the poet's energy in universal relationships. That imaginative dispersal raises difficult questions about Whitman's response. To what extent is Whitman shrinking from sexual contact and from his autoeroticism and sublimating those energies? Does not his consistent resort to a succession of momentary contacts betray his desire to distance experience from his with-held presence? Then is not the poetry itself the principal device in generalizing responses and distancing experience? And, if so, are not the words the very medium of vicarious and self-indulgent gratification? He abstracts himself so habitually that he regularly addresses "you" as "whoever you are." In the last analysis, therefore, is Whitman a narcissist rather than a seer?

The answers to these questions are more complex than a simple yes or no. To begin with, as we have seen, the seer must include all and so must preclude delimitation to specific relationships and identities; and also, it must be admitted, this mode of relationship particularly suits Whitman's own psychological temperament in its weaknesses and vulnerabilities as well as its capacities and strengths. In that case, when does the prophetic role assumed in the poetry become the substitute for the sort of experience that the poems are celebrating and advocating? Since there is no biographical evidence of a physical relationship between Whitman and anyone, man or woman, are the words of the poems a bombastic exercise in self-delusion?

Robert Duncan, another shamanistic poet descendant from Whitman, invokes Freud himself to show such sublimation as a positive force, indeed, as a manifestation of the poet's peculiar prophetic ability:

> Whitman, like Dante, had this vision of Time, of Self and World,
> in his poetic conversion, through the medium of falling-in-love,
> where the inspiration of that falling-in-love being never
> exorcised in a sexual satisfaction, longing has been the seed of
> a creative desiring transforming the inner and outer reality.
> Freud has made us aware, even wary, of such a process of
> sublimation, and simple Freudians, those who do not go along
> with Freud's mythic imagination toward his deeper vision of the
> work of Eros and Thanatos in Creation, think of sublimation as a
> removal from the primary genital fact, which is real, a flight from
> what is sexual and actual into higher thought and abstraction . . .
> But I would see the process at work in Dante's and Whitman's
> falling in love in light of another reading out of Freud, in which
> Eros and Thanatos are primary, at work in the body of the poem
> even as they are at work in the body of the man, awakening in
> language apprehensions of what we call sexuality and spirituality.
> Parts of language, like parts of the physical body, will be
> inspired; syllables and words, like cells and organs, will be

> excited, awakened to the larger identity they belong to. . . . As
> words belong to language and cells to animal bodies, poets
> come to belong to poetry.[26]

In other words, someone like Whitman explores and expresses his sexual-spiritual, feminine-masculine nature in and through the words of the poetry and thereby comes to his deepest realizations of Self and World.

Such a process of sublimation, far from being sick, is the medium of vision—not that Whitman had no neuroses, but that his neuroses provided the occasion for his genius. Any reader may decide to reject Whitman's vision, but he ought not to do so through a facile reduction of prophetic claims to neurotic impulses. In Whitman's case, at least, his neuroses and his genius are associated but not identical, and they are not to be confused. The very character of Whitman's psyche made possible the discovery of himself as seer where a less troubled mind might have remained content with surface calm. That set of complexes led him into the omnific relationships of the prophet, but the poetry testifies that the relationships were genuine: his semidetached presence anchored in momentary identification with a constantly shifting series of concrete particulars, and at the same time drawing those particulars into a coherence which requires the seer to maintain a certain detachment.

A strict Freudian—what Duncan calls a "simple Freudian"—takes Freud's theory of childhood traumas as endemic to the human condition and would argue that unless Whitman digs his way back to all those complications buried in his personal unconscious (and there would seem to be a snarled knot of psychic material to be cleared away in that family with an erratic and irascible father, an ignorant and powerful mother, and a brood of children afflicted with various physical, emotional, and mental illnesses), he will be snared and crippled by his neurotic self-delusions. In Freudian theory human nature is fallen into alienation and neurosis, the psychological analogues to the theologian's original sin, and childhood traumas are its inescapable manifestation and perhaps its inescapable destiny. Later, psychologists and psychiatrists working from basic Freudian principles have sought to modify Freud's emphasis in order to facilitate the individual's passage beyond childhood neuroses. Erik Erikson, for example, claims for himself a "post-Freudian position." However, though he wants to speculate about possibilities after "neurotic resentments end" and "mere readjustment is transcended," he can only conceive of it as *after*; an "ongoing life" is for him built on the previously "resolved crisis."[27] Perhaps no theory which insists on the ego as the source of coherence and meaning in the psyche can trust the impulses of the unconscious, even the conflicts and dislocations within the unconscious, sufficiently to allow them to find their own modes of accommodation and forms of expression. A more broadly humanistic approach might point out that Whitman had turned his anxieties into a positive, notably happy life which was enriching not alone to himself but to his friends and into a book that has moved generation after generation of readers. In this sense his neuroses gave him life instead of trapping him from it. Increasingly psychologists—R. D. Laing is a notable instance—have come to insist that terms like "neurosis" and "psychosis" must be used, when they are used at all, as descriptive terms without judgmental overtones of "bad" or "destructive" or "crippling." It has long been the Jungian view that a so-called neurosis, even a so-called psychosis, could in the end be beneficial by propelling a person into depths that would otherwise remain inert and unexplored. In other words, the psychological complication becomes the dynamism of discovery, pointing the direction and providing the initial but necessary impetus for development.

From that perspective Whitman's psychic bent opened the way for him to express himself as—and to be—the poet-prophet. In a remarkable reversal his neuroses forced his ego from its defensive inhibitions into the turbid, mysterious area where the Self waited to be engaged, waited to emerge for recognition. And Self-awareness transformed not just his vision of "the Me myself" but his vision of the "not-me" as well, both indistinguishably enclosed within and manifesting the ineluctable Life-Mystery.

Clearly, then, the break in the middle of the poem between forward movements was necessary and therapeutic so that all the doubts and self-doubts lurking in the poet's psyche and in the seeming presumptuousness of the "Song" could be confronted and faced out. Contact without surrender of ego-control, extension without absorption of identity—so subtle was the balance that Whitman found himself in constant adjustment and counter-adjustment. The danger that first broke the surface in Section 25 and pressed home in Section 28 was overcome by the end of Section 30. The affront to ego-identity which the sunrise suddenly seemed to present, the loss of ego-control which his polymorphous eroticism unexpectedly brought to a head, were transcended not by reassertion of the ego but instead by acquiescence in the instinctual energies of the unconscious; the psyche, agonizingly aware that it must not want to resist those energies, is driven ("herded," to pick up the word the passage uses) to an almost unbearable point of concentration—and then breakthrough, diffusion. And another pulsation of the poem.

In signification of that fact, Section 31 returns to the symbol of the "leaf of grass" and connects it, and any other humble miracle of life, with the sublimest reaches of time and space. In a startling series of imaginative empathies the poet rehearses within himself the entire evolutionary process of creation: from inorganic substances ("gneiss, coal," "plutonic rocks") through plants ("long-threaded moss, fruits, grains, esculent roots") to animals ("stucco'd with quadrupeds and birds all over") to human consciousness aspiring to the cosmic consciousness of deity—all this "incorporated" in his body-self. By Section 32 the revulsion against animality implicit in the diction of Sections 28 and 29 ("udder," "graze," "herd," "sheath'd hooded sharp-tooth'd touch") has been sufficiently conquered so that the beautiful unconsciousness of animals fulfilling their natures in simple existence seems, for the moment, preferable to the conflicts and anxieties that bedevil ego-consciousness. Recapturing the sense of himself "stout as a horse" (Section 3), the poet sums up his hymn to animals in the "gigantic beauty of a stallion." But unable to rest long in brute unconsciousness, he immediately realizes how far he surpasses the stallion: "I but use you a minute, then I resign you, stallion,/ Why do I need your paces when I myself out-gallop them?" To what? Not a return to ego-consciousness, but an ascension to superconsciousness, to all that is held in "Space and Time!" By absorbing all, he has not lost but found himself; he has not died in it, it lives in him.

So Section 33 returns again to the generating vision, adumbrated in Section 1 and dramatized in Section 5. By now the poet knows "what I guess'd at while I lay on the grass," and the recovered knowledge stimulates the second great sequence of catalogues, Sections 33 through 37, balancing a similar sequence in the first half of the poem. The catalogues begin as rapid, momentary identifications in one-line images. But as Section 33, the longest in the poem, runs on, the "I" becomes gradually more deeply identified with the objects observed, so that the images are suffused with expressions of imaginative projection and negative capability: "All this I swallow, it tastes good, I like it well, it becomes mine,/ I am the man, I suffer'd, I was there"; "All these I feel or am"; "I do not ask the wounded person how he feels, I myself become the wounded person,/ My hurts turn livid upon me as I lean on a cane and observe"; "I am the mash'd fireman with breast-bone broken"; "I am the old artillerist, I tell of my fort's bombardment,/ I am there again"; "I take part, I see and hear the whole." This penetration beyond the mere "show or resonance" of things makes the poet not only an observer but a participant, if only imaginatively. The deepening involvement leads to the most extended episodes in the whole poem: the mass slaughter of the soldiers at Goliad, Texas, recounted in Section 34; and the sea fight during the Revolution between the *Bon Homme Richard* under John Paul Jones and the *Serapis*, occupying both Sections 35 and 36.

The catalogues begin to taper off in 37 with briefer vignettes, but they are all so distressing (a prisoner, a mutineer, a criminal, a cholera victim, a shamefaced beggar) and the poet's imagination by now so sensitively exposed that he finds himself on the verge, once again, of losing his ego-center in circumference:

> Enough! enough! enough!
> Somehow I have been stunn'd. Stand back!
> Give me a little time beyond my cuff'd head,
>   slumbers, dreams, gaping,
> I discover myself on the verge of a usual mistake.

Keats had sought to escape the trap of the "egotistical sublime" which he felt at times in Wordsworth through "negative capability," that is, through negating the ego and identifying as completely as he could with the real or imagined object of his attention. Whitman engaged in the same psychological dialectic for much the same reason, but here he finds himself in the danger opposite to the "egotistical sublime"; namely the rapid dissipation of ego-consciousness both through the dispersive sweep of the catalogue and, more urgently, through the depth of empathetic identification with the vivid and painful particulars. "I am possess'd," he cried out, as he was being raped by the "red marauder" in Section 28. Nevertheless—and this is the sign of growing strength and health—he has come so far along in negotiating a mode of relationship between himself and his circumambience, so cognizant is he of excessive negative capability as a mistake that by the end of Section 38, in the matter of a few lines, the poet has recovered—in fact, resurrected himself beyond extinction eager to "troop forth replenish'd with supreme power, one of an average unending procession."

This last sally—the concluding movement of the poem—begins with the reintegration of the Self, at once immanent and transcendent, individual and inclusive, around the ego-center in four archetypal roles. The first (Sections 39 and 40) is the universal lover ("the friendly and flowing savage") so phallic that his touch strengthens impotent old men: "You there, impotent, loose in the knees,/ Open your scarf'd chops till I blow grit within you"; so multiphallic as to couple plurally with women: "On women fit for conception I start bigger and nimbler babes,/ (This day I am jetting the stuff of far more arrogant republics.)" This boast may seem another instance of the ludicrous exaggeration that Richard Chase thinks must be deliberate comic deflation until myth provides such analogues as the many-breasted statue of Diana of Ephesus and the multiplication of phalluses on statues of fertility deities. So potent a life-force is he in this transcendent dimension that his embrace brings resurrection: "lovers of me" are transformed into "bafflers of graves." Matching the archetype of Lover is the archetype of Deity, so that in Section 41 the Self reveals itself not merely as God but as the God of man's many gods. The other two archetypes of the Lover-God specify his social and communal responsibilities: Guru-Wise Man (Section 42) and High Priest to all priesthoods (Section 43). This quaternity of archetypes justifies the poet in celebrating the Self in Section 44 as center of the cosmos-in-process:

> I am an acme of things accomplish'd, and I am
> encloser of things to be.

> My feet strike an apex of the apices of the stairs,
> On every step bunches of ages, and larger bunches
> between the steps,
> All below duly travel'd, and still I mount and mount.

There is a danger for the individual in equating his limited and fallible psyche with the archetypes in the excitement of realizing that he is giving particular form to their transcendent qualities, and it is here that the ego's awareness of weaknesses and limitations and the ego's consequent tenacity in asserting itself serve a redemptive function in calling the person back to himself without denying the efficacy of the archetypes. Whitman is and is not Lover-God-Wise Man-Priest, and the ego, for all its anxieties, serves to save the psyche from delusory inflation in order to integrate it into a personality. Ego-constrictions have occurred and will recur, but at this point in the poem the ego is able to sustain the Self in its most exalted expansiveness. So, in Section 45, escaping the suffocating presence of objects, even the claims of lovers, the poet presses beyond even the furthest circumference to meet what Emerson called the "aboriginal Self" who is the source and goal for each individual Self:

> My rendezvous is appointed, it is certain,
> The Lord will be there and wait till I come on
> perfect terms,
> The great Camerado, the lover true for whom I pine
> will be there.

In the end, the poet anticipates, he will find the features of "the Me myself" in those of "the great Camerado," just as he had come to find the Lord's visage in his own human face.

To what extent is this anticipation of an afterlife inconsistent with the previously stated acceptance of Materialism (for example, in Section 23), which gives process precedence over personality and for which the religious dimension is Pantheism? It is difficult to say, since Whitman experienced and so was convinced of both beliefs at different times and even at the same time. The poems written mostly in the fifties and sixties but gathered together under the rubric "Whispers of Heavenly Death" in 1881 pose the question and the alternative answers. The first alternative is the sense that *"matter is conqueror—matter, triumphant only, continues onward"* as individual corporeal entities metamorphose into new corporeal entities, the same atoms reassembling in other modes of vital activity. The second is the sense of the indestructibility of the Self, which survives the corpse as "yourself spiritual bodily," or what Christians call the resurrected body. "Thoughts," written in the same year as the lines above, concludes that "the vehement struggle so fierce for unity in one's-self" forges an immortal personal identity; and this conviction, most rhapsodically presented in "Passage to India" (1868), came over the years to be more strongly asserted than Pantheism. In other words, Whitman gradually revised and superseded his notion of the body-self—that is, of an identity inseparable from its material form—as with age and experience he unearthed the spiritual resources of the Self. The poem "Eidólons," first published in 1876, makes the point concisely when it speaks of

> Thy body permanent,
> The body lurking there within thy body,
> The only purport of the form thou art, the real I myself,
> An image, an eidólon.

However, as we have seen, this idea is not merely a late development; "Song of Myself"—at least in some of the sections of the concluding movement—already seems to posit from the outset a personal immortality as the end of life's journey to Selfhood.

In its fullest realization, as elaborated in these sections of "Song of Myself," the Self reveals itself mythologically as the Cosmic Man, one of the recurrent images of psychological wholeness in dreams and legends throughout history. In *Man and His Symbols* Marie-Louise von Franz described the Cosmic Man as he has appeared in various cultures. He takes different forms, but always he is "a gigantic, symbolic human being who embraces and contains the whole cosmos." His appearance denotes the fact that the individual has come to realize that what is most uniquely himself is also what transcends himself; he is part of the Cosmic Man at the same time that he embodies the Cosmic Man. In this way, states Dr. von Franz, the Cosmic Man is "more an inner psychic image than a concrete outer reality." Through his gradual emergence "this inner Great Man redeems the individual human being by leading him out of creation and its sufferings, back into his original eternal sphere"; this psychic "redemption" transpires as the individual draws the Cosmic Man out of himself, personifies the Cosmic Man in himself:

> In practical terms this means that the existence of human beings will never be satisfactorily explained in terms of isolated instincts or purposive mechanism such as hunger, power, sex, survival, perpetuation of the species, and so on. That is, man's main purpose is not to eat, drink, etc., but *to be human*. Above and beyond these drives, our inner psychic reality serves to manifest a living mystery that can be expressed only by a symbol, and for its expression the unconscious often chooses the powerful image of the Cosmic Man.[28]

At the same time, realization of some of the individual's mythic potentiality does not remove him from time and place, as Whitman's biography and his writings confirm; on the contrary, such realization allows him to occupy his place in the world and in society more truly, since his mythic potentiality is what links him to his fellow-humans. The Cosmic Man is rooted in organic nature and in man's sexuality. Mircea Eliade has pointed out that often the experience of the divine light is associated with the body, sometimes projecting a vision of ethereal light-bodies but sometimes settling explicitly in the genitals as emanations of a power both sexual and spiritual. Similarly, in myth the semen of Gayomart, the Persian First Man, sprang up from the earth as two rhubarb shrubs; the Chinese P'an Ku was "depicted covered by leaves like a plant"; the Western Cosmic Man is the unfallen Adam in the green garden. Whitman, displaying himself as a plant-man in the leaves of his book, also identified himself with Adam in the poems of *Children of Adam;* that section opens with the identification of America as the new Eden for the sexual union of Adam and Eve and concludes with "As Adam Early in the Morning":

> As Adam early in the morning,
> Walking forth from the bower refresh'd with sleep,
> Behold me where I pass, hear my voice, approach,
> Touch me, touch the palm of your hand to my body
>   as I pass,
> Be not afraid of my body.

Whitman, the First Man of the New Society, addressed the American people so that each can join with the embodied archetype, be inspirited by him, and take his place in society. Dr. von Franz has reproduced the title page of Hobbes' *Leviathan*, personifying the Commonwealth as the Cosmic Man composed of ("stucco'd all over" was Whitman's descriptive verb in Section 31) his myriad citizens. So the shaman-bard must draw his people magnetically and, as second Adam, name them in his catalogues. Moreover, the Cosmic Man, as Dr. von Franz points out, is not merely a masculine projection; he is often not only sexual but bisexual or hermaphroditic, as many images of the Self are. In other words, the Self is finally beyond sexuality: all oppositions, including sexual oppositions, have found accommodation and resolution. James Hillman, another psychologist, has shown that the figure of Dionysus is important for a man because he symbolizes the androgynous nature of the fully realized psyche—specifically, the openness of ego-consciousness to the unconscious and the possibility in man of recovering and expressing the feminine aspects of his inner nature. Commenting on Whitman's "bisexual wholeness," Adrienne Rich concluded that even the poetry of Whitman which could be described as homoerotic "does not represent a flight from woman but a recognition of woman, and of the being in himself and in his beloved that is capable of tenderness, vulnerability, mutuality." Psychological androgyny does not determine sexual activity or habit any more than a more sexually polarized psyche would. A psychologically androgynous person could be continent or incontinent, faithful or faithless, heterosexual or homosexual or, for that matter, asexual. In Whitman's case, his sexual doubleness, which at times caused his ego many stresses and anxieties, also came to yield such a sense of Self-possession that after seeing the Cosmic Man in himself he seemed, for the most part, not to have needed or desired any particular sexual relationship.[29]

Now, projecting the Cosmic Man in a four-fold mandala of wholeness (Sections 39–43) and conjoining center and circumference in this Self, Whitman has confounded the riddling intellect's logic with magic and squared the circle as the sign of the psyche. Then, with Sections 46 and 47, he can return to the temporal process, again expressly engaging "you" in relation to the achieved "I" and sending "you" forth on a progress that moves beyond any single life or poem. As the Cosmic Man contains us all, as the *Brahman* contains each *atman*, so "I" contain each of "you" in your nascent Self-realization. The very last sections reassert Whitman's Pantheism and his Transcendentalism together, not resolved intellectually but felt simultaneously: "Do I contradict myself?/ Very well then I contradict myself,/ (I am large, I contain multitudes.)" The Self is preeminent, godlike, God: "And nothing, not God, is greater to one than one's self is" (Section 48), ascending to heaven from the entombed corpse, like Jesus in His risen body (Section 49). Yet, at the same time "the soul is not more than the body," and God manifests Himself as flux "in every object" in "each hour" (Section 48); consequently "if you want me again look for me under your boot-soles" because "I bequeath myself to the dirt to grow from the grass I love" (Section 52). Although he has said that at last "it is time to explain myself" (Section 44), he cannot satisfactorily or consistently explain; he can say nothing more than: "There is that in me—I do not know what it is—but I know it is in me" (Section 50). The secret of the life-process is "without name . . . a word unsaid . . . not in any dictionary, utterance, symbol"; it surpasses articulation in human terms. Just as "prophetical screams" and then silence were the alternatives to speech in Section 25 at the middle of the poem, so "Song of Myself" ends in Section 52 with the poet sounding his "barbaric yawp over the roofs of the world" and disappearing, as it had begun with his breaking out of the perfumed houses and rooms into the "atmosphere." Like the weeks in a year, he has come full circle. "Untranslatable" to the end, "I depart as air," and yet "I stop somewhere waiting for you"; and the poem whose first word was "I" concludes, fifty or sixty pages later, with the word "you."

3

Thus far we have been considering "Song of Myself" as an epitome of *Leaves of Grass*. It is important, however, to take some account of the book as a whole. To begin with, there is great variety in the shape, thematic emphasis, and emotional tone of the poems. Besides the long, loosely episodic chants ("The Sleepers,"

"Starting from Paumanok" and "Song of the Open Road" would be other examples) there are more tightly knit pieces, some of which have been widely admired and discussed by academic critics: poems organized around a single image, like "A Noiseless Patient Spider," "Sparkles from the Wheel," and "The Dalliance of the Eagles"; poems strung along a single narrative line, like "Crossing Brooklyn Ferry," "Out of the Cradle Endlessly Rocking," and "When Lilacs Last in the Dooryard Bloom'd"; poems rendered without comment though images, like the most anthologized of the *Drum-Taps* poems, "A Prairie Sunset," and "Unseen Buds."

Almost all Whitman poems end on an upbeat, but this does not mean, as we have already seen, that darkness—sin, death, violence, despair—are excluded or overlooked. The *Sea-Drift* section makes the mother-sea the grave as well as the womb. "Out of the Cradle Endlessly Rocking," the first poem in the section, marks the poet's vocation from his first realization of death as a boy, and that sourcing of poetry in Thanatos stands beside his sourcing of poetry in Eros in "Song of Myself." "As I Ebb'd with the Ocean of Life," another *Sea-Drift* poem, sees the flux as a "type" not of process but disintegration, at least for the individual; and the image of flotsam and sea-wrack as the universal symbol so shakes the poet's prophetic vision of unity that even his most skeptical critic could not call into question the arrogance of his boasts more damningly than he does here. *Whispers of Heavenly Death* weighs the question of personal immortality and seems to answer it positively at last, but the specter of extinction persists throughout the book. The tragedy of the Civil War, for the individuals slain and maimed and for the nation torn bloodily apart, produced *Drum-Taps*, which Whitman came to view as the pivotal section of the book; its validation lay in its ability to survive and surmount such a categorical challenge to its fundamental premises. Although the great Lincoln elegy, "When Lilacs Last in the Dooryard Bloom'd," moves to affirmation, as the funeral train progresses healingly through the mourning cities and across "the breast of the spring" in the rebirth of the slain Redeemer-President's native land, its affirmation is an admission of violence and malice. Whitman's later poems tended to compensate for the venality and corruptions of the Reconstruction and the Gilded Age by becoming more didactically optimistic. Nevertheless, to the end he so resisted any fastidiousness about vice in the name of virtue that when he heard such a simplistic sermon the year before his death, he countered with a poem ironically titled " 'The Rounded Catalogue Divine Complete,' " filling out the minister's list with an accounting that begins: "The devilish and the dark, the dying and diseas'd,/ The countless (nineteen-twentieths) low and evil, crude and savage. . . ."

Moreover, *Leaves of Grass* defined itself not just in variety but in metamorphosis. As Whitman lived through those decades of crisis and change, the shape and structure of his book changed as it grew through many editions to the "Deathbed Edition" in the year of Whitman's death, with still another section added later. The first volume of Roger Asselineau's *The Evolution of Walt Whitman* gives a detailed description of the design, organization, and composition of each of the editions. The main features of the early development of the book are the dramatic expansion of the 1855 edition the next year; the addition of *Children of Adam* and *Calamus* in 1860, along with some of the poems that would comprise the sections later called *Sea-Drift* and *Whispers of Heavenly Death*; and the inclusion in 1865 of *Drum-Taps and Sequel*, with the war poems and Lincoln elegies. By 1872 Whitman was calling *Leaves of Grass* complete and beginning a "Supplementary Volume" to celebrate the *"Democratic Nationality"* as a balance to the primary emphasis on the *"Democratic Individual"* in the first volume. However, during the following year a series of strokes nearly killed him and left him crippled and much reduced in poetic as well as physical vitality for the rest of his life. Consequently, by 1876 he had abandoned the notion of the complementary second volume, although he now described the idea of it in religious rather than political terms as songs of "Death, Immortality, and . . . the Spiritual world" to balance "the songs of the Body and Existence" in *Leaves of Grass*.[30] Nevertheless, each new edition of *Leaves* contained new poems, and rearranged the order of poems. The 1881 edition established the final organization of the poems as a series of sections suggestive of the cycle of the day, the seasons and the life-span, and thereafter that organization remained constant, expanded only by annexes at the end: *Sands at Seventy* (1888); *Good-Bye My Fancy* (1892), the year of his death; and the posthumous *Old Age Echoes* (1897).

Sometimes, after he had become "the good gray poet," Whitman talked grandly as though the design of *Leaves of Grass* were grasped from the initial vision, its determined form merely to be executed as more poems came. But the book's growth, as Asselineau has copiously demonstrated, is a search for form as the design gradually and hesitatingly tested itself out. And, in point of fact, Whitman himself recognized this groping for an emergent design —only to be drawn out through the agency of the poet—as one of the distinctive aspects of his experiment. From the perspective of 1876: "Though from no definite plan at the time, I see now that I have unconsciously sought, by indirections at least as much as by directions." Near the end in "A Backward Glance O'er Travel'd Roads" (1888): "[poems] grow of circumstances, and are evolutionary. The actual living light is always curiously from elsewhere—follows unaccountable sources, is lunar and relative at the best." Or again,

> After completing my poems, I am curious to review them in the light of their own (at the time unconscious, or mostly unconscious) intentions, with certain unfoldings of the thirty years they seek to embody. These lines, therefore, will probably blend the weft of first purposes and speculations, with the warp of that experience afterwards, always bringing strange developments.

Consequently, the design, even of the "Deathbed Edition," had to be an unfinished and open-ended *"sortie,"* the process to be continued (but not even then completed) in each reader's experience: "I round and finish little, if anything; and could not, consistently with my scheme."[31]

Robert Duncan summed up the necessity for a shape metamorphosing through time:

> The Creative Self at work in Creation toward the realization of Self asks, who learns my lesson complete? *Leaves of Grass* was itself a lesson not to be learned complete. The poet returned to his work there in edition after edition. Not addition after addition, but furnishing forth each time a life of the book. . . . The grand

Maker or Poet makes his Self come real—realizes Himself—as
he makes the field of the Real. We learn who we are by living
—we are ourselves the mass of our individualities. Lesson
undoes lesson.

Materials coalescing, dissolving, reforming—such is "at once the
very kinetics of Whitman's own line structure within the poem, of
poem structure within the Leaves of Grass, of edition upon edition
of that book, and of his sense of the essential informing motion
of the life of Man and of the Universe."[32]

So insistent was Whitman on the coexistence of art and life,
so immoral did the nineteenth-century aesthete's distinction between art and life seem to him that he could declare his art anti-
aesthetic: "No one will get at my verses who insists upon viewing
them as a literary performance, or attempt at such performance,
or as aiming mainly toward art or aestheticism."[33] Closing out
Leaves of Grass in 1881 with "So Long!" he reiterated the point:

Camerado, this is no book,
Who touches this touches a man,
(Is it night? are we here together alone?)
It is I you hold and who holds you,
I spring from the pages into your arms—decease
    calls me forth.

Friends and disciples clustered round him in an extraordinary
demonstration of personal devotion, and in the 1870s Anne Gilchrist, the English widow of William Blake's biographer, moved
with her children to the United States in order to be near Whitman and return to him the love she felt in his poems.

No wonder that after the hundred years that Whitman had
said it would take to assess his experiment, William Carlos Williams could see Leaves of Grass as a revolutionary challenge to the
very idea of what a poem is.[34] Yet, without real inconsistency,
Whitman once mused in his old age to Horace Traubel that sometimes he thought of Leaves of Grass as primarily a "language experiment." If "the personal urge and form for me" is "not merely
paper" but "automatic type and ink," if the experience of mystery
in Self and Cosmos is a "flight into the wordless," then it is
simultaneously and equally true that "the words of my book [are]

nothing—the drift of it everything" and that "the words of true poems give you more than poems."[35] Language can only be a gesture toward, but it is *the* gesture toward. Consequently the shaman must enrich and expand his medium in order to make it as expressive, as magical, a gesture as possible.

Hence the tremendous range of diction and rapid shifts of levels and tone of diction in Whitman's poetry, blending slang and philosophical abstractions with coinages and foreign borrowings to strive—sometimes gloriously, sometimes clumsily—for an all-inclusive language to convey the mystery of identity in the eternal flow of bodies. Whitman had thoroughly absorbed the grandiloquence of Shakespeare, the vigor of Homer, the austere sublimity of the Bible and the unabashed emotional flights of opera. In addition to Transcendental Idealism, Yankee homespun in Emerson and Scots-German crosshatch in Carlyle, he came to find in historians like Michelet and philosophers like Hegel, as well as in the religions of the Near East and the Orient, other articulations of his intuitions. He incorporated the oddity and energy of foreign locutions into a "melting pot" language to match the national character. He made up words when he found none to hand, and he deliberately drew on the trenchant volatility of colloquial speech. Whitman saw slang as "an attempt of common humanity to escape from bald literalism, and express itself illimitably" by tapping "the lawless germinal element, below all words and sentences, and behind all poetry" and thus participating in "the wholesome fermentation and eructation of those processes eternally active in language."[36] Although "Slang in America" is a late statement, appearing in *The North American Review* in 1885, Whitman must have had in mind the "Language" chapter of Emerson's *Nature*, which he had known from the beginning. Not only do many of his illustrations repeat Emerson's; there is the same sense of language as symbolic, the same sense of every new relation as requiring a new word.

The prophet and myth-maker speaks in slang, and his method is "indirection": "to approach a meaning not directly and squarely, but by circuitous styles of expression." When language is constantly remade organically ("like some vast living body"), speech projects a vital "Suggestiveness." In other words, a language fann'd by the breath of Nature, which leaps overhead, cares mostly for impetus and effects, and for what it plants and invigorates to grow—tallies life and character, and seldomer tells a thing than suggests or necessitates it. In fact, a new theory of literary composition for imaginative works of the very first class, and especially for highest poems, is the sole course open to these States.

Oddly enough, the suggestion of something is what makes it necessary, bringing it into being. It is true that "Poetic style, when address'd to the Soul, is less definite form, outline, sculpture, and becomes vista, music, half-tints, and even less than half-tints"; but the very lack of finish is what validates the new theory by engaging the reader creatively in the thrust toward completion again and again. The passage from *Democratic Vistas* quoted above went on to reject the notion that the engagement with the poem, however much it moves into the half-tints of suggestiveness and musical vistas, is the sort of reverie which Poe envisioned as an escape from jumbled experience into a dream of a lost ideal. Suggestiveness and indirection could be more strenuous and healthy and life-enhancing than Poe knew. So Whitman described the reader's participation in the creative process:

> The process of reading is not a half-sleep, but, in highest sense, an exercise, a gymnast's struggle; . . . the reader is to do something for himself, must be on the alert, must himself or herself construct indeed the poem, argument, history, metaphysical essay—the text furnishing the hints, the clue, the start or framework.[37]

So, as with Emerson, there is less contradiction than might at first appear between Whitman's anti-aestheticism and his attention to his medium and method as a language experiment. The conviction that art and life are inseparable does not subvert art; rather, it specifies its field of relation and activity. In fact, it makes art indispensable to life. If, as he wrote to Emerson in 1856 at the outset, "the work of my life is making poems," the uses of language to new ends were crucial to his ongoing existence, and Whitman did live more passionately through his imagination in his poetry than in his external relationships. Moreover, if Mrs.

Gilchrist, among others, felt the man when she touched the book, that was only because the words on the page comprised (call it that or not) a successful literary performance. When Mrs. Gilchrist pressed her claims, Whitman warned her not to confuse "the actual W.W." with "an unauthorized & imaginary ideal Figure" and found her a place to live in Philadelphia across the river from his place in Camden, where she could be a friend but nothing more. That distinction leads Roger Asselineau, along with most Freudians, to conclude that the success of the book is a gauge of the neurotic failure of the sick author for which it serves to compensate. Whitman was seemingly candid in admitting to Mrs. Gilchrist that the biographical W.W. is truer somehow than the poetic "I" and "Me myself," but his strategy was defensive rather than confessional. Yes, his poetic identity is in a sense a creation, imaginary and ideal, sublimated from his biographical situation and masking it. But is not the poet's exploration of his highest and deepest possibilities a truer expression of his identity than the observable data of his existence? Whitman, then, was deliberately misleading Mrs. Gilchrist out of the exigencies of his practical, external arrangements, and he was much closer to the truth when he claimed with pride and an earned sense of satisfaction in his later years that he had "put *a Person*, a human being (myself, in the latter half of the Nineteenth Century, in America,) freely, fully and truly on record."[38] We may want to gloss the adverbs some, but the claim still stands. In its "suggestiveness" and "indirection" his book was—literally—Self-creative and Self-expressive. Art became not a death-oriented substitute for life, as it was for Baudelaire, Oscar Wilde, and the aesthetes, but a way of living, even beyond death. His exploration may not have been a literary performance in the notion accepted then, but his words would not have had their enormous effect if his language experiment had not been successful enough to have remained an inspiration, potent and alive, in a future fraught with more violent threats to the individual and to society than Whitman could have suspected.

VI
EMILY DICKINSON:
The Self as Center

In April 1862 Thomas Wentworth Higginson, who considered himself liberal in matters literary as well as in matters theological, social, and racial, received a request from an unknown woman-poet to serve as her mentor as she evaluated and revised her poems. The letter was a puzzling yet winning combination of reserve and directness; it was unsigned but revealed the author's name on a calling card in a separate envelope. It was one of several letters, mostly from eccentrics, addressed to Higginson in the wake of his "Letter to a Young Contributor," published in that month's *Atlantic Monthly* to encourage incipient talent in new writers. But when he answered this note, agreeing to become her preceptor, Higginson could have had no notion of what it meant: Emily Dickinson, living in deeper and deeper seclusion in her father's house in Amherst, was beginning to take herself so seriously as a poet that she felt compelled, against the grain of habit, to open up converse with the outside world at least enough to approach this respectable man of letters. She was at once seeking approval from the literary establishment and serving modest notice of her presence. Dickinson wrote Higginson much later that his acknowledgment of her, coming as it did at a decisive time, constituted the gesture that saved her life.

She had been writing verse since the early 1850s and had begun to refer to herself as a poet in letters to her "literary" brother and to the equally "literary" young woman, Sue Gilbert, who would become her sister-in-law. In the late fifties she began to make fair copies of the poems she liked and bind them into neat, uniform packets. Samuel Bowles, the family friend who edited the *Springfield Daily Republican* and was at that point her sole literary acquaintance of any sort, had published two of her pieces in his newspaper, but even those few verses were subjected to scrutiny and change without so much as a courteous consultation with the poet before blue-penciling. Now Higginson seemed to be sufficiently intrigued by the poems she sent him to write her about them.

But what was he to make of such odd poems, and what was she to make of his response? The rhythms were irregular and jerky ("spasmodic" and "uncontrolled" were his words)[1]; the lines would not always scan; the rhymes often jangled imperfectly against one another; the convolutions and compressions of language sometimes proved impenetrable. In trying to grasp the enigmatic person who could spin out these strange but striking pieces, Higginson asked in his first reply whether she had read Whitman. His "Letter to a Young Contributor" had called for genuine originality but condemned willful eccentricity, and in the Whitman chapter we heard Higginson intoning that Whitman's shame lay not so much in having written *Leaves of Grass* as in not burning it afterward. However powerful and therapeutic the Whitman poems were, they did not have the formal and moral qualities that distinguish art from crude self-expression. Now, in trying to figure out the woman whom he would later call "my partially cracked poetess at Amherst," Higginson thought of the possible effects of reading Whitman's willful free verse. Her reply was evasive: "You speak of Mr. Whitman—I never read his Book—but was told that he was disgraceful—" Her answers to all his searching questions were cryptic, but she sent more poems. Perhaps she had been warned against Whitman; perhaps she had read about him in the *Daily Republican*. An editorial of March 1860 denounced the appearance of "Bardic Symbols," later called "As I Ebb'd with the Ocean of Life," in the *Atlantic Monthly*: "we didn't suppose anybody admired them [Whitman's poems] but Emerson, and that fact was the only really bad thing we ever knew of him." The *Daily Republican*'s review of the 1860 edition of *Leaves of Grass*, which included the *Children of Adam* and *Calamus* poems, intoned phrases like "befouled with filth," "defaced by vulgarity," "a sea of foul impurities." The next year Dr. J. G. Holland, who with his wife would later become an acquaintance of Dickinson, wrote a piece labeled " 'Leaves of Grass'—Smut in them" arguing that this "scandalous volume" was "about as much like poetry as tearing off a rag, or paring one's corns."[2]

Dickinson may not have learned her eccentricity from Whitman, but Higginson advised that her poems were not deserving of publication. She immediately concurred, and whether or not at that point she had lingering hopes for a contemporary public, she thereafter resisted publication as resolutely as she entrusted herself to the fame she expected after her death. If Bowles and Higginson met her with incomprehension, what would she receive from less gifted contemporaries? As a woman poet of the twentieth century, Adrienne Rich has written of the need for male approval bred into the woman writer and of the disastrous inhibitions which those fears inculcated:

> . . . to a lesser or greater extent, every woman writer has written for men even when, like Virginia Woolf, she was supposed to be addressing women. If we have come to the point when this balance might begin to change, when women can stop being haunted, not only by "convention and propriety," but by internalized fears of being and saying themselves, then it is an extraordinary moment for the woman writer—and reader.[3]

Long before American society had reached such a point of liberation for women poets, Emily Dickinson had demanded it for herself. She maintained the connection with Higginson, and they remained friends at a distance till his death. For a while he offered kindly advice and she sent him poems; but she resolved almost from the outset to pay no heed to his cautions about form and technique. Although he remained a kind of link with the masculine world of letters, she knew what she was doing and, with the professional self-assurance which underlay her personal insecurity, wrote her poems accordingly.

The association of Dickinson with Whitman seems on the face of it merely a sign of Higginson's obtuseness. He saw eccentricity and undisciplined lack of form in petto in the one where it was writ large in the other. But what else, we might ask, was there to connect them? Whitman sounded his "barbaric yawp" and advertised himself, and Dickinson hid her poems in a drawer in her room in the family home. Where his verse expands to include everyone and everything, her taut, short poems turn on discrete internal experiences. Where his poems grow toward a single organic design, her almost 1800 pieces stand as distinct and contradictory statements. Where he sought to delineate "a simple separate person" in terms of "the word Democratic," she took as her exclusive materials the scope of her single separate consciousness. Where Whitman became a type of the public bard, she became a type of the poet who clears for herself a place of polar privacy.

At the same time Higginson's inquiry had a certain point, whether or not it was his point. Both were distinctly, if differingly,

American poets; the link is Emerson. In many ways the decisive figure in nineteenth-century America, Emerson stood behind both Whitman and Dickinson, facing in different directions; each of them is a version of the self-reliant consciousness exploring individual identity. Behind Whitman stood the Emerson who called for the national poet to transmute American barbarism and materialism into vision, and behind Dickinson stood the Emerson who believed that "nothing is at last sacred but the integrity of your own mind." For Emerson these two faces—the public and the private, the gaze in and the gaze out—were, or ought ideally to be, consonant. The contrast between the Emerson who moved Whitman and the Emerson who moved Dickinson is symptomatic of the critical split in the American consciousness that had yawned wide by the end of the nineteenth century. In *Representative Men* Emerson had made this basic observation: "Two cardinal facts lie forever at the base; the one, and the two.—1. Unity, or Identity; and, 2. Variety. . . . Oneness and Otherness. It is impossible to speak or to think without embracing both." However, where Whitman characteristically moved to specify Identity in Variety, Dickinson characteristically found variety in her uniqueness. As a result, despite the fact that Whitman boasted with good cause that he had put a person down on paper, the sum total of Dickinson's tiny poems comprises, in many respects, a more complete and immediate expression of an individual consciousness than Whitman ever achieved or, in a sense, wanted to achieve. The corpus of Dickinson's poems represents a complex psyche struggling to press her inner conflicts and contrarieties to clarity from moment to moment through the creative and reflective act of language. There is much more fundamental inconsistency in Dickinson than in Whitman, for all his talk about self-contradiction, precisely because she accepts interplay and counterplay as the condition of consciousness and takes the risks involved in living them out. Indeed, Emerson's description of the Transcendentalist describes Emily Dickinson's temperament more accurately than Whitman's:

> They [Transcendentalists] are lonely; the spirit of their writing
> and conversation is lonely; they repel influences; they shun
> general society; they incline to shut themselves in their chamber
> in the house, to live in the country rather than in the town, and to

find their tasks and amusements in solitude. . . . Meantime, this retirement does not proceed from any whim on the part of these separators; but if any one will take pains to talk with them, he will find that this part is chosen both from temperament and from principle; with some unwillingness too, and as a choice of the less of two evils . . . they have even more than others a great wish to be loved.

The need for love and the fact of alienation; as a result the new breed of artists seemed "born with knives in their brain, a tendency to introversion, self-dissection, anatomizing of motives."[4]

In fact, Emerson was an inspiration and model—perhaps the inspiration and model—for Dickinson when she was choosing to be a poet. And for her it was a life-decision that affected her commitments from then on: a choice between being a strict Christian or a poet, between the Calvinist God and the Spirit in man and nature that she heard about from Emerson and her friend Dr. Holland; between this world, whatever it might yield, and the next, whatever that might be. From the evidence of Dickinson's letters written during the late 1840s and 1850s to women friends, the alternatives stood out as clearly as they did to Yeats in his poem "The Choice":

> The intellect of man is forced to choose
> Perfection of the life, or of the work,
> And if it take the second must refuse
> A heavenly mansion, raging in the dark.

Since most people would not see perfection of the life and perfection of the work as alternatives, how did Emily Dickinson come to see them so categorically?

She lived all her life in the Connecticut River Valley which remained religiously conservative and remote from the Unitarian and (worse) the Transcendentalist heresies of Boston and Concord. The Valley had been the stronghold of Solomon Stoddard and later of his grandson Jonathan Edwards in the eighteenth century, and their staunch Calvinist spirit still ruled the pulpit and hearthside. Throughout her lifetime, the Valley and the town were swept by revivals, harvesting uncommitted souls for Christ. The spiritual ferment of her one year at Mount Holyoke Female Seminary, beneath the unsparing eye of its founder, Mary Lyon, pushed her to the breaking point, and she stumbled home in 1848 not to return the next year. The fervent soul-searching at Mount Holyoke was the more disturbing to her because friends, one after another, answered the call of Christ, made a profession of faith and formally joined the church as believing Christians. At home she found member after member of the family following her mother's earlier decision to profess Christianity. Part of her longed for the security of religious faith, but she did not have the conversion experience that would yield conviction. Against mounting pressures all around she remained unpledged and self-sustained. Again and again she explained to her peers that she could not forfeit the enticements of this life for some problematical Heaven. If heavenly bliss required detachment from the here and now, she preferred instead to try to realize her own potentialities, and the fullest cultivation of consciousness as an artist became, for as much as it would bring, its own election.

Significantly enough, it was a series of men who encouraged and confirmed her in this pursuit. First was Benjamin Newton, a clerk in her father's law firm just when she retreated in disarray from Mount Holyoke. He made her believe that she could be a poet and sealed the commitment with a copy of Emerson's *Poems*, which became for her a treasured possession, even a talisman, after Newton's departure, marriage, and early death. Contemporaries like George Humphrey and Henry Vaughan Emmons were followed by older men: Bowles and the Higginson, himself a poetaster of blandly Trancendental leanings. Emily Fowler Ford, a close friend of Emily Dickinson during these formative years, recalled later that she was "steeped" in Emerson's essays and poems. In his detailed study of her reading Jack Capps reports that Dickinson had surely read at least the following titles at some point during her life: *Nature, Essays: First Series, Essays: Second Series*, and *Representative Men*, as well as the *Poems* Newton gave her.[5] Her reclusiveness kept her from hearing him speak on any of his visits to Amherst, nor did she meet him when he spent the night at Austin and Sue's house next door. But his presence from the outset of her career was so deep that his death in April, 1882, came to her as a personal shock. Frequently her poetry enunciates an Emersonian attitude or idea, and epiphanies constituted her supreme moments. But even through her doubts and difficulties Emerson represented, if not then a philosophical or religious attitude, still a call to the life of consciousness so exacting that it made the vocation, otherwise secular and egoistic, religious.

At the same time, despite her uncertainty about Calvinist doctrines, her experience seemed to confirm the vision of life to which the doctrines gave intellectual formulation. Monist first and last, Emerson posited duality as the mundane operation of unity, and Dickinson could feel, at least for the moment of ecstasy, such harmony within and without. But always she came back to a world riven from the root: creation from Creator, man from nature, each from other, each in his own psyche. Emerson described the veerings of experience as a boat's tacking to race most directly from origin to goal. For Dickinson the extremes of experience were so violent that it was difficult to rise to the elation which would reveal zigzags as a straight line, as Emerson said an overview would, and more difficult still to hold that vision once we fell again into contradictions. Here is Dickinson's harrowing version of Emerson's "Compensation," through which he had resolved contradiction comfortingly into process:

> The Soul has Bandaged moments—
> When too appalled to stir—
> She feels some ghastly Fright come up
> And stop to look at her—
>
> Salute her—with long fingers—
> Caress her freezing hair—
> Sip, Goblin, from the very lips
> The Lover—hovered—o'er—
> Unworthy, that a thought so mean
> Accost a Theme—so—fair—
>
> The soul has moments of Escape—
> When bursting all the doors—
> She dances like a Bomb, abroad,
> And swings upon the Hours,
>
> As do the Bee—delirious borne—
> Long Dungeoned from his Rose—
> Touch Liberty—then know no more,
> But Noon, and Paradise—

The Soul's retaken moments—
When, Felon led along,
With shackles on the plumed feet,
And staples, in the Song,

The Horror welcomes her, again,
These, are not brayed of Tongue—

(P512 II 393-394)*

In her study of feminine psychology, Ann Belford Ulanov argues that the woman's sense of time is qualitative rather than quantitative, each perception having its own character and shading, like phases of the moon.[6] The observation certainly describes Dickinson's time-sense as opposed to Emerson's or Whitman's. There are imprisoned moments, moments of escape and moments of recapture: distinct, yet because of the fragility of each, transpiring in a continuum of oppositions. This tenuous reversability is implied even in the metaphors which characterize the moment of escape. In a Poe-like metamorphosis the lover has become a necrophilic ghoul, and the transmogrification is suggested in the suffocating heaviness of the internal rhymes of "The Lover— hovered—o'er—," as if the speaker were already buried alive. "Dances like a Bomb" is a startling figure for her escape, but while Bomb suggests the explosive flash of the soul's release, it also suggests, as does the word "bursting," the self-destructive conclusion of such a spectacular display. Even the conditions of freedom are paradoxical. Is that Bee borne from the dungeon of his Rose into Liberty, or has he been "Long Dungeoned *from* his Rose," so that in fact he finds "Noon, and Paradise" buried in the flower's dark bosom? It is hard to tell the prison or tomb from escape; each moment threatens to turn into its opposite; the negation is doubled in "know no" and then reversed in the spelling of "Noon."

---

*The poems are identified in the text by Thomas H. Johnson's three-volume edition, *The Poems of Emily Dickinson* (Cambridge, Mass: Harvard University Press, 1955). The references give the number of the poem preceded by P, followed by the volume and page numbers. This variorum edition gives all variants to words and phrases in the manuscript of the poems, and these variants are often revealing.

The lyrics, 1775 in all, do not compose themselves in a linear development or a self-enclosing circle but remain a complex field of zigzags. The drama of consciousness moved to no resolving design. Consequently, where the critic can take a major Whitman poem as symptomatic of the whole work, he must select contradictory fragments from here and there to pose the tensions which are the coherence of Dickinson's work. Nor does chronology provide a line of development; minor variations at different periods of her writing are far less important than the consistent recurrence of unresolved conflicts. The ensuing discussion, therefore, does not imply that the sequence of pieces approximates the prevailing trend in Dickinson's responses. As the poem already cited indicates, each moment can reverse itself in the next, and there is no safe place to stand for a fixed perspective. In her poem on Emily Dickinson, Adrienne Rich describes Dickinson's "hoard of dazzling scraps" as a "battlefield."[7] The aim of the following discussion is to define the issues over which battle was joined.

Dickinson felt Thoreau an essentially kindred spirit. In declaring "I have travelled a good deal in Concord," he made restriction and limits the lens for concentrated focus. A note from Emily Dickinson made the identical declaration of purpose: "Area—no test of depth." In explaining the goal of his *purely* sensuous life," Thoreau wrote:

> I wished to live deliberately, to front only the essential facts of life, and see if I could not learn what it had to teach, and not, when I came to die, discover that I had not lived. I did not wish to live what was not life, living is so dear; nor did I wish to practise resignation, unless it was quite necessary. I wanted to live deep and suck out all the marrow of life, to live so sturdily and Spartan-like as to put to rout all that was not life, to cut a broad swath and shave close, to drive life into a corner, and reduce it to its lowest terms, and if it prove to be mean, why then to get the whole meaness of it, and publish its meanness to the world; or if it were sublime, to know it by experience.[8]

The primacy of experience over presumptions, the openness to the exactions of experience, link Thoreau and Dickinson with one another more genuinely, in some ways, than either is linked with Emerson. And this more experimental, experiential allegiance to consciousness, Dickinson was convinced, could transpire in her room and garden as well as in the woods, if she steeled herself to be independent enough and tenacious enough in her dedication to that ideal.

2

In her reclusiveness Emily Dickinson maintained at least remote contact with the intellectual world of her day, mainly through the books, newspapers, and middle-brow journals that came into her father's study; for example, she came to know at least in general about the controversies over Darwinism and over the Higher Biblical Criticism, and had a sense of the popular poets and writers of her time, many of them long forgotten. But as a provincial New Englander who only ventured outside the region once on an enforced journey with her family to Washington and Philadelphia when her father was a congressman, Dickinson was most deeply responsive to the little world she lived in. In many ways Amherst was a microcosm of that world, and her father's home was an epitome of Amherst. She might dissent from some of its assumptions and practices, but it was acknowledged as the given. Much Dickinson scholarship has gone into the detailed reconstruction of that ambience—the Dickinson household, Amherst, mid-nineteenth-century New England.*

If in that New England world Emerson was the man of imagination who validated for Dickinson her vocation as poet, and if Thoreau mediated Transcendental optimism into something more concrete and complex, her choice of vocation was nonetheless made against the authority and will of the Calvinist patriarchy. Since Calvinism had continued to hold an especially strong grip on the Connecticut Valley, her refusal to conform

---

*Instead of rehearsing the intellectual and social backgrounds here in any detail, let me cite the appropriate sources: George Frisbie Whicher's biography *This Was a Poet* (New York: Charles Scribner's Sons, 1938); Thomas H. Johnson's critical biography *Emily Dickinson* (Cambridge, Mass.: Harvard University Press, 1955); Millicent Todd Bingham's *Emily Dickinson's Home* (New York: Harper & Bros., 1955); Jay Leyda's two-volume chronicle *The Years and Hours of Emily Dickinson* (New Haven: Yale University Press, 1960); the Dickinson chapter in Hyatt H. Waggoner's *American Poets* (Boston: Houghton Mifflin, 1968); and my study of the poet in different religious, intellectual, and aesthetic contexts, *Emily Dickinson: The Mind of the Poet* (Cambridge, Mass.: Harvard University Press, 1965).

constituted an act of particular bravery which could not but cause profound concern even to herself. Her father was the patriarch in residence, but behind him stood a long procession best epitomized in the lingering presence of Jonathan Edwards, the most powerful man in the religious life of the Connecticut Valley.[9]

She had almost certainly not read Edwards, but her two allusions to him indicate that she took him as the embodiment of the Calvinism which shaped her temperament even after doctrinal conviction had faltered. Though swayed by Transcendentalism, she, like Thoreau, would surely have understood Edwards when he wrote:

> ... almost all men, and those that seem to be very miserable, love
> life, because they cannot bear to lose sight of such a beautiful
> and lovely world. The ideas that every moment whilst we live
> have a beauty that we take not distinct notice of, brings a pleasure
> that, when we come to the trial, we had rather live in much pain
> and misery than lose.[10]

She shared Edwards' love of earthly existence for all the anguish it necessitated, and, as some poems show, she could at times anticipate heaven in orthodox terms. But because she knew, too, that Edwards would have condemned as unregenerate her refusal to accept the church and its creed, she had to cling to earth the more for another vision.

> Some keep the Sabbath going to Church–
> I keep it, staying at Home–
> With a Bobolink for a Chorister—
> And an Orchard, for a Dome—
>
> Some keep the Sabbath in Surplice—
> I just wear my Wings—
> And instead of tolling the Bell, for Church,
> Our little Sexton–sings.
>
> God preaches, a noted Clergyman–
> And the sermon is never long,
> So instead of going to Heaven, at last—
> I'm going, all along.

(P324 I 254)

The poem is Dickinson's redaction—and reduction—of Transcendentalism, in which the wry archness is made possible by the diminution of religious references to the feminine world of house and garden. It is the sort of serious humor in the handling of religious questions that Robert Frost enjoyed and expressed at a later stage in the disintegration of Calvinist piety. But just as area is no test of depth, so irony is no sign of insincerity—only of insecurity in affirming Emerson against the condemnation from Edwards which she knew in her bones.

In the following quatrains she could weigh earth against heaven with opposite conclusions and mean each when she wrote it:

> In thy long Paradise of Light
> No moment will there be
> When I shall long for Earthly Play
> And mortal Company–

(P1145 II 803)

> God is indeed a jealous God–
> He cannot bear to see
> That we had rather not with Him
> But with each other play.

(P1719 III 1159)

She could claim that "The Fact that Earth is Heaven/ Whether Heaven is Heaven or not" makes Heaven, even should it exist, an affront (P1408 III 977). Such a claim takes Nature as paradisal, but what if that sense of things resides less in Nature than in the mind of the viewer? Then "Heaven" becomes, as it does in some Dickinson poems, less a place, whether natural or supernatural, than a psychological state. But when does state of mind become mere mood or predilection? Like other Romantics from Poe to Stevens, Dickinson found herself wondering if a subjective ideal was not an unattainable fiction. Poe's "supernal Beauty," imaged in the dead woman in Paradise, is a tragic conception, and Stevens' "Sunday Morning" is an extended meditation on that same quandary. Here is the beginning of one Dickinson poem on this theme:

"Heaven"–is what I cannot reach!
The Apple on the Tree–
Provided it do hopeless–hang–
That–"Heaven" is–to Me!

(P239 I 172)

Perhaps, but the quotation marks express the qualification. Is an unreachable Heaven unreal? Then, as Poe said in "Israfel," real "flowers are merely—flowers": a conclusion too disturbing to rest in. Another poem says:

Paradise is that old mansion
Many owned before—
Occupied by each an instant
Then reversed the Door--

(P1119 II 787)

But could she rest in the hope that a Paradise so lost could be regained, especially by an infidel like herself?

Even the blandishing wit of a phrase like "God preaches, a noted Clergyman–" in poem 324 above betrays her uneasiness with the Deity and a characteristic strategy in response to her uneasiness. Some of the ironic juxtaposition is at the expense of the workaday preacher, but through a reverse turn God is reduced to "Clergyman," like the neighboring pastor who did not intimidate her at all. She had to safeguard her heretical position through seeming guilelessness. The impersonal, transpersonal force which Emerson wrote about might be heedless of her rebellious will, but for her the personal God was not the humanly compassionate Son but the awesome Father, the Jehovah-Judge who absorbed all the legalism of the Old Testament into the Calvinist creed. By all accounts, including her own, her lawyer-father was a formidable man whom she loved and feared, and the legal language which she used throughout the poetry, usually with some irony, indicates how deeply she had imbibed the masculine principle, human and divine, through which and against which she had to define her own nature. Masculine in the rigor of mind and will which made the whole endeavor possible, she quickly found that her endeavor was precisely to define her distinctness from the masculine principle: neither simple rejection nor simple dependence, but the translation of her masculine nature into her own identity. But that would have to come in time, if at all; now faced with charges that would condemn her in court, she maneuvered, as a daughter might, through a coy appeal to paternal sentiment:

> Were Himself–such a Dunce–
> What would we–do?
> Love the dull lad–best–
> Oh, wouldn't you?

(P267 I 190)

Another early poem is a bad little good girl's parody of the Lord's Prayer:

> Papa above!
> Regard a Mouse
> O'erpowered by the Cat!
> Reserve within thy kingdom
> A "Mansion" for the Rat!
>
> Snug in seraphic Cupboards
> To nibble all the day,
> While unsuspecting Cycles
> Wheel solemnly away!

(P61 I 46)

The outrageous play is calculated, beginning with the reduction of "Our Father Who art in Heaven" to "Papa above" and concluding with "pompously," the variant to "solemnly" in the last line, which repeats the sound of "Papa" while giving a humorous turn to the conceit of a clockwork universe. At the same time, Dickinson's unworthiness of Papa's "Regard" manifests itself when the pitiable Mouse, helpless in the paws of the devilish Cat, turns out instead to be a Rat, the blunt rhyme establishing in the ear the connection between herself and Satan. As she well knows, rats are exterminated from dwellings, not welcomed snugly inside, but Dickinson's identification with the rat persists

in a poem, written almost twenty years later, which serves as a
coda to the poem above by explicitly noting the rat's vices as
virtues:

> The Rat is the concisest Tenant.
> He pays no Rent.
> Repudiates the Obligation–
> On Schemes intent
>
> Balking our Wit
> To sound or circumvent–
> Hate cannot harm
> A Foe so reticent–
> Neither Decree prohibit him–
> Lawful as Equilibrium.

(P1356 III 937)

The poem pretends to a critical distance, but admiration fills the
description of a creature whose situation is recognizably like her
own vis-à-vis the Dickinson household and her heavenly Father's
mansion. The rat's wit is as resourceful as her own learned to be
in maintaining its position by serving as its own law and
equilibrium.

Sometimes Dickinson's complaints against Providence ef-
fected a temporary reversal of roles and allowed her to charge
God Himself with chicanery in dealing with His creatures. So in
poem 49 the loss of loved ones forces an exclamation which is as
much accusation as plea: "Burglar! Banker—Father!" Does God
steal from the already impoverished, and does He then store up
things in heaven for us? Is He a criminal or a respectful pillar of
society? Can we tell the difference? The punctuation shows that
burglar and banker are the twin faces of father, neither displaying such soft, womanly virtues as love or pity. In other poems
Dickinson identifies herself with a masculine persona; for example, in this direct challenge to God's authority:

> He outstripped Time with but a Bout,
> He outstripped Stars and Sun
> And then, unjaded, challenged God
> In presence of the Throne.

And He and He in mighty List
Unto this present, run,
The larger Glory for the less
A just sufficient Ring.

(P865 II 646)

The poem depicts the contention between God and man (or God
and Satan, man's defender) as a chivalric contest, in which the
knightly challenger so nearly matches the King ("And He and
He") that the battle is still raging, not won but not lost yet either.
This titan, unlike Melville's Ahab or Enceladus in *Pierre*, manages to hold his own and continue the struggle.

In another poem (P597 II 458) the poet becomes the impassioned advocate for the prophet Moses himself, his long service of
God ending in defeat when God allowed him to see but not to
enter the Promised Land. Even if the Bible be only a "Romance,"
as German biblical criticism was claiming, still in the story Moses
endured more mocking abuse even than Saints Stephen and Paul;
them God merely martyred in return for their faith, but Moses
He toyed with maliciously. In the following lines the echoes of
the lines "As flies to wanton boys, are we to th' gods; They kill
us for their sport" add the force of Lear's tragedy to Moses':

. . . God's adroiter will

On Moses—seemed to fasten
With tantalizing Play
As Boy—should deal with lesser Boy—
To prove ability.

In the record Moses did not complain when God punished His
servant for the godlessness of the other Israelites, but Dickinson
seizes Moses' cause in the name of human justice, rhetoric mounting with her outrage:

The fault—was doubtless Israel's—
Myself—had banned the Tribes—
And ushered Grand Old Moses
In Pentateuchal Robes

234

Upon the Broad Possession
'Twas little–He should see–
Old Man on Nebo! Late as this–
My Justice bleeds–for Thee!

The glorious vindication of Moses becomes her own. But rhetoric,
no matter how righteous, cannot alter the outcome; her justice
can only bleed in sympathy. Another poem from the early sixties,
years of special crisis which produced a flood of outcries, extends
the image of God as bully victimizing His creatures:

But–should the play
Prove piercing earnest–
Should the glee–glaze–
In Death's–stiff–stare–

Would not the fun
Look too expensive!
Would not the jest–
Have crawled too far!

(P338 I 270)

"Crawled" suggests both the cravenness of the "Joke" or "fun"
(the variants for "jest") as well as its crippling results. The
absolute sovereignty to which Puritans like Edwards and Taylor
submitted rapturously devolved for her into capriciousness; pre-
destination into vindictiveness. The difference in her was the
absence of a reliable sense of grace transforming the fallen human
condition.

What standard could she raise against the Calvinism that
still held such sway over her? The poet's powers of transformation. In her last years she reiterated the alternatives in an archly
wicked poem sent next door to her young nephew Ned, because
he shared her free-thinking tendencies:

The Bible is an antique Volume–
Written by faded Men
At the suggestion of Holy Spectres–
Subjects–Bethlehem–
Eden–the ancient Homestead–
Satan–the Brigadier–

Judas–the Great Defaulter–
David–the Troubadour–
Sin–a distinguished Precipice
Others must resist–
Boys that "believe" are very lonesome–
Other Boys are "lost"–
Had but the Tale a warbling Teller–
All the Boys would come–
Orpheus' Sermon captivated–
It did not condemn–

(P1545 III 1065–1066)

A draft of the poem with the title "Diagnosis of the Bible, by a
Boy—" masks the parodic irreverence of the masculine persona
as the innocent ignorance/wisdom of a child. But again the fun
is serious; the unmistakable implication is that a "lost" infidel
seems hardly worse off than a "lonesome" believer. Besides,
would an infidel be lost if he had the power and vision of
Orpheus' song? The artist's "Sermon" affirmed life against damnation: a message she could hope that the "noted Clergyman"
who preached outside the church walls would accept, even if the
God of the Fathers did not.

In another late poem to Ned, humor darkens into mordant
irony:

"Heavenly Father"–take to thee
The supreme iniquity
Fashioned by thy candid Hand
In a moment contraband–
Though to trust us–seem to us
More respectful–"We are Dust"–
We apologize to thee
For thine own Duplicity–

(P1461 III 1009–1010)

Like the early "Papa above!" poem, this is also a parody of the
Lord's Prayer, but the defiant condescension toward the Deity in
the name of human dignity is so blasphemous that one has to
turn to anguished unbelievers like Melville and Hardy for analogues. The anti-prayer means the opposite of what it seems to

be saying. The quotation marks deprive God of paternal love and call into question the pious verse from Genesis that would invoke our mortality to enforce humble subjection: "Man, dust thou art and to dust thou shalt return." The violent juxtaposition of words—"supreme" with "iniquity," "candid Hand" with "contraband," "trust" and "respectful" with "Duplicity"—prepares for the inversion of roles at the conclusion, in which mortal creatures rise to apologize to their Creator for the double-dealing that foredooms them. The scorn for God, almost olympian itself, carries the weight of one of Captain Ahab's speeches compressed into four jagged couplets.

This ambivalence—defensiveness and assertiveness oscillating and almost coexisting—is for Dickinson the primary rhythm of consciousness confronting an alien world. Freud posited a fall from an original state of psychic wholeness as one of the causes of anxiety endemic to the human situation. Closer to Emily Dickinson, Emerson too described paradise lost as a fall into consciousness; in "Experience" we find:

> It is very unhappy, but too late to be helped, the discovery we
> have made that we exist. That discovery is called the Fall of
> Man. . . . Once we lived in what we saw; now, the rapaciousness
> of this new power [consciousness], which threatens to absorb
> all things, engages us. Nature, art, persons, letters, religions,
> objects, successively tumble in, and God is but one of its ideas.[11]

The question arises whether this original unsundered wholeness is fact or postulation. Since experience makes an impression only if we are in some way reflexively aware of it, our first perceptions split perceiver from perceived and enact the fall. Unprovable as Paradise is, Freud took the almost-memory of such bliss as evidence of our psychic needs, however unsatisfiable, just as Wordsworth and Emerson took it as evidence of our spiritual origins. Dickinson once imaged this precious state as a jewel grasped and then gone:

> I held a Jewel in my fingers—
> And went to sleep—
> The day was warm, and winds were prosy—
> I said, " 'Twill keep—"

I woke—and chid my honest fingers,
The Gem was gone—
And now, an Amethyst remembrance
Is all I own—

(P245 I 176)

The "prosiness" of temporal experience has destroyed the
"poetry" of her initial possession. The dispossession fell so early
that she cannot specify the "something" lost except in images
like "Amethyst remembrance" or Eden:

A loss of something ever felt I—
The first that I could recollect
Bereft I was—of what I knew not
Too young that any should suspect

A Mourner walked among the children
I notwithstanding went about
As one bemoaning a Dominion
Itself the only Prince cast out—

(P959 II 694–695)

The last stanza of this poem goes on to make the pious suggestion
that although she is looking vainly for heaven on earth, paradise
lost will prove to be kingdom come; but the first part of the poem
is clearer and more convincing in its apprehension of failure. All
she can say with certainty is that a fundamental flaw condemns
her to contingency and in the end to obliteration. Her contingency stems from her inability to find a fixed center in herself
and nature; the something lost is her connection with the All.
"The Missing All," she wrote in poem 985 (II 711) shortly after
the poem cited above, "prevented Me/ From missing minor
Things" such as a world or a sun, the irony again serving to keep
the anguish manageable by understatement. "Compensation" was
Emerson's way of accounting for the "inevitable dualism" that
"bisects nature" and thus mending the "crack in every thing God
has made," but Emily Dickinson found that she could compensate
for the divisions riven into her psyche and her world only by
asserting her own psychic resources: a desperate gamble on self-
reliance.[12]

A poem, written in the middle sixties when the poems above were also composed, describes her strategy:

> Growth of Man—like Growth of Nature—
> Gravitates within—
> Atmosphere, and Sun endorse it—
> But it stir—alone—
>
> Each—it's difficult Ideal
> Must achieve—Itself—
> Through the solitary prowess
> Of a Silent Life—
>
> Effort—is the sole condition—
> Patience of Itself—
> Patience of opposing forces—
> And intact Belief—
>
> Looking on—is the Department
> Of it's Audience—
> But Transaction—is assisted
> By no Countenance—

> (P750 II 571)

The first line links man and nature provisionally, but the reiteration of the "gr" alliteration internalizes the growth of "Each," whose individuality is insisted upon by "alone," "Itself," "solitary," "Silent," "sole," "Itself," "intact." "Patience" indicates the "receptivity" and "tenacity" as well as the "suffering" which the "Effort" will impose. "Intact Belief" sustains the psyche ("Patience of Itself") as it contends with contradictions ("Patience of opposing forces"), and, in the quatrain, "Effort" and "Belief" bracket the twin patience they demand. "Belief" in what? In the capacity of the psyche to "achieve Itself." The variant for "difficult Ideal" is "absolute Ideal," and "absolute" refers both to the irrevocability of the commitment to growth and to the ideal selfhood toward which growth gropes. The language of the poem remains abstract but emphatic; other poems would specify the oppositions and the possibilities of reconciliation. Poem 384 (I 304), written a little earlier, declares that "Captivity is Consciousness—/ So's Liberty," or, rephrased, that if consciousness is a trap it is also one's passage to freedom "Except Thyself may be/ Thine Enemy–".

The love poems of Emily Dickinson grow out of the missing something and All. Quickened to an outpouring during the early to middle sixties but running throughout her poetic career, the love poems constitute the effort to fill her emptiness with reception of and receptivity to "the other." A poem of 1861 personifies the desire for, and in this case the failure of, completion; the sexual distinction between the male Sun and the female Morning provides a favorite metaphor:

> The *Sun–just touched* the Morning–
> The *Morning*–Happy thing–
> Supposed that He had come to *dwell*–
> And Life would all be *Spring!*

The middle section of the poem, a double quatrain, anticipates the Sun-King's power to elevate and spiritualize her into "a *Raised–Etherial Thing!*" and then undercuts it as the Sun withdraws, abandoning her to "a *new nescessity* [sic]/ The *want* of Diadems!"

> The Morning–*fluttered–staggered*–
> *Felt feebly–*for Her *Crown*–
> Her *unannointed forehead*–
> *Henceforth*–Her *only* One!

(P232 I 168)

"Want" suggests her desire and her lack; "Her *only*," bare forehead would have to compensate for the Crown He did not confer. The erotic dimension of the poem is even given decorous acknowledgment in the editors' title for the 1891 *Poems*, where it first appeared: "The Sun's Wooing." Dickinson frequently used such imagery to depict her need for a completing love, most openly perhaps in an 1852 letter, long before any surviving poems, to her dear friend and future sister-in-law, Sue. She spins out to Sue a breathless picture of the woman's dilemma: their virginal existence, isolated and intact, must seem dull to "the bride, and the plighted maiden, whose days are fed with gold, and who gathers

pearls every evening"; but it must seem enviable "to the *wife,/*
. . . sometimes the wife *forgotten.*" She confesses the mixed feelings of the morning-flowers before the onslaught on the sun:

> you have seen flowers at morning, *satisfied* with the dew, and
> those same sweet flowers at noon with their heads bowed in an-
> guish before the mighty sun; think you these thirsty blossoms
> will *now* need naught but–*dew?* No they will cry for sunlight,
> and pine for the burning noon, tho' it scorches them, scathes
> them; they have got through with peace–they know that the
> man of noon, is *mightier* than the morning and their life is
> henceforth to him.

The masculine "spirits mightier" than the "simple trusting
spirits" of women are both irresistible and necessarily to be
resisted: "I tremble lest at sometime I, too, am yielded up."[13]
The satisfaction craved in "cry" and "pine" and fulfilled in the
violence of "scorches" and "scathes" turns into the passive and
sacrificial "am yielded up." The interpenetration of spiritual and
erotic aspirations and anxieties, admitted candidly in this early
letter, provides a clue to the ambiguity of the love poems.

In many, perhaps most, of the love poems it is impossible
to determine whether the lover is a man or God or Jesus the God-
man, because in no mere figurative or casual sense the lover is
any and all of them. Love, as distinguished from lust or charity,
would satisfy her entire nature, and in that single, harmonious
fulfillment sex and spirit would be called out by the same activating stimulus. Some of the poems make an explicit linking
between sexuality and divinity in preparation for the great love
poems. For instance, poem 357 (I 357) facetiously calls God "a
distant–stately Lover" and explicates the relationship between
Father and Son in terms of the love triangle of Miles Standish,
John Alden, and Priscilla Mullins; the wooers, Standish and
Alden, were "Synonyme" in their double approach to the favored
maiden. Poem 817 (II 618) presents the poet in mystic marriage as
"Bride of the Father and the Son/ Bride of the Holy Ghost." The
association of the amatory and (in a loose sense) the mystical—
as God becomes lover-bridegroom or lover manifests praeter-
natural or deific qualities—is too persistent to be dismissed. For
instance:

Wild Nights—Wild Nights!
Were I with thee
Wild nights should be
Our luxury!

Futile—the Winds—
To a Heart in port—
Done with the Compass—
Done with the Chart!

Rowing in Eden—
Ah, the Sea!
Might I but moor—Tonight—
In Thee!

(P249 I 179)

It is possible—and pertinent—to read these lines in the mystical tradition which always stresses the erotic element in spiritual union. But the erotic element is here so dominant that it worried Higginson in preparing the first selection of poems, "lest the malignant read into it more than that virgin recluse ever dreamed of putting there."[14] She knew what she was putting there, and her point is that love was for her an experience that had something to do with man and something to do with God: the masculine "other" filling what her female nature lacked, ached for, and, at the same time, feared.

The poem above is perhaps the most unabashedly passionate poem that Dickinson wrote (though there are many other erotic poems by the "virgin recluse" which Higginson chose to overlook in his avuncular concern). Nevertheless, a second look indicates something of the difficulties in Dickinson's emotional life. The luxuriating in wild nights is cast throughout in the subjunctive mood: "Were I"; "should be"; "Might I but," the "might" qualifying the "Tonight" at the end of that line. Not only is every verb a wish-fulfillment, but the sexual roles are blurred. She is the hero-voyager seeking a haven from the wind and waves; he (or she?) is the harbor and paradisal garden in which her struggling heart-ship will nestle.

Something more subtle than an inversion of sexual roles is at work here, and the point is not that Emily Dickinson was homosexual, as Rebecca Patterson and John Cody have argued.[15] Only a configuration of poems can outline Dickinson's psychology of love. Poem 303, written in the same years as "The Sun's Wooing" and "Wild Nights," points the direction:

> The Soul selects her own Society—
> Then—shuts the Door—
> To her divine Majority—
> Present no more—
>
> Unmoved—she notes the Chariots—pausing—
> At her low Gate—
> Unmoved—an Emperor be kneeling
> Upon her Mat—
>
> I've known her—from an ample nation—
> Choose One—
> Then—close the Valves of her attention—
> Like Stone—

(P303 I 225)

The negotiations of the feminine soul with outside "Society" is again a wooing, but here the thrust is turned inward. The chosen one, with all the overtones of Calvinist election, is drawn into the chamber of her mind, and the variant for "present"—"obtrude no more"—suggests, along with the shut door and the valves of a heart turned stone and a rhythm that clenches a longer line almost spasmodically into a shorter, an exclusiveness that unwittingly sounds rather like solitary confinement: a dungeon or tomb. Another poem, written in the same year, 1862, begins: "Of all the Souls that stand create—/ I have elected—One—"; and the poem goes on to transmogrify him into a spirit beyond "this brief Tragedy of Flesh": "Behold the Atom—I preferred—/ To all the lists of Clay!" (P664 II 511). The female mind and will which are capable of handling the "other"—either an individual "him" or patriarchal society—becomes a motif repeated sufficiently in the poetry to establish it as an axiom of her consciousness. The purpose is to obviate external relationships, but the result of that maneuver, as it turns out, is to link love by election with the grave.

Poem 322, also written in 1862, might seem to contradict this conclusion. It celebrates an experience of deep communion between her and the lover, and the intimation of an actual man, coupled with a description of the love relationship in religious terms with the climax on Calvary, has led some critics to identify the lover in this poem as the Reverend Charles Wadsworth, whom Dickinson presumably met in Philadelphia in the mid-fifties and who left his pastorate there to be minister of the Calvary Church in San Francisco in 1862. But even in this poem, allowing (so it seems) more contact and reciprocity than most, the psychological restrictions noted above are the decisive factors. Despite the fact that the two are "Permitted to commune this—time—" (the dashes emphasize the fragility of the singular moment), "Each was to each The Sealed Church," and the seal indicates the closed doors which, by further extension, recall the seals only to be broken at the Apocalypse. The poem that began:

> There came a Day at Summer's full,
> Entirely for me—
> I thought that such were for the Saints,
> Where Resurrections—be—

ends up finding that fulfillment comes only through death and resurrection:

> And so when all the time had leaked,
> Without external sound
> Each bound the Other's Crucifix—
> We gave no other Bond—
>
> Sufficient troth, that we shall rise—
> Deposed—at length, the Grave—
> To that new Marriage,
> Justified—through Calvaries of Love—

> (P322 I 249–250)

Since the variant for "Resurrections" in the first stanza is "Revelations," the suggestions of the Apocalypse at the conclusion are intimated from the start, and specified in the quotation from

Revelations in the second stanza and the reference to seals in the fourth. The pun on "Bond," placed between "Each bound the Other's Crucifix–" and "Sufficient troth" epitomizes the hope-lessness of the present situation which must seek the grave's justification (again a Calvinist term) for future union. Though the poem says that speech is a profanation of a sacred communion, the image of the lovers as sealed even to each other adds to the breathless claustrophobia. In fact, the solipsism is covertly noted from the first stanza with the admission that this day of summer's full was "entirely for me–".

Thus internalized and at the same time projected into the future, marriage became indistinguishable from a death-marriage and from a mystic marriage: "Mine–by the Right of the White Election!/ Mine–by the Royal Seal!" (P528 II 405). Marriage suc-ceeds Apocalypse, and death is the *rite de passage*—this configu-ration is drawn repeatedly in the poems. Romantic poetry is filled with death-marriages all the way from Poe's verse to John Crowe Ransom's "Emily Hardcastle" and "Piazza Piece" and Allen Tate's "The Robber Bridegroom." But of all those poets, probably Emily Brontë, whose verse Dickinson loved, would best have under-stood her particular development of the theme. The first stanza of the following poem states the virgin's nervous anticipation of sexual fulfillment, but in the second stanza the lover eerily reveals himself as death, then Eternity, personalized as Christ the Savior.

A Wife–at Daybreak I shall be–
Sunrise–Hast thou a Flag for me?
At Midnight, I am but a Maid,
How short it takes to make it Bride–
Then–Midnight, I have passed from thee
Unto the East, and Victory–

Midnight–Good Night! I hear them call,
The Angels bustle in the Hall–
Softly my Future climbs the Stair,
I fumble at my Childhood's prayer
So soon to be a Child no more–
Eternity, I'm coming–Sir,
Savior–I've seen the face–before!

(P461 I 355)

In two other poems of 1862 these lines occur: "Baptized—this Day—A Bride—" (P473 I 363) and "Brides—an Apocalypse—" (P300 I 222). Baptism and Apocalypse: Alpha and Omega in one fierce, remote concentration.

Poem after poem asserts in an agony of triumph that this love by "White Election" was predestined to other than the usual sort of consummation.

> Title divine—is mine!
> The Wife—without the Sign!
> Acute Degree—conferred on me—
> Empress of Calvary!
> Royal—all but the Crown!
> Betrothed—without the swoon
> God sends us Women—
> When you—hold—Garnet to Garnet—
> Gold—to Gold—
> Born—Bridalled—Shrouded—
> In a day—
> "My Husband"—women say—
> Stroking the Melody—
> Is *this*—the way?

(P1072 II 758)

The fact that one copy of this poem was sent to Bowles has been taken by some commentators as evidence that he was Dickinson's secret (or not-so-secret) love, but since another copy was sent to Sue, after quarrels between the two women had cooled the girlish confidences of earlier years, it is not clear that the poem points to any person. Its references are in fact all self-references, and it is better read as a concise statement of Emily Dickinson's experience of love: elevation to royalty, to near-divinity, coupled with denial and renunciation; love admitted and lived out imaginatively as the basic human need and the transforming human experience without ever the possibility of external confirmation. In short, the drama of passion and separation all within the arena of her consciousness, itself at once perilously engaged and safely detached; the entire love-experience—baptism to apocalypse, "Born—Bridalled—Shrouded—/ In a Day—" with no real risk of contact or surrender to the "other" out there. The dashes are cracks or fissures in the verses; the lines break in the middle, and the affirmation is qualified or negated by the other side of the schism. Yet living exclusively for and within one's own consciousness has its advantages as well as its restrictions. Dickinson made sure not to miss the experience but at the same time not to be "yielded up" to the stress and possible ravages of an actual relationship. Such is the very ecstasy of this defeat; the "Victory" of poem 461 above becomes, in the version of the poem sent to Sue, "Tri Victory," the word inserted between the day's cycle of birth-copulation-death and the faltering attempt at the end to mimic saying "My Husband" in the way wives should. The Bowles version dates from 1862 and Sue's from perhaps as late as 1866; possibly the intervening years of crisis had brought Dickinson into sufficient accommodation with her anomalous position to see it as the "Tri Victory" she added to Sue's version.

Who, then, is the lover in Emily Dickinson's poems? Most commentators have assumed with Thomas Johnson that the Reverend Charles Wadsworth was the likeliest person. Emily Dickinson had probably met him on that single visit to Philadelphia after Washington in the mid-fifties; his departure to San Francisco for several years coincides roughly with Dickinson's time of near-breakdown and prodigious creativity during the sixties. One brief note from Wadsworth to Dickinson, written with the distant solicitude of a pastor for a troubled soul, dates roughly from this period; the two exchanged letters later, none of which have survived. More recently, other commentators, notably David Higgins and Ruth Miller, have nominated Bowles as the man in the poems, and Theodora Ward rejects both those suggestions and postulates another man about whose identity we have no clue. John Cody's Freudian analysis argues that the marriage of Austin and Sue precipitated a crisis between Dickinson's homosexual and heterosexual attachments to them both. The very diversity of interpretations[16] and the intriguing but inconclusive evidence advanced in the cause of each confirm the fact that the "other" in Dickinson's love poems is finally none of the candidates, is finally "no one" at all. The poems describe a subjective drama, and both figures in the drama are first and last psychological factors. This is not to say that the drama is totally self-induced with no catalytic agent in Dickinson's biographical experience; but it is to conclude that even if there was an external agent and even if he (or she) served as a catalyst to arouse the poet's craving for erotic and spiritual satisfaction, the experience as played out in the poems is imaginary as well as vividly imagined; the "other" is a projected personification of the poet's emotional and religious needs much more than any person she has known and loved. "He" is real but not actual, and his reality is self-referential. "He" is a protagonist/antagonist in the drama of identity.

Emily Dickinson admitted as much, however slyly and indirectly. Here is the text of an unusually long poem written about 1860:

> We dont cry—Tim and I,
> We are far too grand—
> But we bolt the door tight
> To prevent a friend—
>
> Then we hide our brave face
> Deep in our hand—
> Not to cry—Tim and I—
> We are far too grand—
>
> Nor to dream—he and me—
> Do we condescend—
> We just shut our brown eye
> To see to the end--
>
> Tim—see Cottages—
> But, Oh, so high!
> Then—we shake—Tim and I—
> And lest I—cry—
>
> Tim—reads a little Hymn—
> And we both pray—
> Please, Sir, I and Tim—
> Always lost the way!
>
> We must die—by and by—
> Clergymen say—
> Tim—shall—if I— do—
> I—too—if he—
>
> How shall we arrange it—
> Tim—was—so—shy?
> Take us simultaneous—Lord—
> I—"Tim"—and—Me!

(P196 I 141)

This early poem contains many of the motifs scattered through-out the love poems: a passion linked to religion, withdrawn into exclusive association, resistant to the death it is doomed to, un-certain of the eternity which offers the only chance for genuine union. The seriousness of the poem is no more betrayed by the witty playfulness than it would be in a poem of Robert Frost or John Crowe Ransom. The poet is employing the resources of the little-girl persona to distract us at first from what she is revealing, but the nursery-rhyme quality, the singsong rhythms, the repeti-tions and refrains ("We are far too grand–"; "Tim and I"; "he and me"; "by and by"; "if I–do– . . . if he"), the puns on "eye-I" and "Hymn-him" and "Tim-Hymn" all lead up to the last lines, spaced out with dashes to heighten the recognition. How can we, Tim and I, arrange for simultaneous death? Because we are one and the same person: "I–'Tim'–and Me!" The fact that it is not "I and Thou" (to use Martin Buber's phrase) but "I and Me" catches up the refrains and puns, so that now we can notice retro-spectively those odd singular-plurals in the first half of the poem as anticipating the revelation at the end: "our brave face," "our hand," "our brown eye."

Another poem of the same year comes to much the same self-awareness:

> I'm "wife"–I've finished that–
> That other state–
> I'm Czar–I'm "Woman" now–
> It's safer so–

> (P199 I 142)

The passage from virgin to wife is not a matter of maidenhead but of psychological depths. And the activation of inert potentiali-ties, the summoning of the unconscious to consciousness, make the poet realize herself simultaneously, almost equally as mascu-line and feminine: "I'm Czar–I'm 'Woman' now–". Becoming Czar is not the opposite of becoming Woman; on the contrary, it is part of becoming Woman. One's incompleteness becomes whole by finding the "other" in one's self; it is not only "safer so," it is necessary.

The "lover" in Emily Dickinson's poetry, therefore, reveals

himself not so much as a person or God or Jesus but rather as an essential component of her personality. Jung's term for the masculine elements in the female psyche is the animus. The animus mediates, to put it crudely, the woman's capacity for abstract form, rational thought, and pure spiritual enlightenment, as well as her relationship with the masculine (God and man conjoined again), just as the anima, or feminine elements in the male psyche, mediates his connection with the body, nature, emotion, and instinct, as well as his relationship to the opposite sex. Thus the "other"—even if a person actually precipitated the crisis, indeed even if the "masculine" catalyst were a woman—exists in the poetry and in Dickinson's emotional life chiefly as a mask for aspects of herself, potentialities within herself struggling for expression and accommodation within the psyche.

This conclusion is no debunking or even unriddling of the love poems, only a specification of their real nature. Theodora Ward identified the lover with the animus casually, without pursuing the implications of her insight. The recognition of the lover as Dickinson's own animus and of the complications of her relationship to the animus lets us see more accurately what is happening in these poems. For while it is true that Dickinson wrote some of the most poignant and moving love poems in English, they all spell out love of a sort peculiarly and inevitably doomed: a love inseparable from—in fact characterized by—separation, pain, sickness, and finally death. This love-death could conceivably have had some basis in a failed love affair, but the absence of any convincing evidence despite the unflagging efforts of several generations of biographers, combined with the overwhelming evidence from the poems of how internalized the experience is made to be, points to the conclusion that love was lived out, in ecstasy and travail, as the drama of a divided consciousness. The "Missing All" made her aware of the necessity of filling the void but it made her equally wary of the risks that openness would require. Consequently she contrived—partly through calculated design, partly through the inhibitions of her personality—to convert (with all the religious connotations of that word) her need into an active psychological fact and thus to experience the whole range of love-emotions within herself. The hopelessness of her claustrophobic situation, her consciousness shut on itself like stone, invested the poems, as she knew full well, with their particular tragic urgency and appeal.

The "man within" serves, roughly speaking, two major functions in the woman's psyche. "He" should be the mediating point for the integration of the dualistic components within the psyche into individual identity; and, secondly, "he" should serve as the mediating point through which the woman understands and so relates to a man or men. This second outer-directed act of accommodation should match and complement the subjective integration, and vice versa. The woman's animus (like the man's anima) is, then, the major point of connection and reconciliation in the individual's development toward androgynous wholeness. However, since "he" opens up this unique opportunity for completion, "he" can also seem to the insecure individual to stand as a menacing challenge. If the difficulties are severe enough, the point of crossover can become the sticking-point, and the frustration of one of the animus-functions indicated above could be a sign of difficulty in the other area as well.

For Emily Dickinson the animus which should effect a resolution of anxieties did come to seem at times the source of anxiety: the presence within herself of that "other" which she most resisted and with which she most wanted to identify. The danger in such an animus relationship was that she might not be able to assimilate "him" into herself. As a Freudian clinician, John Cody argues in detail that Emily Dickinson's confused sexual identity stemmed not just from the dominating presence of her stern but loving father but, even prior to that, from the failure of her weak mother to present a clear and attractive model of womanhood for Emily's acute sensitivity to identify with. Certainly the ambivalence about sexual roles is already there in the early poetry. Imaging the masculine as the sublime immensity of the Alps and the feminine as the humble daisies below, she asks: "Which, Sir, are you and which am I/ Upon an August day?" (P124 I 89). These verses date from about 1859, but the same juxtaposition of images for the sexual roles, as well as the uncertainty of her relationship to each, runs throughout the poetry. And ambivalence of course ended in a conflict which, because of her double identification, it would be difficult for her to resolve. She could not win, no matter what the result. In another early poem:

He was weak, and I was strong—then—
So He let me lead him in—
I was weak, and He was strong then—
So I let him lead me—Home.

. . . .

Day knocked—and we must part—
Neither—was strongest—now—
He strove—and I strove—too—
We didn't do it—tho'!

(P190 I 137)

Didn't do what? It is not clear, but if the referent is, as seems most likely, "part," then the contention continues in the seclusion of Home, neither able to vanquish or submit to the other.

The ambivalence can assume various kinds of imbalance. To begin with, abasement to the masculine principle. One poem ends by saying that, though forgotten and denied, "I'll do thy Will" (P438 I 339); another (P738 II 562–563) expatiates on the contingency with which it begins:

You said that I "was Great"—one Day—
Then "Great" it be—if that please Thee—
Or Small—or any size at all—
Nay—I'm the size suit Thee—

But such demeaning self-denial can turn at times into a fantasy of a masochistic vindication:

No matter—now—Sweet—
But when I'm Earl—
Wont you wish you'd spoken
To that dull Girl?

. . . .

I shant need it—then—
Crests—will do—
Eagles on my Buckles—
On my Belt—too—

Ermine—my familiar Gown—
Say—Sweet—then
Wont you wish you'd smiled—just—
Me upon?

(P704 II 542)

These poems are not especially interesting as verse, but they indicate how fully dramatized the love plot with the animus was. The projection of the conflict into poems reflects the rapid shifts of mood as they afflicted her. In the lines just quoted it is clear that her ultimate victory will come when she assumes masculine power, tricked out in protective royal armor; and the rhyme of "dull Girl" against "Earl" catches the contrast between sexual roles at the same time that it states the possibility of reversal or resolution.

Other poems rehearse a similar transition. Poem 616, for example, inverts the fairy-tale situation of Sleeping Beauty or Snow White by having the "fainting Prince" die instead of her, while she arrogates to herself his physical and moral strength. It begins and concludes with the following lines:

I rose—because He sank—
I thought it would be opposite—
But when his power dropped—
My Soul grew straight.

I cheered my fainting Prince—
I sang firm—even—Chants—
I helped his Film—with Hymn—

And when the Dews drew off
That held his Forehead stiff—
I met him—
Balm to Balm—

. . . .

And so with Thews of Hymn—
And Sinew from within—
And ways I knew not that I knew—till then—
I lifted Him—

(P616 II 473–474)

253

The lack of any felt sorrow and the growing sense of vigor and assurance indicate that this poem does not memorialize anyone's death but enacts her absorption of the animus into her psyche. Read as dream, the poem tells how he died into her ("I rose— because He sank—"), investing her with a strength both "phallic" and spiritual. "Thews of Hymn" joins physical and religious strength, with a pun on "Him," the rhyming word for "Hymn." His thews are then matched by "Sinew from within—" to become the psychic muscle and fiber through which she can lift him in "ways I knew not that I knew—till then—"

So in many poems she becomes not just Queen to someone else's King, but herself King, Emperor, Monarch, Czar. Two poems of 1862, both in the same manuscript packet, illustrate the challenge which the animus presented. Poem 506 glories in her dependence on "him":

> He touched me, so I live to know
> That such a day, permitted so,
> I groped upon his breast—
> It was a boundless place to me
> And silenced, as the awful sea
> Puts minor streams to rest.
>
> And now, I'm different from before,
> As if I breathed superior air—
> Or brushed a Royal Gown—
> My feet, too, that had wandered so—
> My Gipsy face—transfigured now—
> To tenderer Renown—

> (P506 II 388)

Her identification of renown with him, her submission to his superiority, her basking humbly in his reflected glory, provide her point of rest, and the last stanza goes on to say that her obeisance is more enviable than that of Jewish or Persian women worshipping their Gods. But despite what the poem wants to say, she cannot rest in him, and the variants for the phrase "permitted so./ I groped upon his breast—" demonstrate her uneasiness: "persuaded so,/ I perished" and "accepted so, I dwelt." Poem 508 takes up the image of her on his breast and rejects such subservience. It appeared in *Poems* (1890) under the title "Love's Baptism," and it contrasts her first baptism as a baby, which imposed a name on her and left her crying on her father's chest, and a second baptism which she chooses herself and which gives her a conscious identity. The last stanza reads:

> My second Rank—too small the first—
> Crowned—Crowing—on my Father's breast—
> A half unconscious Queen—
> But this time—Adequate—Erect,
> With Will to choose, or to reject,
> And I choose, just a Crown—

> (P508 II 390)

In the metaphorical context of baptism as a psychological event (Emily Dickinson was never baptized) she moves from subordination to authority. The variants are revealing: for "Crowing," "whimpering" and "dangling"; for "half unconscious," "too unconscious" and "insufficient"; for "Will," "power"; for "Crown," "Throne." The Queen becomes fully conscious, sufficient and erect not by elimination of the masculine from her psyche but rather by an assumption of his powers into her wholeness. As we saw in the poem discussed earlier, the virgin must become a Czar to become a Woman. The difficulty came when the Czar blocked the way, making the woman project her yearning on him and accept something less than full womanhood. But as many poems like the one above testify, it was a difficulty that she learned increasingly to trust herself to surmount. As a result, the animus could bring her to experience completion within herself, even when restrictions, in part at least self-imposed, inhibited the animus from leading her into a confirming relationship with a man.

The existence of the three "Master letters"[18] has whetted the eagerness of biographers to detect the man in the love poems through these documents. The letters are drafts, and there is no evidence that they were ever sent. One, written in a fairly controlled tone, dates from the late fifties; the other two, convulsed with passion and rejection, date from the early sixties when she was also writing many of the love poems. But the existence of these drafts does not undermine the theory advanced above. Emily Dickinson's penchant for viewing all men as father, tutor, preceptor, and master only generalizes the man addressed in the letters instead of specifying him. Moreover, these may well not have been letters at all in the sense of communications intended to be mailed to a recipient. It is convincing to read the letters as diary-like addresses to a troubled aspect of herself.

The suggestion is not farfetched; the journals of Margaret Fuller, another remarkable woman who could find no adequate place or outlet in the American patriarchy, served a similar purpose for her. All of Margaret Fuller's passion and frustration, her mind and will and wild emotions thrown back on their own self-doubt and self-assertion, tumbled out on those private pages, and she found relief and clarification in such thwarted auto-communication. Here, for example, is a "letter" from the journal, addressed to Beethoven in 1843, the almost-twenty years since the composer's death diminishing not at all his immediate presence to her. Her relationship to "Beethoven" stands as a projection of those masculine characteristics which she experienced as her torment and her glory:

MY ONLY FRIEND,
How shall I thank thee for once more breaking the chains of my sorrowful slumber? My heart beats. I live again, for I feel that I am worthy audience for thee, and that my being would be reason enough for thine.

Master, my eyes are always clear. I see that the universe is rich, if I am poor. I see the insignificance of my sorrows. In my will, I am not a captive; in my intellect, not a slave. Is it then my fault that the palsy of my affections benumbs my whole life?

. . . .

But thou, oh blessed master! dost answer all my questions, and make it my privilege to be. Like a humble wife to the sage, or poet, it is my triumph that I can understand and cherish thee; like a mistress, I arm thee for the fight; like a young daughter, I tenderly bind thy wounds. Thou art to me beyond compare, for thou art all I want.[19]

Her fantasy of Beethoven acted out the anomalies of her condition; her sexual and maternal maturity as a woman included those "masculine" faculties of mind and spirit for which she had found no satisfying means of development and expression in Concord, Boston, or New York and for which Beethoven served as measure and tally.

Less impelled than Margaret Fuller toward an external relationship, Emily Dickinson adopted a less peremptory and haughty tone, adopted in fact the cringing coyness which was her usual strategy under stress. Still, the "Master" letters, like the apostrophe to Beethoven, expressed a need, if only to the sufferer, and to some extent relieved the suffering through the admission of it. This passage is from the second of the "Master" letters:

> I am older–tonight, Master–but the love is the same–so are the moon and the crescent. If it had been God's will that I might breathe where you breathed–and find the place–myself–at night–if I (can) never forget that I am not with you–and that sorrow and frost are nearer than I–if I wish with a might I cannot repress–that mine were the Queen's place –the love of the Plantagenet is my only apology–To come nearer the presbyteries–and nearer than the new Coat–that the Tailor made–the prank of the Heart at play on the Heart– in holy Holiday–is forbidden me–You make me say it over– I fear you laugh–when I do not see–[but] "Chillon" is not funny.[20]

This excerpt comes from the last "Master" letter:

> Low at the knee that bore her once into wordless rest Daisy kneels a culprit–tell her her fault–Master–if it is small eno' to cancel with her life, she is satisfied–but punish dont banish her–shut her in prison, Sir–only pledge that you will forgive –sometime–before the grave, and Daisy will not mind–She will awake in your likeness.[21]

The diction and imagery are so much an extension of the poetry that these letters are best read (as are many of Dickinson's letters) as prose poems or free verse, and the situation is no more fictionally dramatized here than, for example, in the poems imagining his death or her death.

Poems in which the animus relationship is crucial are as much to be expected from women poets as are the anima-poems from men which make an unbroken procession down literary history. Animus-poems are rarer only because not until the twentieth century have women poets been numerous enough and strong enough to find in their new status the mind and will to be sufficiently candid and exploratory. In fact, the breakthrough came after Marianne Moore and even Elizabeth Bishop and Louise Bogan with the women born in the twenties—Denise Levertov and Adrienne Rich, for instance—and women after them—Sylvia Plath, Jean Valentine, Robin Morgan, and others. In *The Motorcycle Betrayal Poems* (1971) Diane Wakoski invented a moustachioed motorcyclist as the figure of her animus, and in an imaginative strategy that Margaret Fuller and Emily Dickinson would have recognized she addressed other poems as "letters" to George Washington and Beethoven. In fact, her obsessive theme is the animus-relationship in all its potential destructiveness and creativity. From a poem "In Gratitude to Beethoven":

> At times, you who look at me with so much tenderness,
> you make me cry.
> Where are you when I need you?
> This is all literary invention, a way of
> talking when there is no life.

From a sequence "To the Man in the Silver Ferrari":

> I talked to you this evening,
> by phone, realizing again I only love men I make up
> in my head, wishing for your presence,
> yet once more feeling that by word we do not communicate.[22]

Adrienne Rich's poem about Emily Dickinson speaks to her as "you, woman, masculine/ in single-mindedness," centering on the animus-drive behind her creativity and defining her "single-mindedness" not as undivided female placidity but as an unswerving dedication to language as the "battlefield" where she could have her conflicts "out at last/ on your own premises."[23] It would have been extraordinary for a woman as fiercely sensitive and aware as Emily Dickinson not to have at the heart of her psychological life an active and complex animus-connection.

The poems and letters, then, develop the same theme: a love whose desperation is part of its exaltation, a love inconceivable

apart from prison and the grave. In the same year as the last of
the "Master" letters she admitted once again the association of
love with death and eternity which we have noted in other poems:

> Love is like Life—merely longer
> Love is like Death, during the Grave
> Love is the Fellow of the Resurrection
> Scooping up the Dust and chanting "Live"!

(P491 I 374)

By extension death appears consistently in the poems as a man,
specifically as a lover with authority and often with royal rank.
A late poem sums the figure up:

> Death is the supple Suitor
> That wins at last—
> It is a stealthy Wooing
> Conducted first
> By pallid innuendoes
> And dim approach
> But brave at last with Bugles
> And a bisected Coach
> It bears away in triumph
> To Troth unknown
> And Kinsmen as divulgeless
> As throngs of Down—

(P1445 III 1001)

So, too, in poem 665 the journey by carriage to death is "Riding
to meet the Earl—" (P665 II 512); in "I heard a Fly buzz—when
I died—" Death comes as a King "For that last Onset—" (P465 I
358). The famous poem beginning "Because I could not stop for
Death—" (P712 II 546) is another version of dying as coronation-
procession or carriage-ride to eternity; here death is the most
tactful and courteous of gentlemen-callers, but there is no possibility of refusing his invitation.

Consequently many poems turn on the erotic satisfaction of
a death-marriage after years of a repressed life. Poem 577 is one
of several which imagine fondling the beloved's corpse; it begins:

If I may have it, when it's dead,
I'll be contented–so–
If just as soon as Breath is out
It shall belong to me–

Until they lock it in the Grave,
'Tis Bliss I cannot weigh–
For tho' they lock Thee in the Grave,
Myself–can own the key–

Think of it Lover! I and Thee
Permitted–face to face to be–
After a Life–a Death–We'll say–
For Death was That–
And This–is Thee–

(P577 II 441)

The contortions of the last lines seem to be saying that while the terms of our life were death-like in their passionless isolation, death comes as "Thee" to be loved and accepted, and the grave joins them at last. Poem 648 (from 1862 again) opens:

Promise This–When You be Dying–
Some shall summon Me–
Mine belong Your latest Sighing–
Mine–to Belt Your Eye–

Not with Coins–though they be Minted
From an Emperor's Hand–
Be my lips–the only Buckle
Your low Eyes–demand–

(P648 II 498–499)

The poem goes on punctuated by a refrain: "Mine to stay–when all have wandered–"; "Mine–to guard Your Narrow Precinct –"; "Mine to supplicate Madonna–". Another 1862 poem, "Mine–by the Right of the White Election!", rings even more ecstatically with the chorus of "Mine," as the privileges of death and resurrection are passionately proclaimed (P528 II 405–406).

So eternity comes as an erotic awakening. One poem from the mid-sixties reads:

'Tis Anguish grander than Delight
'Tis Resurrection Pain—
The meeting Bands of smitten Face
We questioned to, again.

'Tis Transport wild as thrills the Graves
When Cerements let go
And Creatures clad in Miracle
Go up by Two and Two.

(P984 II 710)

A late poem about resurrection begins "The Thrill came slowly
like a Boon for/ Centuries delayed" and goes on to use words like
"sumptuous," "Rapture," "ravished Holiness" (P1495 III 1032).
All that Eternity holds for her became personified, like Love and
Death, in the man in her mind. A poem of 1863 introduces this
secret, silent figure:

Conscious am I in my Chamber,
Of a shapeless friend—
He doth not attest by Posture—
Nor Confirm—by Word—

. . . .

Presence—is His furthest license—
Neither He to Me
Nor Myself to Him—by Accent—
Forfeit Probity—

(P679 II 525)

"He to Me" and "Myself to Him" recall other pairings we have
quoted earlier: "Tim and I," "Each . . . to each," "Balm to Balm,"
"I and Thee," "face to face," "Two and Two." Consequently,
by the time the last lines reveal Him as "Immortality," we recognize "Him" as an aspect, along with Love and Death, of the same
psychological configuration. The pattern is traced out over and
over; for example, in these poems from the mid-sixties: "The
Test of Love—is Death—" (P573 II 437); "Love—is that later Thing
than Death—/ More previous—than Life—" (P924 II 674); "Love—is

anterior to Life–/ Posterior to Death–" (P917 II 671); "Unable are the Loved to die/ For Love is Immortality,/ Nay, it is Deity–" (P809 II 611).

Another poem from these years (P640 II 492–493) is particularly revealing because it pushes the pattern of life-death-eternity to a frightening conclusion. It is notably long for a Dickinson poem and strikes familiar notes from the beginning:

> I cannot live with You–
> It would be Life–
> And Life is over there–
> Behind the Shelf

> . . . .

> I could not die–with You–
> For One must wait
> To shut the Other's Gaze down–
> You–could not–

However, more than half of the poem is spent explaining why eternity is just as empty of hope as are life and death:

> Nor could I rise–with You–
> Because Your Face
> Would put out Jesus'–
> That New Grace

> Glow plain–and foreign
> On my homesick Eye–
> Except that You than He
> Shone closer by–

> They'd judge Us–How–
> For You–served Heaven–You know,
> Or sought to–
> I could not–

> Because You saturated Sight–
> And I had no more Eyes
> For sordid excellence
> As Paradise

And were You lost, I would be–
Though My Name
Rang loudest
On the Heavenly fame–

And were You–saved–
And I–condemned to be
Where You were not–
That self–were Hell to Me–

So We must meet apart–
You there–I–here–
With just the Door ajar
That Oceans are–and Prayer–
And that White Sustenance–
Despair–

(P640 II 492–493)

The argument moves with unflinching logic, eliminating possibility after possibility. The lover would outshine Jesus in heaven (an assertion which many poems make and which matches her initial choice of earth over heaven in electing to be a poet); he will be saved as a professing Christian, whereas she could not; if he were lost, then heaven could mean nothing without him; if they were separated, her "self," wherever it was, "were Hell to Me–". At last nothing remains but the pair of them "You there—I— here—" with the void yawning between. Line by line she has reconstructed the trap she had devised for herself. The "White Election," signified in the white dresses that she wore from the early sixties like a costume or habit, ends up here as "that White Sustenance—Despair—". Neither the ambiguity of Melville's white whale nor the white apocalypse that confronts Poe's A. Gordon Pym is more damning.

Did Emily Dickinson's exclusive dedication to consciousness imprison her psyche in a labyrinth? It certainly seemed so at times. In the face of metaphysical doubt she was unable to live conditionally with an "if" and seek solace in society, as Melville's Ishmael finally learned to do. Consciousness, therefore, remained for her the only substitute for the missing absolute, and so, despite all, constituted her only security. After all, as she said in poem 384, if consciousness sometimes spelled "Captivity," it could also spell "Liberty" on its own terms. She could not be sure about a life after death, although at times the comforting doctrine seemed to have to be true; but even without heaven eternity could be, she knew from experience, a dimension of temporal experience. The psyche could—if only for fragile moments—hold heaven, and, for as long as those moments lasted, the ache of love and the ecstasy of death were transfigured into an experience in which the individual, body and soul, sex and spirit, masculine and feminine, met completion.

Now we can look back and read Dickinson's poems about death and resurrection in a new light. Without denying that many of those poems describe the renunciations and deprivations of her actual existence and her projections of fulfillment into another order of existence, it is possible as well to see that at least some of the poems describe the death psychologically as the painful passage from deprivation into glorious realization. She—often she and "he" together—die into a transfigured self, much as Blake says, "I have died twenty-nine times" or Keats in "The Fall of Hyperion" speaks of the passage from lower to higher stages of consciousness as "dying into life." Such "Superior instants" made it all, even the anguish and longing, not just bearable but worth an unstinting commitment of will. Even in the midst of her worst time, she never lost sight of that fact:

The Soul's Superior instants
Occur to Her—alone—
When friend—and Earth's occasion
Have infinite withdrawn—

Or She—Herself—ascended
To too remote a Hight
For lower Recognition
Than Her Omnipotent—

This Mortal Abolition
Is seldom—but as fair
As Apparition—subject
To Autocratic Air—

Eternity's disclosure
To favorites—a few—

Of the Colossal substance
Of Immortality

(P306 I 227–228)

From the same year comes this poem:

Heaven is so far of the Mind
That were the Mind dissolved–
The Site–of it–by Architect
Could not again be proved–

'Tis vast–as our Capacity–
As fair–as our idea–
To Him of adequate desire
No further 'tis, than Here–

(P370 I 294)

Even without a postulated Heaven after death, Heaven is a leap
of the imagination and so a measure of our capacity not just to
receive but to conceive, much as Wallace Stevens would come to
say: "We say that God and the imagination are one."[24] As a psychological state, "Heaven" is the furthest dimension of selfhood.

However, even in inferior moments the life of consciousness
was worth the struggle precisely because her identity would be
fought out, if at all, through those conflicts, as several poems,
again from the terrible years 1862 and 1863, make clear:

Me from Myself–to banish–
Had I Art–
Invincible my Fortress
Unto All Heart–

But since Myself–assault Me–
How have I peace
Except by subjugating
Consciousness?

And since We're mutual Monarch
How this be
Except by Abdication–
Me–of Me?

(P642 II 494)

"I–'Tim'–and–Me!"; now phrases that sound like the opposite: "Me from Myself–to banish"; "Abdication–/ Me–of Me." But in fact she will countenance no such self-subjugation and self-abdication; she would prefer to press on toward a peace in which the hostile factions within the psyche discover that they are "mutual Monarch." For we are each our own Savior or Betrayer:

> The Soul unto itself
> Is an imperial friend–
> Or the most agonizing Spy–
> An Enemy–could send–
>
> Secure against it's own–
> No treason it can fear–
> Itself–it's Sovreign–of itself
> The Soul should stand in Awe–
>
> (P683 II 529)

Even if God appeared as much Betrayer as Savior at times, even if in the eyes of the faithful she had played Judas to Jesus' call, she would never betray the allegiance to her "Sovreign" self. A poem of 1861 which begins "Why–do they shut Me out of Heaven?" concludes:

> Oh, if I–were the Gentleman
> In the "White Robe"–
> And they–were the little Hand–that knocked–
> Could–I–forbid?
>
> (P248 I 179)

Obviously not. Variants which pluralize a deific "Gentleman" into saintly "gentlemen" and "Robe" into "robes" do not blunt the fact that her difficulty was with the categorical reasoning of the masculine spirit. (Clinical experience has indicated that very frequently the animus is imaged as many men, not just one man.) Another poem of that year which opens

> A solemn thing–it was–I said–
> A Woman–white–to be–
> And wear–if God should count me fit–
> Her blameless mystery–
>
> (P271 I 193)

might seem at first to resolve the problem by admitting her dependence on "Him." But once homage is paid almost perfunctorily to God, the poem turns to what it would be like to penetrate the "blameless mystery" of Womanhood. The last stanza reads:

> And then–the size of this "small" life–
> The Sages–call it small–
> Swelled–like Horizons–in my breast–
> And I sneered–softly–"small"!

In the end, pregnant with her own mystery, she can condescend to those male Sages who thought her small and dependent. Although this poem was assigned the title "Wedded" in *Poems* (1896), it is clearly not about a mystic marriage, much less a nuptial; it is about the mysterious wedding of opposites into identity. Being a woman in white had something to do with the Gentleman, or gentlemen, in white, but Dickinson learned that, for her at least, the way to compensate for her felt deficiency before the masculine "Other" did not lie in capitulation to its superiority. Acceptance of female inferiority would impel her to thwart her womanhood in one of two unsatisfactory ways: either through an unnatural identification with the masculine or through accepting such prescribed female roles as "wife" and "mother," permitted by the patriarchy. The bolder choice—very bold indeed for the mid-nineteenth century, when unwed women became maiden aunts, tending the children and pottering about their house chores—was to adapt the masculine characteristics of mind and will to the achievement of an integral identity as a woman. The variant for "my breast" above is "my *vest*," the word underscored for emphasis.

Another poem describes her "Self" as "Columnar," and the male connotations of the adjective identify the qualities which formed the foundation of her achievement:

> On a Columnar Self–
> How ample to rely
> In Tumult–or Extremity–
> How good the Certainty
>
> That Lever cannot pry–
> And Wedge cannot divide

Conviction—That Granitic Base—
Though None be on our Side—

Suffice Us—for a Crowd—
Ourself—and Rectitude—
And that Assembly—not far off
From furthest Spirit—God—

(P789 II 595–596)

She had described Emerson's *Representative Men* as "a little Granite Book that you can lean upon" (*Letters*, II, 569). Here she assembles around her towering self the sage gentlemen of God. The variant reading for the last two lines produces another acknowledgment of the animus-figure, his masculine power now fully assimilated into herself; the variant is: "And that Companion—not far off/ From furthest Good Man—God—". That "Companion" of hers had all along been in league with the "furthest Good Man—God—" and His Assembly; or so it seems now in the exaltation of her "Columnar Self," when she has nothing to fear from any of them.

Now we can comprehend much more clearly what she meant when she spoke of the "Effort" and "Patience" and "Belief" required to achieve an identity out of the conflicts confronting the psyche. The lines which were cited early in this section as a preliminary indication of what the cultivation of consciousness entailed can stand now as a coda:

Effort—is the sole condition—
Patience of Itself—
Patience of opposing forces—
And intact Belief—

(P750 II 571)

3

The metaphor which Dickinson evolved to describe the activity of consciousness is "Circumference." Other words occur more frequently in her work, but perhaps none is more indicative of her guiding intention. Its imperativeness breaks out in her fourth letter to Higginson in July 1862; sensing his cautious reservations about her poems, she interrupted her circumlocutions with an abrupt declaration that she knew what she was doing and intended to continue on her course: "Perhaps you smile at me—I could not stop for that–My Business is Circumference–"[25]. The tone is peremptory; she had set about her own business as single-mindedly as had her father and her brother.

Several critics, myself included, have commented on "Circumference" in Dickinson's work, but none has grasped adequately the psychological dimension of the symbol. Many religious, mystical, and philosophical writers—East and West— have invoked the circle to symbolize totality, whether of the individual, of creation, of the Life Force, or of God. Emerson's essay on "Circles," which Dickinson would have known, develops the image in neo-Platonic terms: "The eye is the first circle; the horizon which it forms is the second; and throughout nature this primary figure is repeated without end. It is the highest emblem in the cipher of the world. . . . Our life is an apprenticeship to the truth that around every circle another can be drawn."[26] But Emily Dickinson's bent was the poet's, not the philosopher's; and her circles represent not so much a metaphysical system as a human consciousness exploring itself and its place in the world. In other words, just as she had told Higginson in 1862, her circles constitute a metaphor, shifting in emphasis but consistent in cumulative development, for the "Business" which was her exclusive vocation.

The entire process, from its humble point of origin to its anticipated apotheosis, is encapsulated in two quatrains written in the early sixties:

Time feels so vast that were it not
For an Eternity–
I fear me this Circumference
Engross my Finity–

To His exclusion, who prepare
By Processes of Size
For the Stupendous Vision
Of His Diameters–

(P802 II 607)

The abstract language and geometric conceit will be substantiated in the more concrete imagery of other poems, but the implications are all here. The figure is a series of concentric circles in which the poet is the finite center surrounded by the sweep of Time, which is in turn encompassed by the almost unimaginable expanse of Eternity. Characteristically she "sees" time and space in complementary terms. Time seems threateningly large to the individual consciousness; it would sink into the temporal vastness were not that vastness itself given a delimiting shape by the Eternity that rings it round. Oblivion is poised in the suspended "were it not" of the first line, but paradoxically eternity makes time bearable by confining it to a circumference which allows the individual to establish herself within it as the center for her time-space experience. In the overall economy of things containment proves not only positive but necessary. Otherwise the individual, unable to maintain her position in time-space, would thereby never come to know the Him who controls the process; but within the widening series of circumferences the individual can advance through the "Processes of Size" which prepare her for "the Stupendous Vision/ Of His Diameters—". The variants for "Processes" are "Rudiments" and "Prefaces," and the variant for "Vision" is "Volume"; the phrase "Processes of Size" epitomizes the equivalence of time and space. Even from this single poem it is clear that Emily Dickinson is contending with mortality and change in terms of an expansible "inner space" amidst the seeming infinity of "outer space." The phrase "Engross my Finity," which means "absorb my Finity" at the beginning of the poem and indicates her threatened insignificance, comes to mean "enlarge my Finity" by the end, "engross" in the sense of "write in large letters."

Erik Erikson found that the feminine psyche characteristically operates out of a primary sense of its "inner space," at once physical and psychological, in contrast to the masculine psyche which characteristically operates out of a primary impulse toward a linear exploration of "outer space." Erikson was eager to add that any given woman need not be trapped exclusively in her "inner space" and the maternal, domestic role which it in part implies, and even further that a woman of strong mind will naturally engage and enter into "outer space," just as a man, particularly a man of emotion and subjectivity, may occupy his "inner space" more than his "outer." But Erikson still maintained that a woman will probably—and should—negotiate "outer space" differently from men—on different terms and assumptions proceeding from her original sense of "inner space." Moreover, personally and existentially, the "inner space" may be experienced as full or empty, tending toward fullness or emptiness, alternating between fullness and emptiness; as a result, the psychological life of the woman will be governed by that delicate balance or disturbing imbalance. "In female experience," said Erikson, "an inner space is at the center of despair even as it is the very center of potential fulfillment." So although for men, and for the masculine aspect of the woman's mind, the "Ultimate has . . . been visualized as an infinity which begins where the male conquest of outer space ends, and a domain where an 'even more' omnipotent and omniscient Being must be submissively acknowledged," the Ultimate "may well be found also to reside in the Immediate, which has so largely been the domain of woman and of the inward mind."[27] Erikson's statement sums up the two sides—and the inner dialectic—of Emily Dickinson's psyche, but his words (perhaps because he is a man, even more because he is a behavioristic social scientist) convey little of the complexity and dangers of the problem, especially of the metaphysical and mystical dimensions of the problem, for a woman like Emily Dickinson. Her poems record the lived experience, infinity yawning beyond and within the circumference of her psyche.

The circle-image was, centuries before Freud, the woman's symbol. But as the poem under discussion indicates, Dickinson's circles are not biological or genital symbols but images of psychological and spiritual space responding to and negotiating with the "Him" of Time and Eternity. Containment, therefore, makes for space and possibilities ("Area—no test of Depth"), and Dickinson's circumference encloses the totality of expansible psychic activity in contrast to the more characteristically masculine modality in which a stronger and more assertive ego-consciousness conducts its daily business with "outer space."

It is true that the acknowledged point of origin for Dickinson is the individual psyche, navelled in the ego: minuscule and disjunct from other psyches as well as from the world of nature.

Another person, she felt, "carries a circumference/ In which I have no part" and which remains "Impregnable to inquest" from "my slim Circumference."[28] It is nonetheless equally true that any experience deep enough and acute enough exceeds "the minute Circumference/ Of a Single Brain," at once expanding it and concentrating within it "Ages" and "Eternities" (P967 II 699). The expansion and delimitation are, in a sense, synonymous; the mind holds seemingly impossible quantities, but within its enlarged boundaries: not so much a sallying forth (Whitman's repeated phrase) as an absorption.

Yet within her mind there is an imaginative going forth:

I saw no Way—The Heavens were stitched—
I felt the Columns close—
The Earth reversed her Hemispheres—
I touched the Universe—

And back it slid—and I alone—
A Speck upon a Ball—
Went out upon Circumference—
Beyond the Dip of Bell—

(P378 I 300)

In this poem, in contrast to poem 802 above, space and time seem smothering constriction, an implosion of the abyss but equally threatening. The speaker feels herself sealed in and sealed off, the skies stitched shut (the word "Heavens" carrying metaphysical implications as well) and the cloud-columns closed tight. But at the end of the first quatrain a miraculous breakthrough occurs, the rhyme of "Earth reversed" imitating the wrenching motion. At the merest pressure of her touch the confining spheres invert themselves; the skies open out to the "Heavens" and the earth splits into hemispheres. The terse phrasing of the rest of the poem, spaced out by dashes, conveys the tense excitement as the speaker, still "alone" and still "A Speck upon a Ball," veers beyond the partial arcs of bells, marking men's time, to the furthest Circumference. "Upon Circumference"; but in the "Processes of Size" there is no single Circumference, and so in another poem the bird which images the mind in flight begins in arcs and arrives "among Circumference," as though Circumference were an inexhaustible range of possibilities:

She staked her Feathers–Gained an Arc–
Debated–Rose again–
This time–beyond the estimate
Of Envy, or of Men–

And now, among Circumference–
Her steady Boat be seen–
At home–among the Billows–As
The Bough where she was born–

(P798 II 604)

The word play reenforces the tricky ascent; the very sticks of her wings become the stakes of this risky resurrection ("Rose again") as she succeeds "This time" in moving "beyond" the time "of Men."

Circumferences exist, of course, only in relation to centers, and vice versa. So this "Business of Circumference" with all its soaring flights is conducted in terms of "some Centre," as poem 680 recognizes. The center "Exists in every Human Nature" as its essence and "Goal," hidden from the start but needing to be arrived at and located. Most people fail even in a lifetime of quest not just because the individual human center is hidden deep in the psyche but because that deep secret is mysteriously associated with God as Absolute Center or, as Emerson imaged Him in "Circles," as the circle which is all center and no circumference, all Being and nothing apart from Himself. The poem is a complex statement about the individuality of this center ("each" and "every") which is as well the link with and passage to the Absolute. The poem moves in and closes on itself in shape as well as meaning. The alternation of long and short lines moves forward in a repeated rhythm of implosion toward the assertion of the final short lines: "But then–," "Again"; and the rhymes of the short lines, played tightly off against each other, modulate from the dissonances of the slant rhymes to the perfectly corresponding rhymes of the last two stanzas.

Each Life Converges to some Centre–
Expressed–or still–
Exists in every Human Nature
A Goal–

Embodied scarcely to itself–it may be–
Too fair–

For Credibility's presumption
To mar—

Adored with caution—as a Brittle Heaven—
To reach
Were hopeless, as the Rainbow's Raiment
To touch—

Yet persevered toward—surer—for the Distance—
How high—
Unto the Saints' slow diligence—
The Sky—

Ungained—it may be—by a Life's low Venture—
But then—
Eternity enables the endeavoring
Again.

(P680 II 526–527)

Whether or not Dickinson had in mind Robert Browning's expressions of the ethic of striving when she wrote the last quatrains, she would only have been pleased with the association.

Another poem characterizes eternity as "Circumference without Relief—/ Or Estimate—or End—" (P943 II 685). No wonder that at times she felt "My little Circuit" inadequate for "This new Circumference" (P313 I 236). But at other times she knew herself capable of full Circumference. The hearty Browningesque pursuit of life beyond death in poem 680 above is based on the belief that the convergence which penetrated to her center would make her concentric with the All-Center. It is a positive version of Poe's apocalyptic *Eureka*. Pierre Teilhard de Chardin made the same theological point: everything that rises must converge to the Alpha-point and Omega-point which is God. For Emily Dickinson full Circumference was not like grace, which the orthodox said could not be earned or merited; it was, in fact, individual will and choice that activate potentialities and bring them to consciousness. Poem 508, written in the same year and cited in the previous section, conveys her growth through the two contrasting "baptisms": the child's church baptism (which Dickinson in fact did not have) and the coming to consciousness which is self-definition:

Baptized, before, without the choice,
But this time, consciously, of Grace–
Unto supremest name–
Called to my Full–The Crescent dropped–
Existence's whole Arc, filled up,
With one small Diadem.

(P508 II 390)

Then she became "Adequate–Erect,/ With Will to choose" the Crown which signs her Circumference. The imagery reiterates the fact that our supreme moments subsume the polarities which afflict our daily existence. Uplifted, she could feel herself "Duke in a moment of Deathlessness/ And God, for a Frontier" (P1090 II 769). Then God appeared "A just sufficient Ring" for the knight who had outstripped Time and Space (P865 II 646). When ordinary human limitations drop away, Circumference marks the border line between modes of existence, between being and Being, as the human presses into the absolute to enclose more and more within her frontiers. In a conception that anticipates existential theologians like Paul Tillich, God is the totality (Tillich's phrase was "the ground of being") into which the person expands, so that her Circumference measures and defines her capacity for personhood under God.

But never for long could Emily Dickinson feel secure in the expectation of personhood. The confrontation between God and man in poem 865 issued, as we have seen, from bitter antagonism which turned the frontier into a contested battle line. The extreme dangers of her exposed position inform many poems. Poem 1343 (III 928) reads like an ironic comment on the previously cited 798, written more than ten years earlier. In 798 the bird sailed out "among Circumference," "At Home—among the Billows—As/ The Bough where she was born—"; in 1343 the persona is "A Bee I personally knew," suddenly swept by the wind into oblivion:

This harrowing event
Transpiring in the Grass
Did not so much as wring from him
A wandering "Alas"–

(P1343 III 928)

275

Frost would have enjoyed the puns on "harrow" as an agricultural tool to churn up the soil and on "transpiring" in its etymological meaning of "breathing or blowing across," but the second stanza keeps the poem from being merely a grim little joke:

> Twixt Firmament above
> And Firmament below
> The Billows of Circumference
> Were sweeping him away—

Between our earthly atmosphere and heaven is a precarious zone, belied by the word "Firmament," and suddenly "Bumble Bee was not—", as if he had never been. So the line between being and Being becomes the demarcation between life and death, presence and absence. Poem 1084 (II 766) charts the same inexplicable shift from existence to nothingness; "a single Bird," who at half past three tried out his voice and by half past four supplanted the actual scene with his now-perfect song, is nowhere to be found at half past seven. The singer may lose himself in the world his art creates; but mortality breaks off the song, and "Supplanted" becomes a wry comment on the organic efficacy of art. The repeated "Half past" anticipates the bird-artist's extinction, when empty "Place was where the Presence was/ Circumference between."

A poem from the mid-sixties begins to describes a death scene with the words "Crisis is a Hair," and goes on to meditate on this fragile but categorical hairline between life and death:

> Let an instant push
> Or an Atom press
> Or a Circle hesitate
> In Circumference
>
> It—may jolt the Hand
> That adjusts the Hair
> That secures Eternity
> From presenting—Here—

(P889 II 656)

Again, wit and the nursery-rhyme cadences reminiscent of "The House That Jack Built" are verbal strategies to hold horror at bay.

In poem 802 she had warned against "His exclusion, who prepare/ By Processes of Size" for eternity. Now, ironically, our security seems to lie in excluding eternity: its "presenting–Here–" absents us. "Here" Circumference rings center until time's pressure or matter's density breaks the line sealing off the protected area and all the forces arrayed against the individual flood in. So the frontier where Emily Dickinson extended her territory toward God became not just a battle line but a barrier behind which she would hold out against His assaults as staunchly and as long as she could. Imagining a watery grave, she rejected the death-choice for all its alluring enticements:

> Abhorrent is the Rest
> In undulating Rooms
> Whose Amplitude no end invades–
> Whose Axis never ends.

(P1428 III 990)

In self-preservation we need a center for location and a circumference for limits.

Nonetheless, she held out behind her defense-perimeter precisely for those still times when she seemed to reach the secret in the psyche and in nature which saved her from annihilation and delivered her to wholeness. A companion poem to "Some keep the Sabbath going to Church—" is a runic quatrain from 1862:

> When Bells stop ringing–Church–begins–
> The Positive–of Bells–
> When Cogs–stop–that's Circumference–
> The Ultimate–of Wheels.

(P633 II 486)

The clangor of the bells finds its quiet affirmation in the church service; similarly, in the religion of consciousness, completion comes when the psychic machinery, as well as the industry of living, stops the spinning that moves consciousness toward stasis.

Another quatrain, equally condensed and mysterious, sums up the Circumference poems. Sent a few years before her death to the celebrated sculptor, Daniel Chester French, whom Dickinson had known as a boy during a brief residence in Amherst, the lines adopt a tone of oracular finality in speaking, artist to artist, of a fulfillment erotic and religious:

> Circumference thou Bride of Awe
> Possessing thou shalt be
> Possessed by every hallowed Knight
> That dares to covet thee

(P1620 III 1111)

By the strict code of the Commandments coveting was a sin, but the hunger of the imagination that moves the artist-knight confers its own grace. In that marriage, that *hieros gamos*, hallowed if not mystic in the traditional sense, all the distinctions that made for conflict and so for defensive withdrawal—masculine and feminine, possession and surrender, individuality and otherness—fall away or, better yet, meet; and their union stands eternal for a moment in the mind and for longer in the projected aesthetic creation.

The Business of Circumference ended for Emily Dickinson in a conjunction of opposites suggestive of that elusive wholeness of being for which mystics and religious people, ranging all the way from alchemists to her churchgoing neighbors, yearned. It was a sign of her strength and audacity that she dared to try to encounter that mystery alone. She recognized from the outset the renunciations necessary to maintain herself; then she drove herself to the secret frontiers where the mystery waited to be engaged and, in the engagement, to test her out and drive her to the point of dissolution and despair. But in that same engagement she also found access to resources that made her recognize herself as "Bride," "Wife," "Woman," "Queen," "Knight," "Czar," a crowned presence and a worshipped power. Even the Bride of God and consort to the Holy Trinity. In rural, provincial New England, under the forbidding, patriarchal eye of her father and God, in the privacy of her mind-chamber, Emily Dickinson was celebrating her woman's mysteries, while Whitman was singing his masculine mysteries in public print. It is not surprising that she came to see her Self as queen, priestess, goddess; she had experienced her womanhood as fully as she could. Through this risky, strenuous effort Dickinson became a pioneer of her "inner space," a frontierswoman as American as the men who were extending the borders for power or profit, and her work foreshadows the sort of poetry that many women are writing today. As we have seen, Adrienne Rich's poem about Dickinson presents her as the type of the woman-poet in a patriarchal world focusing with clarifying "masculine" consciousness on the exploration of her nature.

References to priestesses and goddesses and woman's mysteries suggest Eleusis more than Amherst, but the association of the Eleusinian mysteries with a Yankee recluse like Emily Dickinson proves not to be as adventitious as it might seem at first. The rites at Eleusis acted out the depth and power of woman's nature through the myth of Demeter-Persephone-Kore as triune aspects of the feminine principle. Kore, the virgin daughter of Demeter, was seduced by the dark brother of Zeus, Kore's father, with Zeus' consent, and was rapt down to the world of the dead, where she was crowned Pluto's queen-wife. In this hierogamy, or sacred marriage, sexual ecstasy and religious exaltation, the conjoined experience of the erotic and the divine through the force of the masculine, come to consummation. There she reigned as Persephone until won back to earth—for only part of the year, as it turned out—by Demeter. The three goddesses are so closely related that they meld into one another. The virgin becomes woman through the death-marriage and becomes pregnant with the divine son, whose birth is a part of the Eleusinian mysteries; she returns again as virgin, though now in more complete identification with the mother who bore her by Zeus. However, in a configuration that recalls Whitman's version of the "Square Deific," the trinity of women is completed in a fourth dimension: the feminine round of Kore-Persephone-Demeter subsumed under the resurrected Kore, Sophia, woman as vessel of Spirit and Wisdom.

Erich Neumann, who has studied feminine psychology more extensively perhaps than anyone so far, has noted that the invasion of the women's psyche by an awareness of the masculine often comes like "an overpowering intoxication, like being seized and laid hold of by a 'ravishing penetrator,' not personally related to a concrete man and projected to him but experienced as a transpersonal numen" or "as the fascinating Spirit Father." But even such transpersonal experience has its erotic aspect. For the woman, the situation is that of the "maiden" delivered "not to a personal man but to a god who overpowers her, now as a cloud, or as rain, as wind, as lightning, as gold, as sun, as moon, and so on." This description confirms the connection between Dickinson's love poems and her strongly erotic nature poems. The first encounter with the masculine may come as a psychic rape or death-marriage, but that is by no means the conclusion. As we have already seen in the poems, the death-marriage can be a transformative awakening. In his discussion of the psychological significance of the Kore myth and of the Eleusinian mysteries, Neumann concluded that only when the full cycle has been "perceived, or emotionally suffered and experienced in the mystery,"

> has the Feminine undergone a central transformation, not so much by becoming a woman and a mother, and thus guaranteeing earthly fertility and the survival of life, as by achieving union on a higher plane with the spiritual aspect of the Feminine, the Sophia aspect of the Great Mother, and thus becoming a moon goddess.
>
> For the renascent Kore no longer dwells as before on the earth, or only in the underworld as Persephone, but in conjunction with Demeter becomes the Olympian Kore, the immortal and divine principle, the beatific light. Like Demeter herself she becomes the goddess of the three worlds: the earth, the underworld, and the heavens.

As a result, "her luminous aspect, the fruit of her transformative process, becomes the luminous son, the divine spirit-son, spiritually conceived and spiritually born." So it is that in the development of the woman the ravisher can come to be the saving hero who delivers her from the dragon-father into her own creative womanhood. Nor need the hero be an actual masculine partner. In the highest forms of feminine development "this masculine element [can] be experienced and understood as something 'inner,' so that the woman is enabled to achieve 'autonomy,' that is, a relative independence from an outer masculine partner." Her "hero" is the "power of consciousness in the woman herself."[29]

No woman will of course embody adequately or consistently all aspects of the archetype, any more than any single man can bring the masculine principle to total and sustained realization.

And at first we might be tempted to object that a myth depicting so grandly the spectrum of the feminine experience has little to do with the narrow experience of Emily Dickinson. However, reflection on the psychological significance of the myth reveals that all of the areas of experience which the story rehearses are concerns crucial to Dickinson's poetry. What was enacted at Eleusis was Emily Dickinson's pain and triumph too, on however stiffly guarded terms.

Yet it is equally true that the terms and limits Dickinson imposed upon her possibilities determined the particular way in which she engaged the archetype and gave it individual expression. Dickinson chose to be Kore the maiden-bride more than Demeter the mother or Persephone the wife. She wanted to restrict herself to that inviolate and inviolable aspect of woman's mystery. The attempt to control by definition and discrimination and thus to break out of the feminine round—all distinctly "masculine" tendencies—invalidates for her aspects of the psychological truth at the heart of the Eleusinian mysteries, namely, that woman is by nature all the goddesses in the cycle of generation and regeneration: Demeter, Kore, Persephone, the Olympian Kore. But the masculine and feminine can be sorted out only conceptually, not in individual or collective experience. Thus myths insist that even the masculine deities became involved in the mystery of sex and procreation—and not just Pluto the dark brother but Zeus himself, the source of light and spirit. So, too, myths tell us that woman joins with the masculine, passing through her connection with man as wife and mother to a distinctive embodiment of the light. Demeter-mother rescues Persephone-wife from the death-marriage with the husband-god and restores her to the life and light of nature. But for only part of the year: she must return to be the god's wife and queen. At the same time, Kore returns impregnated with the divine light-seed of the dark god. Woman bears her daughter, daughter mothers her divine son; the process repeats itself without end. But beyond the process stands the figure of Sophia or the Olympian Kore—beyond, yet comprehending the process in all its essential aspects. Emily Dickinson's concern with consciousness led her away from an immediate involvement with the sexual and maternal dimensions of womanhood and directed her toward the Sophia aspect, for in Sophia the hierogamy which resolves the sexual roles is accomplished in the one eternally inviolate figure.

Sophia is, then, the symbol of the feminine Self, analogous to the figure of the hermaphroditic self or hermaphroditic Wise Old Man for the masculine psyche. It was to the realization of her Sophia-Self* that Emily Dickinson dedicated her imaginative energy, and it was this that she was able to realize during those supreme moments when Circumference and Awe were wed as Bride and Knight. Those moments were associated with the light-principle, with Sun and Noon, with "the man of noon," as she called him in the letter to Sue quoted earlier.

Now if the Sun seemed, as he often did, treacherously "other," his light struck her in the image of the thunderbolt. It was a rape, as Zeus and Pluto had raped. Still, the rape, for all its terrors, was the desired seizure: all-seeing and all-blinding. And the lesson of the myth was that rape restored virginity: Kore shone forth as Sophia. She became more luminous and whole than she had ever known: at once the receiver and dispenser of life-energy.

A late quatrain sums up her relation to and awe of the sun:

> The pattern of the sun
> Can fit but him alone
> For sheen must have a Disk
> To be a sun—

> (P1550 III 1069)

The first two lines associate light-energy with the masculine sun, and the second two lines implicate the sun in the feminine element with the recognition that even the light-spirit needs a material-maternal form to manifest itself: "For sheen must have a Disk/ To be a sun—". Light embodies itself as sun; then light-seed and womb-form, vessel and radiance, establish the full Circumference. So "Disk" stands out as the only specially capitalized word in the poem.

---

*In a poem expressing her deepening experience of woman's mysteries, H.D. spoke of "Santa Sophia, the SS of the Sanctus Spiritus" and added a little later: "She is Psyche, the butterfly,/out of the ocean" (Trilogy [New York: New Directions, 1973], pp. 101, 103). As we have seen, Whitman, too, called the Holy Spirit "Santa Spirita."

But "sheen must have a Disk/ To be a" moon as well, and in the moon Emily Dickinson found the woman's own way of shining. For all her fascination with the sun and her hesitating half-acquiescence in the surrender which the man of noon exacted, her relation with the moon was easier. The identification of the moon with the feminine light, like the identification of the sun with the masculine light, goes back to early Western myths, and Erich Neumann's essay "On the Moon and Matriarchal Consciousness" is a suggestive exploration of the connection. This form of consciousness, not limited to women but characteristic of most women and of men of strongly imaginative bent, "has nothing to do with the abstract logic of the masculine, patriarchal spirit, but belongs to a specifically feminine form of spiritual experience which in mythology is frequently connected with the moon symbol."[30] In other words, the moon symbolizes a consciousness which knows by feeling and whose deepest, most trusted sources of understanding and relationship lie in the rhythms of intuition and the imagination. So the moon fluctuates through the full cycle of light and dark:

Which is the best—the Moon or the Crescent?
Neither—said the Moon—
That is best which is not—Achieve it—
You efface the Sheen.

(P1315 III 910)

Neither is better because both are aspects of the ongoing presence, and she is a creature of that lunar power: "Obedient to the least command/ Thine eye impose on me—" (P429 I 332).

But the difference between the sun and the moon, between patriarchal and matriarchal consciousness remains. And can the moon, even at the full, efface the solar sheen? By ending in dissolution the poem above seems to admit the moon's inferiority:

Not of detention is Fruition—
Shudder to attain.
Transport's decomposition follows—
He is Prism born.

Emily Dickinson's earliest surviving poem, though only a teasing Valentine, seems to invert the primacy of the masculine over the feminine: "Adam, and Eve, his consort, the moon and then the sun" (P1 I 1). Yet despite the splendor of all its phases the moon reflects the sun's light. No wonder that unmindful of our frets and worries ("Life—and Death—/ And Afterward—or Nay—") the moon gazes "engrossed to Absolute—/ With shining and the Sky—" (P629 II 484). It is the moon's staring at the sun that lights it, and so the man in the moon shows in the shadows of her shining disc.

However, if the man in the moon is the masculine source of the moon's light, he is—just as importantly—the man of noon internalized in the woman's nature as her own. Here is a poem about the man in the moon written in 1862 during the time of her profoundest engagement with the animus:

> You know that Portrait in the Moon—
> So tell me who 'tis like—
> The very Brow—the stooping eyes—
> A-fog for—Say—Whose Sake?
>
> The very Pattern of the Cheek—
> It varies—in the Chin—
> But—Ishmael—since we met—'tis long—
> And fashions—intervene—
>
> When Moon's at full—'Tis Thou—I say—
> My lips just hold the name—
> When crescent—Thou art worn—I note—
> But—there—the Golden Same—
>
> And when—Some Night—Bold—slashing Clouds
> Cut Thee away from Me—
> That's easier—than the other film
> That glazes Holiday—

> (P504 II 387)

The vagaries of the man in the moon, his changes and phases, even the dark when his face is blanked out are "easier" than death's final film because they are the repeated cycle of her psyche. In a poem written fifteen or so years later the poet watches a moonlit "Traveller on a Hill":

To magic Perpendiculars
Ascending, though Terrene—
Unknown his shimmering ultimate—
But he indorsed the sheen—

(P1450 III 1004)

The image of her animus, he moves under the moon's sheen, showing her the ascent to the unseen Absolute.

However, she is not a function of the man in the moon; he is a function of her. Just as the woman's masculine qualities should be accommodated to her developing womanhood, just as they should serve as the channel for her conscious comprehension of her womanhood, so the moon encloses the man, and he appears only in her radiance; for within the woman's psyche the moon's light must shine triumphantly. "Fabulous as a Moon at Noon," she wrote in one quatrain (P1250 III 867), and in other places she celebrated woman's apotheosis in "Her [not his] perfect Face":

The Moon was but a Chain of Gold
A Night or two ago—
And now she turns Her perfect Face
Upon the World below—

. . . .

Her Bonnet is the Firmament—
The Universe—Her Shoe—
The Stars—the Trinkets at Her Belt—
Her Dimities—of Blue—

(P737 II 562)

So runs Emily Dickinson's provincial-Yankee version of a mythic figure who carries suggestions of and affinities with the Blessed Virgin in glorious Assumption and the moon-goddess Diana as well as such nineteenth-century descendants as Rossetti's Blessed Damozel. The moon's apotheosis is her own, at least when she is transfixed in its lunar light and becomes its vessel. Then Emily Dickinson of Amherst holds the prerogatives of the moon-goddess herself, as in the following poem:

I make His Crescent fill or lack–
His Nature is at Full
Or Quarter–as I signify–
His Tides–do I control–

He holds superior in the Sky
Or gropes, at my Command
Behind inferior Clouds–or round
A Mist's slow Colonnade–

But since We hold a Mutual Disc–
And front a Mutual Day–
Which is the Despot, neither knows–
Nor Whose–the Tyranny–

(P909 II 668)

During such experiences, the distinction between "Him" and her, between ruling and being ruled becomes irrelevant, because under the sway of her transcendent possibilities she approaches Self-possession. Myth becomes fact, not fable; she is the living myth. Now lines cited earlier display their portentous significance, when, for instance, she boasts of being

Called to My Full–The Crescent dropped–
Existence's whole Arc, filled up,
With one small Diadem.

(P508 II 390)

4

At the same time, the fact that Emily Dickinson embodied the archetype only imperfectly and only at certain times kept her constantly aware of the terms and limits within which she found this possible. And since the practice of her poetic vocation provided the preeminent frame and discipline, the assumptions behind her poetic practice are inseparable from and yet qualify the psychological pattern already outlined. The energy which in most other women would have found expression in their sexual and maternal lives was deliberately channeled, in Emily Dickinson's experience, into the artistic expression which embodied her inner

life. The sublimation of woman's activity into aesthetic creation—
in the most affirmative and substantive sense of sublimation—
is something that women artists have recognized. Anne Bradstreet
spoke of her poems as her babes, and in the mid-twentieth century Adrienne Rich could still speak about being a parent to a
poem. For Emily Dickinson the divine offspring—specifically the
divine son—which in woman's mysteries symbolizes the association of the masculine and feminine in creativity—issued in her
poems: the offspring of Sophia or of the Virgin-Mother or of the
moon-goddess by the man in the moon. And since she succeeded
only by the redirection of libidinal and emotional energy from
external commitments into the gestation of poems of self-explora-
tion, she was as curious about the poetic act itself as about any
of her major thematic concerns. The poetic act included and made
possible all the rest, and without attempting to compose a systematic philosophical aesthetic she tested out the creative experience
and reflected upon what went into it.

Clearly, poetry was the subsuming activity:

I reckon–when I count at all–
First–Poets–Then the Sun–
Then Summer–Then the Heaven of God–
And then–the List is done–

But, looking back–the First so seems
To Comprehend the Whole–
The Others look a needless Show–
So I write–Poets–All–

(P569 II 434)

The pose of nonchalance in the first line is only a facade for the
presumptuous claim that the poet, first and last and "All," comprehends (in the double sense of "understands" and "includes
within himself") paradise in this world and the next. Though a
poem like 1084, quoted earlier, may question the efficacy of art,
this poem goes on, in the subsequent two quatrains, to assert that
the completed poem supplants both the Sun and a problematical
Heaven. It is worth noting that this affirmative poem dates from
the period of her most frustrated anguish.

Not surprisingly, many poems, like the one above, enunciate Emersonian ideas about the poet. The famous piece that begins "I taste a liquor never brewed—" (P214 I 149) is a witty depiction of herself as a ladylike Dionysian reveler, with an arch awareness of how much this "little Tippler" who becomes "Inebriate of Air" and "Debauchee of Dew" is like and unlike a figure like Bacchus or Whitman's "friendly and flowing savage."

The poet assumes a passive-feminine role before the overwhelming possession by the god; the poet is a prophetess, a vessel overflowing to expression, an oracle whose responsibility is to find human expression for the divine wordlessness. Another 1862 poem gives powerful expression to such a divine "rape":

You'll know it—as you know 'tis Noon—
By Glory—
As you do the Sun—
By Glory—
As you will in Heaven—
Know God the Father—and the Son.

By intuition, Mightiest Things
Assert themselves—and not by terms—
"I'm Midnight"—need the Midnight say—
"I'm Sunrise"—Need the Majesty?

Omnipotence—had not a Tongue—
His lisp—is Lightning—and the Sun—
His Conversation—with the Sea—
"How shall you know"?
Consult your Eye!

(P420 I 326)

The experience is visionary and not linguistic; in fact, language is not only secondary but inadequate to the untongued Glory. Emerson and Whitman had said much the same thing; Emerson could even claim for Thoreau that he possessed poetry so intuitively that poems did not concern him much.

Dickinson could not herself forgo poems for poetry; but again and again she experienced poetry as light and heat rather than a craftsman's way with words: the poet seized by the man of noon or by the thunderbolt. The following poem from the same year as the one above conveys the erotic aspect of this epiphanic experience even more strongly:

> He fumbles at your Soul
> As Players at the Keys
> Before they drop full Music on—
> He stuns you by degrees—
> Prepares your brittle Nature
> For the Etherial Blow
> By fainter Hammers—further heard—
> Then nearer—Then so slow
> Your Breath has time to straighten—
> Your Brain—to bubble Cool—
> Deals—One—imperial—Thunderbolt—
> That scalps your naked Soul—
>
> When Winds take Forests in their Paws—
> The Universe—is still—

(P315 I 238)

She told Higginson in her first interview with him in 1870: "If I feel physically as if the top of my head were taken off, I know *that* is poetry."[31] Such a blinding vision is reiterated in a later poem sent to Sue, as was the "man of noon" letter and the poem above:

> To pile like Thunder to it's close
> Then crumble grand away
> While Everything created hid
> This—would be Poetry—

(P1247 III 866)

However, another 1862 poem indicates a different source for the poet's powers. In each of the three stanzas Dickinson seems to be saying that she prefers the humbler, more passive role of audience to the power of the painter, the musician, and the poet; but the disclaimer is merely strategic in order to let the artist stand forth the more forcefully at the end:

> Nor would I be a Poet—
> It's finer—own the Ear—
> Enamored—impotent—content—

The License to revere,
A privilege so awful
What would the Dower be,
Had I the Art to stun myself
With Bolts of Melody!

(P505 II 388)

The auditor's privilege (variant: "luxury") is "awful," filled with
the same sublime Awe to which Circumference was wed. His
humming responsiveness is caught by the resonation of "Enam-
ored—impotent—content—" against each other. But the words are
hobbled together lamely, and since Dickinson is disclaiming the
poet's prerogatives in a lively poem, the ruse falls away: *she*
thunders the lightning bolts; the source and subject of that incandescence is herself. If she felt the top of her head taken off, that
was perhaps because she exercised "the Art to stun myself/ With
Bolts of Melody!"

Consequently several poems describe her as a volcano. Poem
601, written in 1862, images the psyche, smoldering with explosive subterranean materials, as

A still—Volcano—Life—
That flickered in the night—
When it was dark enough to do
Without erasing sight—

A quiet—Earthquake Style—
Too subtle to suspect
By natures this side Naples—
The North cannot detect

The Solemn—Torrid—Symbol—
The lips that never lie—
Whose hissing Corals part—and shut—
And Cities—ooze away—

(P601 II 461)

The puns on "erasing," "Style," "Symbol," "lips" leave no doubt
that she is describing herself as poet, and by naming herself a
secret Vesuvius of the North she takes the light and fire previously ascribed to the phallic thunderbolt into the female land-

scape as "her" eruptive, expressive power. No wonder her poems seemed "spasmodic" and "uncontrolled" to Higginson. Another poem links her again with Naples' volcano:

> Volcanoes be in Sicily
> And South America
> I judge from my Geography
> Volcanoes nearer here

And so "I may contemplate/ Vesuvius at Home" (P1705 III 1153). But the "still," "quiet" volcano does not publish its molten materials abroad: "Dare you see a Soul *at the White Heat?*" (P365 I 289); "The reticent volcano keeps/ His never slumbering plan" (P1748 III 1174);

> On my volcano grows the Grass
> A meditative spot—
> An acre for a Bird to choose
> Would be the General thought—
>
> How red the Fire rocks below
> How insecure the sod
> Did I disclose
> Would populate with awe my solitude

(P1677 III 1141)

Another metaphorical contrast between the poet gripped by transformative power and the poet drawing upon the transforming power of the imagination is rendered in the recurrent imagery of flowers and bees. In the following poem, the poet as flower is metamorphosed from the labeled botanical parts of the first line into the organic entity of the last by the bees' vitalizing touch:

> A sepal, petal, and a thorn
> Upon a common summer's morn—
> A flask of Dew—A Bee or two—
> A Breeze—a caper in the trees—
> And I'm a Rose!

(P19 I 21)

Other poems take the bee's "masculine" perspective, as his potency rouses nature from inertia into life. Where the volcano hoarded its genius in secret, the bee goes abroad vanquishing a world waiting to be touched and taken:

> Like Trains of Cars on Tracks of Plush
> I hear the level Bee—
> A Jar across the Flowers goes
> Their Velvet Masonry
>
> Withstands until the sweet Assault
> Their Chivalry consumes—
> While He victorious tilts away
> To vanquish other Blooms.

(P1224 III 852)

Dickinson did not have to choose between being the bee or the rose, just as the poems composed in the same year quoted above include both the lightningbolt and the volcano. She had felt herself vanquished by superior powers, and she had felt herself the inseminating presence of all that she saw. In "consulting her eye" she knew that at times it had been blinded by vision and that at other times her idiosyncratic vision (in that very different sense of the word) had transformed the world, or at least her perception of it. She had known both experiences:

> Because the Bee may blameless hum
> For Thee a Bee do I become
> List even unto Me.
>
> Because the Flowers unafraid
> May lift a look on thine, a Maid
> Alway a Flower would be.

(P869 II 647)

And again:

> A Bee his burnished Carriage
> Drove boldly to a Rose—
> Combinedly alighting—
> Himself—his Carriage was—
> The Rose received his visit

With frank tranquility
Witholding not a Crescent
To His Cupidity–
Their Moment consummated–
Remained for him–to flee–
Remained for her–of rapture
But the humility.

(P1339 III 925)

With the puns on "burnished" and "alighting," on "Carriage," and on the Bee as Cupid, this is a more fanciful poem than "Circumference thou Bride of Awe," but it too describes a consonance of rose and bee, crescent and moon.

Both these conceptions of the poet proceed from a concern for the source of inspiration from which the poem arises, and they represent the twin aspects of the Transcendental idea of the poet as prophet of another world or genius of this one. Both show only secondary regard for technique because the resort to language is attendant upon and consequent to the perception. However, the rapid and unpredictable shifts of attitude and mood which resulted from Emily Dickinson's bewilderment before metaphysical and religious problems made her unable to sacrifice the poem to a higher faith in the order of things, as Emerson said was possible for Thoreau. Her self-reliance had learned to take itself literally. The integrity of the poem as her unique creation became a paramount concern as it did not have to be for Emerson, Thoreau, or Whitman. Craft and technique forced language into shape in the hope that the design might withstand the wild inconsistencies of experience and the ravages of mortality. It was, put simply, a matter of personal survival. Since even our best moments perished, the poet, in the long run, lasted only as long as his poems. Even a naturalist like Thoreau had saved himself from flux and wrung his personal immortality by contriving his experience of Nature's cycle into the artistic pattern of *Walden*, which outlasts the seasons.

In 1862 the following lines acknowledged the artisan's responsibility to the tools and secrets of his trade; such an acknowledgement, at least as pronounced here, qualifies what has been said about the poetic process so far without necessarily canceling out any of it:

This was a Poet–It is That
Distills amazing sense
From ordinary Meanings–
And Attar so immense

From the familiar species
That perished by the Door–

(P448 I 346)

Dickinson would not want to go as far as Poe's anti-Transcendental statement that "flowers are merely—flowers," but she knew with Poe that art was the human attempt to resist the flow of experience, even of transcendental experience, by extracting and fixing the essence of experience like an elixir of life; "arresting" is the verb used later in the poem. Attar is the "essence" of the rose, but attar can be squeezed from the perishing rose only through the skilled handicraft of the technician. From the next year come these lines elaborating upon the poem above:

Essential Oils–are wrung–
The Attar from the Rose
Be not expressed by Suns–alone–
It is the gift of Screws–

The General Rose–decay–
But this–in Lady's Drawer
Make Summer–When the Lady lie
In Ceaseless Rosemary–

(P675 II 522)

The poem is the attar, not the rose; and here the pun on "essence" is explicit. There could be no rose without nature's creative cycle for which the sun is source and center, but only the human refusal to reside in cycle resists the decay which is nature's way of continuing life. Species, such as the "General Rose," persist, but rose by rose they die. The extraction of the essence into artifice—itself a paradox—makes no difference to the fate of the unmindful rose, but it secures for the conscious artist a sense of transcendence which seemed more than natural and, to Poe and at times to Dickinson, even god-like. The artisan, therefore, was no mere

294

technician, important as that skill was. The artisan was a skilled alchemist or a psychic midwife, transmuting and delivering herself. The poems which Dickinson conceived and birthed out of her woman's nature through the impregnating imagination were her most immediate assurance of at least a quasi-immortality. Playing with women's names, she noted that when Emily lay "In ceaseless Rosemary" (a better phrase than the variant: "Spiceless Sepulchre"), the manuscripts of her poems would be waiting in her dresser drawer, unchanged by a single phrase, pungent still with the summer sun's rose, like the alchemist's *aqua vitae*. Thus the artist must fix upon the rose not merely to see it (or into it) or to light it by his imagination but to take the rose in so metamorphically that his conscious apprehension of it is rendered ("distilled" suggests the alchemical translation, scientific yet mysterious) into the materials of his medium. The experience in language becomes, then, the experience of language, and the artist's use of the given materials and technical conventions invests language with personal expression. From this viewpoint language is not a flawed gesture back to a lost epiphany nor a projection toward divine wordlessness but a deliberate human act of comprehension, preservation, and extension. As part of her training Emily Dickinson pored over the dictionary, relishing the histories and resources of words in order to find ways of making them live anew:

> A word is dead
> When it is said,
> Some say.
> I say it just
> Begins to live
> That day.

> (P1212 III 845)

Focus made for suggestiveness as well as clarity, and word by chosen word, line by terse line, the poem breathed out its shape.

"Your every suggestion is Dimension," she wrote in a letter. Language, like experience, has center and circumference, not only because it reflects, and reflects upon, antecedent experiences but because it is itself an experience so complicated that it must move by a certain kind of circumlocution:

Tell all the Truth but tell it slant—
Success in Circuit lies
Too bright for our infirm Delight
The Truth's superb surprise

(P1129 II 792)

The truth which required slant telling was not necessarily
a platonic or metaphysical absolute; the world within and the
world outside were elusive enough to train the consciousness in
subtlety of maneuver. Indirection, far from being inconsistent
with candor, was its prerequisite. With consciousness as exposed
and vulnerable as it was, the writer depended on the indirections
of language to shield him as he pursued his roundabout explorations: "In all the circumference of Expression, those guileless
words of Adam and Eve never were surpassed, 'I was afraid and
hid myself.'" Paradoxically, hints and intimations were the necessary course, yet the hints and intimations constellate around a
center whose exploratory acts were also attempts at self-location.
The radii proceeding to the circumference all meet at the center.
And just as the individual consciousness seemed to gravitate not
merely to its own center but to an All-Center, so Dickinson recognized not only the uses of circumference but the need to pro-
nounce, at times, as absolutely as she could: "All grows strangely
emphatic, and I think if I should see you again, I sh'd begin
every sentence with 'I say unto you—' The Bible dealt with the
Centre, not with the Circumference—"[32]. The center-language of
the Bible was a categorical, clear statement of Truth so direct that
the individual can be judged by it; the circumferential language
of art strives to tell a slant Truth eccentrically.

In fact, as she also recognized from beginning to end, Orpheus' sermon was so different from the Bible's that it could seem
opposite. If Jesus and the prophets were poets, they were poets of
a particularly emphatic sort. To most artists the poem achieved
through long labor seemed rather a location and confirmation of
center through circumference. The emblem for the poet as maker
was neither the thunderstruck oracle nor the eruptive genius,
neither the rose nor the bee, but the spider. From 1862 again:

The Spider holds a Silver Ball
In unperceived Hands—

And dancing softly to Himself
His Yarn of Pearl—unwinds—

He plies from Nought to Nought—
In unsubstantial Trade—
Supplants our Tapestries with His—
In half the period—

An Hour to rear supreme
His Continents of Light—
Then dangle from the Housewife's Broom—
His Boundaries—forgot—

(P605 II 464)

For Jonathan Swift in "The Battle of the Books," the artist as bee was superior to the artist as spider because the bee gathered his materials far and wide from nature to build his hive, whereas the spider spun his dwelling from the filth of his own guts. But Emily Dickinson had different, even opposite, associations. In a later poem she joins forces with "The Spider as an Artist" against the philistine threat from "every Broom and Bridget": "Neglected Son of Genius/ I take thee by the Hand—" (P1275 III 886–887).

An intervening spider poem draws together other key metaphors to describe the poetic act with concentrated inclusiveness and finality:

A Spider sewed at Night
Without a Light
Upon an Arc of White.

If Ruff it was of Dame
Or Shroud of Gnome
Himself himself inform.

Of Immortality
His Strategy
Was Physiognomy.

(P1138 II 800)

Whitman's "noiseless patient spider . . . launch'd forth filament, filament, filament, out of itself" in order "to explore the vacant vast surrounding." Dickinson's spider, too, pieces out his own luminous circle amidst the engulfing darkness, and his inner capacities and resources, far from being the psychic excrement of his egotism, as Swift saw it, provided rather his own shrewd means for securing his own immortality. The outcome all depended on the web of words he wove from and for himself; she had already observed how fragile the web was before the rude, indifferent sweep of time. All the individual had at hand to use was what he found in his own substance, but he held all he needed perhaps, if he laid out his "Boundaries" cunningly enough and within those boundaries spun as expertly as his training could contrive. In that way "Himself himself inform," not only in the sense that he alone knew his secret but, much more profoundly, in the sense that he defined his form in the projected design of the web. "Physiognomy" refers not only to the conformation of face and body but to the art of reading the character of the person from his features and shape; so the poet's verbal web, woven from his vitals, is his own best creation and revelation. Yet it was a fabric, and since the stakes were no less than life or death, it was the weaver's skill that determined whether he wove a death-sheet ("Shroud of Gnome") or his lady's fancy dress ("Ruff of Dame"). No wonder the words and phrases were tested and placed one by one; no wonder the lean stanzas were tautly delineated from the hymn-quatrains; no wonder the materials were calculated economically and the strenuous effort was to mark the poem as an indelible center for its range of resonance.

The spider is normally a feminine symbol, and for men the spider can symbolize woman in her frighteningly threatening and overwhelming aspect, like the sea or the octopus. It is doubly significant, therefore, that as a woman-poet Emily Dickinson chose the spider as her emblem and that she thought of it as masculine. Nor is there any contradiction between these facts; the spider is the symbol of her androgynous wholeness as a woman-poet. For most poets, male or female, those aspects of the psyche archetypally identified with the opposite sex become the mediating point for the passage to psychic wholeness and for imaginative activity as a principal means thereto. Whitman had to assimilate his feminine nature into himself, and Dickinson had to assimilate her masculine nature into herself. As poets, each had to do this Self-creation through language and each addressed himself to the effort with singular exclusiveness. In that process, then, Whitman's anima and Dickinson's animus became the channels through which their psychic energy found characteristic form and expression in words. In Whitman the poetic process turned upon his fleshing the imagination not only in the body but in his passions and intuitions; his validation came from the nonrational life of the instincts. His poems issued from that "feminine" part of himself, and he had to entrust his poems and his identity to "her" amorphous and ongoing fluidity. He gave birth to his book again and again as it grew. In direct contrast, Emily Dickinson, surrounded by the dark despite flashes of supreme self-realization, depended on the poet's capacity for conscious control and discrimination to illuminate a design around "himself" and to organize "himself" into a tight design. Her identity and survival turned on "his" ability to make each strand of the design, each line of the stanza, each poem of the corpus, resilient enough to stand as both defining boundary and extension.

In the following poem the familiar ring of light signifies the success which she anticipated for her strategy to assure immortality:

> The Poets light but Lamps—
> Themselves—go out—
> The Wicks they stimulate—
> If vital Light
>
> Inhere as do the Suns—
> Each Age a Lens
> Disseminating their
> Circumference—
>
> (P883 II 654)

The double reference of the pronoun "their" shows that in the end—in the long run of the future, at least—the poet's circumference and the circumference of the poems are coextensive and equally abiding.

NOTES

INDEX

Notes

I: The American as Artist

1. *The Works of the Rev. Sydney Smith* (Boston: Phillips, Sampson & Co., 1856), p. 141.

2. Ibid., p. 112.

3. William Cullen Bryant, *Prose Writings*, ed. Parke Godwin (New York: D. Appleton, 1884), I, 24–25.

4. Ibid., pp. 32–33, 34–35.

5. John Trumbull, *M'Fingal* in *The Connecticut Wits*, ed. V. L. Parrington (New York: Harcourt Brace, 1926), p. 150.

6. Ibid., p. 310.

7. *The Poems of Freneau: Poet of the American Revolution*, ed. F. L. Pattee (Princeton: University Library, 1902–1907), I, 49; II, 94; I, 281; II, 280.

8. Ibid., II, 281.

9. Ibid., I, 82; III, 121; II, 303.

10. Ibid., III, 393.

11. Ibid., III, 228.

12. Ibid., II, 298.

13. Ibid., II, 333.

14. Ibid., I, 208.

15. Hawthorne's "Preface" to *The Marble Faun* (1860), *Works* (Boston: Houghton Mifflin, 1888), VI, 15.

16. All the quotations here are from Melville's review "Hawthorne and His Mosses" (1850) which is reprinted in full in *The Shock of Recognition*, ed. Edmund Wilson (New York: Farrar, Straus & Cudahy, 1955), pp. 187–204.

17. James's *Hawthorne* is reprinted in full in *The Shock of Recognition*, pp. 427–565. The quotations cited here can be found on pp. 450–451, 428, 550, and 538.

18. "Dr. Williams' Position," *Literary Essays of Ezra Pound*, ed. T. S. Eliot (New York: New Directions, 1954), pp. 390–392.

19. *The Selected Letters of William Carlos Williams*, ed. John C. Thirwall (New York: McDowell, Oblensky Inc., 1957), p. 69.

20. Ibid., pp. 313, 302–303.

21. "Edgar Poe's Significance," *Specimen Days*, *Prose Works 1892*, I, ed. Floyd Stovall (New York: New York University Press, 1963), 232.

II: EDWARD TAYLOR: Types and Tropes

1. *The Works of Anne Bradstreet*, ed. Jeannine Hensley (Cambridge, Mass.: Harvard University Press, 1967), p. 241.

2. William Bradford, *Of Plymouth Plantation 1620–1647*, ed. Samuel Eliot Morison (New York: Alfred A. Knopf, 1952), p. 3.

3. *The Works of Anne Bradstreet*, p. 240.

4. John Bulkeley, "Preface to Wolcott's *Poetical Meditations*" (1725), *The Puritans*, ed. Perry Miller and Thomas H. Johnson (New York: American Book Co., 1938), pp. 683–684.

5. "Preface to *The Bay Psalm Book*" (1640), *The Puritans*, pp. 671–672.

6. Thomas Hooker, "Preface to *A Survey of the Summe of Church-Discipline*" (1648), *The Puritans*, pp. 672-673.

7. Cotton Mather, "Preface to *Psalterium Americanum*" (1718), *The Puritans*, pp. 678-680.

8. Cotton Mather, "Of Poetry and Style" (1726), *The Puritans*, pp. 685–688.

9. Mather Byles, "Bombastic and Grubstreet Style: A Satire" (1745), *The Puritans*, pp. 689–694.

10. Cotton Mather, "Of Poetry and Style," *The Puritans*, p. 686.

11. Jonathan Edwards, *Representative Writings*, ed. Clarence H. Faust and Thomas H. Johnson (New York: American Book Co., 1935), p. 39.

12. Kenneth B. Murdock, *Literature and Theology in Colonial New England* (Cambridge, Mass.: Harvard University Press, 1949), p. 29.

13. Jean Senault, *The Use of Passions* (1649), quoted in Perry Miller's *The New England Mind: The Seventeenth Century* (Cambridge, Mass.: Harvard University Press, 1939, 1954), p. 257.

14. The authoritative edition is *The Poems of Edward Taylor*, ed. Donald E. Stanford (New Haven: Yale University Press, 1960). All quotations from Taylor's poetry use this text.

15. I am very grateful to my colleague, Donald Davie, for suggesting that I look at Isaac Watts in this connection.

16. *The Letters of Ralph Waldo Emerson*, ed. Ralph L. Rusk (New York: Columbia University Press, 1939), II, 43; Ezra Pound, "Patria Mia," *Selected Prose 1909–1965*, ed. William Cookson (New York: New Directions, 1973), p. 123.

17. An undergraduate honors thesis by Evan Prosser (Harvard College, 1964), written when he was a student of mine, provided the stimulus for my own investigation of the metaphorical patterns in the *Meditations*.

18. Ezra Pound, "I Gather the Limbs of Osiris," *Selected Prose 1909–1965*, p. 29.

19. Brother Antoninus, "Annul in Me My Manhood" in *The Crooked Lines of God* (Detroit: University of Detroit Press, 1959), p. 86; and "The Song the Body Dreamed in the Spirit's Mad Behest" in *The Hazards of Holiness* (New York: Doubleday, 1962), pp. 68, 70.

20. An address by John Livingston Lowes on "Religion and the

Arts," printed in the *Harvard Alumni Bulletin,* January 13, 1927; Robert Frost *In the Clearing* (New York: Holt, Rinehart & Winston, 1962).

21. *The Works of Anne Bradstreet,* pp. 307ff, 309, 318, 256, 249ff. The verses are from "Contemplations," p. 250.

22. Jonathan Edwards, *Images or Shadows of Divine Things,* ed. Perry Miller (New Haven: Yale University Press, 1948), p. 44.

23. Quoted in *Images or Shadows of Divine Things,* p. 27, from *Works,* ed. Sereno Dwight (New York, 1830), IX, 110–111.

24. Edward Taylor, *Christographia,* ed. Norman S. Grabo (New Haven: Yale University Press, 1962), pp. 341, 354, 253.

25. *Ibid.,* pp. 182, 192, 273.

26. Quoted in *Images or Shadows of Divine Things,* p. 36.

27. *Ibid.,* pp. 6–7.

28. "The Poet," *Essays: Second Series, The Complete Works of Ralph Waldo Emerson,* Centenary Edition, ed. Edward Waldo Emerson (Boston: Houghton Mifflin, 1903–1904), III, 26; *Images or Shadows of Divine Things,* p. 18.

29. *The Collected Letters of Samuel Taylor Coleridge,* ed. Earl Leslie Griggs (Oxford: Clarendon Press, 1956), II, 864.

III: RALPH WALDO EMERSON: The Eye of the Seer

1. *The Journals and Miscellaneous Notebooks of Ralph Waldo Emerson* (Cambridge, Mass: Harvard University Press, 1960–   ), II ed. William H. Gilman, Alfred R. Ferguson and Merrell R. Davis, 3–4. Henceforth in the notes this edition of the journals will be abbreviated as JMN with the appropriate citations of volumes and pages.

2. "Art," *Essays First Series, The Complete Works of Ralph Waldo Emerson,* ed. Edward Waldo Emerson, Centenary Edition (Boston: Houghton Mifflin, 1903–1904), II, 368. This edition is being superseded by a new, authoritative scholarly edition, the first volume of which, *Nature, Addresses and Lectures,* has already been published. Consequently, in the notes to this chapter citations to that volume will refer to the new Harvard University Press edition, abbreviated after the full reference in note 5 below to *Collected Works,* and the citations to other volumes will perforce be to the old Centenary Edition, abbreviated hereafter as *Works. Essays First Series* will be abbreviated in the notes to *Essays I.* Robert Frost, "The Gift Outright," *Complete Poems 1949* (New York: Henry Holt, 1949), p. 467.

3. "The Poet," *Essays Second Series, Works,* III, 19. This volume will henceforth be abbreviated in the notes to *Essays II.*

4. "Poetry and Imagination," *Letters and Social Aims, Works,* VIII, 34.

5. "American Civilization," *Miscellanies, Works,* XI, 299; "Literary Ethics," *Nature, Addresses and Lectures, The Collected Works of Ralph Waldo Emerson,* ed. Alfred R. Ferguson et al. (Cambridge,

Mass.: Harvard University Press, 1971), I, 100. Henceforth *Nature, Addresses and Lectures* will be abbreviated in these notes as *NAL*, and this edition as *Collected Works*.

6. "The Method of Nature," *NAL, Collected Works*, I, 121; *JMN*, IX ed. Ralph H. Orth and Alfred R. Ferguson, 83; *The Heart of Emerson's Journals*, ed. Bliss Perry (Boston: Houghton Mifflin, 1926), p. 262; *JMN*, VII ed. A. W. Plumstead and Harrison Hayford, 200.

7. *JMN*, V ed. Merton M. Sealts, Jr., pp. 210–211.

8. "The Transcendentalist," *NAL, Collected Works*, I, 207, 210–211. See also "Historic Notes of Life and Letters in New England," *Lectures & Biographical Sketches, Works*, X, 325–327.

9. "Historic Notes of Life and Letters in New England," *Lectures & Biographical Sketches, Works*, X, 325; "Self-Reliance," *Essays I, Works*, II, 50; "The Transcendentalist," *NAL, Collected Works*, I, 208.

10. "The Poet," *Essays II, Works*, III, 41.

11. *Poems, Works*, IX, 228, 76, 77.

12. "Literary Ethics," *NAL, Collected Works*, I, 109.

13. *JMN*, VIII ed. William H. Gilman and J. E. Parsons, 379–380.

14. "The Lord's Supper," *Miscellanies, Works*, XI, 24, 23, 20–21; "The Divinity School Address," *NAL, Collected Works*, I, 81; *Poems, Works*, IX, 6; Nature, *NAL, Collected Works*, I, 7.

15. *Nature, NAL, Collected Works*, I, 9, 12; "Beauty," *The Conduct of Life, Works*, VI, 281.

16. *Nature, NAL, Collected Works*, I, 9.

17. "Poetry and Imagination," *Letters & Social Aims, Works*, VIII, 35.

18. *Nature, NAL, Collected Works*, I, 10.

19. "Swedenborg; or, the Mystic," *Representative Men, Works*, IV, 137; *JMN*, III ed. William H. Gobson, and Alfred R. Ferguson, 304; "Experience," *Essays II, Works*, III, 75; *Poems, Works*, IX, 14.

20. "Plato; or, the Philosopher," *Representative Men, Works*, IV, 47–48; "Experience," *Essays II, Works*, III, 84; *Nature, NAL, Collected Works*, I, 30; *Poems, Works*, IX, 15.

21. "The Transcendentalist," *NAL, Collected Works*, I, 213, 203; *Nature, NAL, Collected Works*, I, 42; *JMN*, VII, 342.

22. "The Poet," *Essays II, Works*, III, 6; see also p. 5.

23. "The Divinity School Address," *NAL, Collected Works*, I, 84; "The Poet," *Essays II, Works*, III, 21, 37, 5, 7.

24. *Nature, NAL, Collected Works*, I, 17.

25. "The Poet," *Essays II, Works*, III, 18, 20–21; "Walking," *Excursions, The Writings of Henry David Thoreau*, Walden Edition (Boston: Houghton Mifflin, 1906), V, 232.

26. Nature, *NAL, Collected Works*, I, 29; "Beauty," *The Conduct of Life, Works*, VI, 283; "The Divinity School Address," *NAL, Collected Works*, I, 90; "Literary Ethics," *NAL, Collected Works*, I, 104; "The Poet," *Essays II, Works*, III, 8.

27. "Beauty," *The Conduct of Life*, Works, VI, 304; "Literary Ethics," *NAL, Collected Works*, I, 105; "The Poet," *Essays II, Works*, III, 24–26; *Nature, NAL, Collected Works*, I, 28; *Poems, Works*, IX, 359; "Art," *Essays I, Works*, II, 363.

28. "The Poet," *Essays II, Works*, III, 40; "The Over-Soul," *Essays I, Works*, II, 287.

29. "The Poet," *Essays II, Works*, III, 8–10; "Thoreau," *Lectures & Biographical Sketches, Works*, X, 474–476.

30. "The Poet," *Essays II, Works*, III, 9–10; "Circles," *Essays I, Works*, II, 304; *Poems, Works*, IX, 127.

31. "The Poet," *Essays II, Works*, III, 10, 24; *Poems, Works*, IX, 298; "Poetry and Imagination," *Letters & Social Aims, Works*, VIII, 42.

32. "The Poet," *Essays II, Works*, III, 26.

33. *Nature, NAL, Collected Works*, I, 23, 38; "The Poet," *Essays II, Works*, III, 33, 40; "Self-Reliance," *Essays I, Works*, II, 63–64; "The Over-Soul," *Essays I, Works*, II, 277; "The American Scholar," *NAL, Collected Works*, I, 55.

34. *Writers at Work: The Paris Review Interviews, Second Series* (New York: Viking, 1963), pp. 171–173.

35. Denise Levertov, "Some Notes on Organic Form," *The Poet in the World* (New York: New Directions, 1973), pp. 7–9; "The Poet," *Essays II, Works*, III, 14, 24.

36. "The Poet," *Essays II, Works*, III, 3, 26–27; 32ff, 40; *Poems, Works*, IX, 125–127, 360.

37. *Poems, Works*, IX, 312, 335.

38. *Nature, NAL, Collected Works* I, 28, 23, 19; *JMN*, IX ed. Ralph H. Orth and Alfred R. Ferguson, 267; *Poems, Works*, IX, 87.

39. *JMN*, IX, 18, 236; *The Heart of Emerson's Journals*, p. 33; "The Poet," *Essays II, Works*, III, 27–29. See also "Circles," *Essays I, Works*, II, 322.

40. Yvor Winters, *Forms of Discovery: Critical and Historical Essays on the Forms of the Short Poem in English* (Denver: Alan Swallow, 1967), p. 318; *In Defense of Reason* (New York: Swallow Press and William Morrow, 1947), p. 55; "Critical Foreword," *The Complete Poems of Frederick Goddard Tuckerman* (New York: Oxford University Press, 1965), p. ix.

41. *Heart*, p. 240; "Montaigne; or, the Skeptic," *Representative Men, Works*, IV, 168; "Poetry and Imagination," *Letters and Social Aims, Works*, VIII, 46–50.

42. Denise Levertov, *The Poet in the World*, p. 11.

43. "Experience," *Essays II, Works*, III, 58; *Poems, Works*, IX, 360.

44. Denise Levertov, *The Poet in the World*, p. 11; Charles Olson, "Projective Verse," *New American Poetry 1945–1960*, ed. Donald M. Allen (New York: Grove Press, 1960), p. 390.

45. *JMN*, V, ed. Merton M. Sealts, Jr., 476.

46. "Poetry and Imagination," *Letters & Social Aims, Works*,

VIII, 17, 28–29; *Representative Men, Works,* IV, 11, 115–116; "The Poet," *Essays II, Works,* III, 13.

47. "Circles," *Essays I, Works,* II, 301; *Nature, NAL, Collected Works,* I, 10, 18, 22; *Poems, Works,* IX, 322.

48. *Nature, NAL, Collected Works,* I, 19, 21, 22.

49. "Swedenborg; or, the Mystic," *Representative Men, Works,* IV, 120–121; "The Poet," *Essays II, Works,* III, 34; "Beauty," *The Conduct of Life, Works,* VI, 293–294.

50. *Nature, NAL, Collected Works,* I, 29; "Experience," *Essays II, Works,* IV, 52, 60; Whitman, "Of the Terrible Doubt of Appearances"; Robert Duncan, *Roots and Branches* (New York: Charles Scribner's Sons, 1964), p. 3.

51. "Poetry and Imagination," *Letters & Social Aims, Works,* VIII, 11, 15; *Representative Men, Works,* IV, 121; "The Poet," *Essays II, Works,* III, 21, 40; *Nature, NAL, Collected Works,* I, 31–32, 19–20; Robert Frost, "The Over Bird," *Complete Poems 1949* (New York: Henry Holt, 1949), p. 150; Wallace Stevens, "A High-Toned Old Christian Woman" and "The Idea of Order at Key West," *Collected Poems* (New York: Alfred A. Knopf, 1954), pp. 59, 129.

52. "Poetry and Imagination," *Letters & Social Aims, Works,* VIII, 15; *Nature, NAL, Collected Works,* I, 17; "The Poet," *Essays II, Works,* III, 14.

53. *Nature, NAL, Collected Works,* I, 10; "Self-Reliance," *Essays I, Works,* II, 50; *JMN,* VII, 342; Section 23 of Whitman's "Song of Myself"; William Carlos Williams, "Paterson," *Collected Earlier Poems* (New York: New Directions, 1951), p. 233; Ezra Pound, *Cantos* (New York: New Directions, 1970), pp. 438, 796–797; Charles Olson, "Letter to Elaine Feinstein," *New American Poetry 1945–1960,* p. 399; "Experience," *Essays II, Works,* III, 55.

IV: EDGAR ALLAN POE: The Hand of the Maker

1. Herman Melville, *Pierre; or, the Ambiguities* (New York: Hendricks House, 1957), p. 402.

2. "A Chapter of Suggestions," *The Complete Works of Edgar Allan Poe,* ed. James A. Harrison (New York, 1902; reprinted in facsimile: New York: AMS Press, 1965), XIV, 186; "Marginalia," *Works,* XVI, 165. With the exceptions noted below, references to Poe's writings will cite this edition, known as the "Virginia Edition," as above by giving the appropriate volume and page references after the word *Works.* The "Virginia Edition" will be superseded by a new, authoritative edition, the first volume of which has already been published: *The Collected Works of Edgar Allan Poe,* I (*Poems*) ed. Thomas Ollive Mabbott (Cambridge, Mass.: Harvard University Press, 1969). The text of Poe's poems cited in the chapter refer to this edition; page references for the poems are not given in the notes.

3. "Marginalia," *Works*, XVI, 165–166; "A Chapter of Suggestions," *Works*, XIV, 190.

4. "The Philosophy of Composition," *Works*, XIV, 201.

5. "The Poetic Principle," *Works*, XIV, 289; "Byron and Mary Chaworth," *Works*, XIV, 151–152.

6. Allen Tate, "Our Cousin, Mr. Poe" and "The Angelic Imagination," *Essays of Four Decades* (Chicago: Swallow Press, 1968), pp. 385–423. The words quoted here are on pp. 411 and 403.

7. "Preface" to *Poems* (1845), *Works*, VII, xlvii.

8. Walt Whitman, *Specimen Days, Prose Works 1892*, ed. Floyd Stovall (New York: New York University Press, 1963), I, 231.

9. Ibid., pp. 232–233.

10. Ibid., p. 232.

11. T. S. Eliot, "American Literature and the American Language," *To Criticize the Critic* (New York: Farrar, Straus & Giroux, 1965), p. 55.

12. Ellen Glasgow, *A Certain Measure: An Interpretation of Prose Fiction* (New York: Harcourt, Brace, 1943), pp. 132–133.

13. Edmund Wilson, *The Shock of Recognition* (New York: Farrar, Straus & Cudahy, 1955), p. 79; William Carlos Williams, *In the American Grain* (first published, 1925; reprinted: New York: New Directions, 1956), pp. 216, 217, 220, 223.

14. "A Few Words About Brainard," *Works*, XI, 15; "Drake and Halleck," *Works*, VIII, 277; "Marginalia," *Works*, XVI, 122; "Fifty Suggestions," *Works*, XIV, 182; "Mr. Griswold and the Poets," *Works*, XI, 148–149.

15. "Exordium," *Works*, XI, 2.

16. "Orion," *Works*, XI, 252–253; "The Poets and Poetry of America," *Works*, XI, 229.

17. "Poems by William Cullen Bryant," *Works*, IX, 297.

18. "Marginalia," *Works*, XVI, 6–7.

19. "The Philosophy of Composition," *Works*, XIV, 195.

20. "Marginalia," *Works*, XVI, 87–88; "The Poems of William Cullen Bryant," *Works*, IX, 292.

21. "Letter to B—," *Works*, VII, xliii; "The Poetic Principle," *Works*, XIV, 274–275.

22. Robert Frost, *Complete Poems 1949* (New York: Henry Holt, 1949), pp. 328–329; Wallace Stevens, "The Man Whose Pharynx Was Bad," *Collected Poems* (New York: Alfred A. Knopf, 1954), p. 96; Robert Frost, *Selected Prose*, ed. Hyde Cox and Edward Connery Latham (New York: Holt, Rinehart & Winston, 1966), p. 18; J. V. Cunningham, *The Exclusions of a Rhyme* (Denver, Col.: Alan Swallow, 1960); Edgar Bowers, *The Form of Loss* (Denver, Col.: Alan Swallow, 1956).

23. "The Philosophy of Composition," *Works*, XIV, 193, 194–195; "Marginalia," *Works*, XVI, 100.

24. "The Poetic Principle," *Works*, XIV, 273–275; "New Notes on Edgar Poe," *Baudelaire on Poe*, trans. and ed. Lois & Francis E. Hyslop Jr. (Bald Eagle State College, Pa.: Bald Eagle Press, 1952), pp. 140–141.

25. "Marginalia," *Works*, XVI, 128; "The Philosophy of Composition," *Works*, XIV, 196, 197, 198, 203.

26. "The Philosophy of Composition," *Works*, XIV, 207–208; "The Poetic Principle," *Works*, XIV, 271.

27. "Marginalia," *Works*, XVI, 111; "The Poetic Principle," *Works*, XIV, 272, 275.

28. "N. P. Willis," *Works*, XII, 37; "Marginalia," *Works*, XVI, 164; "Fifty Suggestions," *Works*, XIV, 176; "A Chapter of Suggestions," *Works*, XIV, 190.

29. "Marginalia," *Works*, XVI, 99.

30. "The Domain of Arnheim," *Works*, VI, 182, 188.

31. *Eureka, Works*, XVI, 185–205.

32. *Ibid.*, p. 183; "Letter to Alphonse Toussend, Jan. 21, 1856," *Baudelaire: A Self-Portrait*, ed. and trans. Lois and Francis E. Hyslop Jr. (London: Oxford University Press, 1957), pp. 104–105.

33. *Eureka, Works*, XVI, 185–186, 309, 292; Edgar Allan Poe, *Key Writings*, ed. Margaret Alterton and Hardin Craig (New York: Hill & Wang, 1962), p. 549.

34. *Eureka, Works*, XVI, 311, 312, 314–315.

35. *Ibid.*, p. 206; "Marginalia," *Works*, XVI, 89–90.

36. David Halliburton, *Edgar Allan Poe: A Phenomenological View* (Princeton: Princeton University Press, 1973), p. 418.

37. T. S. Eliot, "From Poe to Valéry," *To Criticize the Critic*, p. 40.

38. "Letters, Conversations and Recollections of S. T. Coleridge," *Works*, IX, 51–52.

V: WALT WHITMAN: The Self as Circumference

1. *The Complete Works of Ralph Waldo Emerson*, Centenary Edition, ed. Edward Waldo Emerson (Boston: Houghton Mifflin, 1903–1904), III, 37–38.

2. Roger Asselineau, *The Evolution of Walt Whitman* (Cambridge, Mass.: Harvard University Press, 1960), I, 56–62.

3. Bronson Alcott, *Journal*, quoted in Gay Wilson Allen's *The Solitary Singer: A Critical Biography of Walt Whitman* (New York: New York University Press, 1967), p. 204; J. T. Trowbridge, *My Own Story* (Boston, 1903), p. 367.

4. *Leaves of Grass*, Comprehensive Reader's Edition, ed. Harold W. Blodgett and Sculley Bradley (New York: New York University Press, 1965), pp. 709, 711, 712, 727, 717, 713, 714. All page references to the poems and prefaces will be from this edition.

5. *Ibid.*, pp. 712, 729.

6. Ibid., pp. 729–730; *The Shock of Recognition*, ed. Edmund Wilson (New York: Farrar, Straus & Cudahy, 1955), pp. 249, 252; Asselineau, *The Evolution of Walt Whitman*, I, 29.

7. *Leaves of Grass*, pp. 730, 731, 739.

8. *Prose Works 1892*, ed. Floyd Stovall (New York: New York University Press, 1964), II, 516; Asselineau, *The Evolution of Walt Whitman*, I, 52–53.

9. *Leaves of Grass*, pp. 715, 732, 734, 737, 716, 719.

10. *Prose Works 1892*, II, 516; Gay Wilson Allen, *The Solitary Singer: A Critical Biography of Walt Whitman*, pp. 202, 203, 372.

11. *Prose Works 1892*, ed. Floyd Stovall (New York: New York University Press, 1963), I, 250.

12. Charles Olson, *Selected Writings*, ed. Robert Creeley (New York: New Directions, 1966), pp. 15–26; William Carlos Williams, *The Autobiography* (New York: New Directions, 1951), pp. 329–332; Robert Duncan, "Changing Perspectives in Reading Whitman," *The Artistic Legacy of Walt Whitman*, ed. E. H. Miller (New York: New York University Press, 1970), pp. 99–100. Hugh Kenner provides an illuminating approach to spatial poetry in a chapter called "Space-Craft" in *The Pound Era* (Berkeley and Los Angeles: University of California Press, 1971), pp. 23–40.

13. *Leaves of Grass*, p. 712.

14. *Prose Works 1892*, II, 391, 407, 405, 366; *Prose Works 1892*, I, 248; *Leaves of Grass*, pp. 570, 574.

15. *Leaves of Grass*, p. 564.

16. Erik H. Erikson, "Once More the Inner Space," *Women and Analysis: Dialogues on Psychoanalytic Views of Femin150ity*, ed. Jean Strouse (New York: Grossman, 1974), p. 337; Norman O. Brown, *Life Against Death: The Psychoanalytical Meaning of History* (Middletown, Conn.: Wesleyan University Press, 1959), pp. 30, 29, 27.

17. *The Correspondence*, ed. Edwin Haviland Miller (New York: New York University Press, 1969), IV (1886–1889), 70.

18. *Leaves of Grass*, p. 572; *Prose Works 1892*, II, 493.

19. Robert E. Ornstein, *The Psychology of Consciousness* (New York: Viking, 1972), pp. 128–129.

20. Robert Duncan, "Changing Perspectives in Reading Whitman," p. 95.

21. Mircea Eliade, *The Two and the One* (New York: Harper & Row, 1965), pp. 19–77 but esp. pp. 26, 34, 40–41, 58, 70; Erich Neumann, *The Great Mother: An Analysis of the Archetype* trans. Ralph Mannheim (Princeton, N.J.: Princeton University Press, 1955), pp. 277–278; Norman O. Brown, *Life Against Death*, p. 31; *The Correspondence*, IV, 70.

22. *Democratic Vistas, Prose Works 1892*, II, 371.

23. *Leaves of Grass*, pp. 750, 559.

24. Norman O. Brown, *Life Against Death*, pp. 45, 46, 49.

25. Erich Neumann, *The Origins and History of Consciousness*, tr. R. F. C. Hull (Princeton, N.J.: Princeton University Press, 1954), pp. 122, 123, 307–308; Erich Neumann, "Narcissism, Normal Self-Formation, and the Primary Relation to the Mother" in *Spring 1966* (New York: Analytical Psychology Club, 1966), pp. 85–86, 92–95, 101–103.

26. Robert Duncan, "Changing Perspectives in Reading Whitman," p. 74.

27. Erik H. Erikson, "Womanhood and the Inner Space," *Women and Analysis: Dialogues on Psychoanalytic Views of Femininity*, ed. Jean Strouse (New York: Grossman, 1974), pp. 302–305, 318.

28. Marie-Louise von Franz, "The Process of Individuation," *Man and His Symbols*, ed. C. G. Jung (New York: Doubleday, 1964), pp. 200, 202.

29. Ibid., pp. 200–203; Mircea Eliade, *The Two and the One*, pp. 31–43; James Hillman, *The Myth of Analysis* (Evanston, Ill.: Northwestern University Press, 1972), pp. 258–298; Adrienne Rich, "Poetry, Personality and Wholeness: A Response to Galway Kinnell," *Field: Contemporary Poetry and Poetics*, 7 (Fall, 1972), 17.

30. *Leaves of Grass*, pp. 739, 743, 744, 746.

31. Ibid., pp. 750, 565, 562, 563, 570.

32. Robert Duncan, "Changing Perspectives in Reading Whitman," pp. 91, 94.

33. "A Backward Glance o'er Travel'd Roads," *Leaves of Grass*, p. 574.

34. William Carlos Williams, "An Essay on *Leaves of Grass*," *Leaves of Grass One Hundred Years After*, ed. Milton Hindus (Stanford, Cal.: Stanford University Press, 1955), p. 22.

35. A collage of quotations from the following Whitman poems: "Now Precedent Songs, Farewell," "A Clear Midnight," "Vocalism," "Song of the Answerer," "Shut Not Your Doors."

36. *Prose Works 1892*, II, 572, 573.

37. Ibid., pp. 573, 574, 577, 424–425; *Leaves of Grass*, pp. 570, 753.

38. *Leaves of Grass*, pp. 731, 573–574; *The Correspondence*, ed. Edwin Haviland Miller (New York: New York University Press, 1961), II (1868–1875), 170.

VI: EMILY DICKINSON: The Self as Center

1. *Letters of Emily Dickinson*, ed. Thomas H. Johnson and Theodora Ward (Cambridge, Mass.: Harvard University Press, 1958), II, 409. Henceforth this three-volume edition will be designated in the notes as *Letters* with the appropriate volume and page references.

2. *Letters*, II, 404; Jay Leyda, *The Years and Hours of Emily Dickinson* (New Haven: Yale University Press, 1960), II, 213, 263;

cited in Ruth Miller, *The Poetry of Emily Dickinson* (Middletown, Conn.: Wesleyan University Press, 1968), pp. 64, 65 and in Jack L. Capps, *Emily Dickinson's Reading 1836–1886* (Cambridge, Mass.: Harvard University Press, 1966), p. 139.

3. Adrienne Rich, "When We Dead Awaken: Writing as Re-Vision," *College English* (October 1972), p. 20.

4. "Self-Reliance," *Essays: First Series, The Complete Works of Ralph Waldo Emerson,* Centenary Edition, ed. Edward Waldo Emerson (Boston: Houghton Mifflin, 1903–1904), II, 50; *Representative Men,* ibid., IV 47–48; "The Transcendentalist," *Nature, Addresses and Lectures, The Collected Works of Ralph Waldo Emerson,* ed. Alfred R. Ferguson et al. (Cambridge, Mass.: Harvard University Press, 1971), I, 208; "Historic Notes on Life and Letters in New England," *Lectures & Biographical Sketches, Works,* X, 329. See note 2 of Chapter III for an explanatory note on editions of Emerson.

5. George Frisbie Whicher, *This Was a Poet: A Critical Biography of Emily Dickinson* (New York: Charles Scribner's Sons, 1939), pp. 190ff; Jack L. Capps, *Emily Dickinson's Reading 1836–1886,* pp. 113–118.

6. Ann Belford Ulanov, *The Feminine in Jungian Psychology and Christian Theology* (Evanston, Ill.: Northwestern University Press, 1971), pp. 175–177.

7. Adrienne Rich, " 'I am in Danger–Sir–,' " *Necessities of Life* (New York: W. W. Norton, 1966), p. 33.

8. For Dickinson's relation with Thoreau, see Albert J. Gelpi, *Emily Dickinson: The Mind of the Poet* (Cambridge, Mass.: Harvard University Press, 1965), esp. pp. 62–63, 105–106; *Letters,* III, 767; *Walden,* Walden Edition (Boston: Houghton Mifflin, 1906), pp. 4, 100–101.

9. For Dickinson's place in the New England tradition, particularly in relation to Edwards and Emerson, see Gelpi, *Emily Dickinson: The Mind of the Poet,* pp. 55–93.

10. Jonathan Edwards, *Images or Shadows of Divine Things,* ed. Perry Miller (New Haven: Yale University Press, 1948), p. 126.

11. "Experience," *Essays: Second Series, The Complete Works of Ralph Waldo Emerson,* III, 75–76.

12. "Compensation," *Essays: First Series, The Complete Works of Ralph Waldo Emerson,* II, 97, 107.

13. *Letters,* I, 210.

14. *Poems,* I, 180.

15. Rebecca Patterson, *The Riddle of Emily Dickinson* (Boston: Houghton Mifflin, 1951); John Cody, *After Great Pain: The Inner Life of Emily Dickinson* (Cambridge, Mass.: Harvard University Press, 1971).

16. For the arguments in favor of the interpretations outlined see: Thomas H. Johnson, *Emily Dickinson: An Interpretive Biography*

(Cambridge, Mass.: Harvard University Press, 1955); David Higgins, *Portrait of Emily Dickinson: The Poet and Her Prose* (New Brunswick, N. J.: Rutgers University Press, 1967); Theodora Ward, *The Capsule of the Mind: Chapters in the Life of Emily Dickinson* (Cambridge, Mass.: Harvard University Press, 1961); Ruth Miller, *The Poetry of Emily Dickinson*; John Cody, *After Great Pain*. The bibliographical information for the last two books is given in their initial citation above.

17. Theodora Ward, *The Capsule of the Mind*, p. 70.

18. *Letters*, II, 333, 373–374, 391–392.

19. *The Transcendentalists: An Anthology*, ed. Perry Miller (Cambridge, Mass.: Harvard University Press, 1950), pp. 335–336.

20. *Letters*, II, 374.

21. Ibid., p. 391.

22. Diane Wakoski, *The Motorcycle Betrayal Poems* (New York: Simon & Schuster, 1971); *Inside the Blood Factory* (New York: Doubleday, 1968), pp. 29, 39.

23. Adrienne Rich, *Necessities of Life* (New York: W. W. Norton, 1966), p. 33.

24. Wallace Stevens, "Final Soliloquy of the Interior Paramour," *Collected Poems* (New York: Alfred A. Knopf, 1954), p. 524.

25. *Letters*, II, 412.

26. "Circles," *Essays: First Series, The Complete Works of Ralph Waldo Emerson*, II, 301.

27. Erik Erikson, "Womanhood and the Inner Space," *Women and Analysis: Dialogues on Psychoanalytic Views of Femininity*, ed. Jean Strouse (New York: Grossman, 1974), pp. 291–319. The quotations appear on pp. 305 and 318–319.

28. P1663 III 1134; *Letters*, III, 690.

29. Erich Neumann, *The Great Mother: An Analysis of the Archetype*, trans. Ralph Manheim (Princeton: Princeton University Press, 1955), pp. 319–320; Erich Neumann, "The Psychological Stages of Feminine Development," trans. and rev. Hildegard Nagel and Jane Pratt, in *Spring 1959* (New York: The Analytical Psychology Club, 1959), pp. 71, 73, 77.

30. Erich Neumann, "On the Moon and Matriarchal Consciousness," *Dynamic Aspects of the Psyche*, trans. Hildegard Nagel (New York: The Analytical Psychology Club, 1956); "The Psychological Stages of Feminine Development," p. 72.

31. *Letters*, II, 474.

32. *Letters*, III, 847, 850, 858; P680 II 526–527.

Index

Index

Beauty, perception of: Coleridge on, 107; Poe's "supernal," 134, 136, 137, 230

"Because I could not stop for Death-(Dickinson), 259

"Because the Bee may blameless hum" (Dickinson), 292

bee imagery: Dickinson's, 291–293

"Beethoven" letter (Fuller), 256–257

Bible, 16, 45; Song of Solomon, 28, 30, 36; St. John's Gospel, 29; and Taylor, 37, 40; St. Paul, 40, 182; St. Augustine, 182n; Moses, 234–235; and Dickinson, 234–236, 245, 296; *Revelations*, 245

Biblical Criticism, Higher, 228

Bingham, Millicent Todd, 228n

Biographia Literaria (Coleridge), 150

bisexuality of psyche, *see* androgyny

Blackmur, R. P., 132

Blake, William, 69, 79, 164, 175, 181, 213, 264; human form divine, 190–191

blank verse: Emerson's use of, 95–98

"Blessed Damozel, The" (Rossetti), 123, 285

"Blight" (Emerson), 95–96

body-self, 182–183; and Whitman, 183, 186–187, 190, 206

body/spirit: union, 35–37, 167, 180–181, 182, 190n, 206; conflict, 120–122, 190n

Bowers, Edgar, 135

Bowles, Samuel, 219, 220, 224, 246, 247

Bradford, William, 15, 16, 19, 22

Bradstreet, Anne, 15, 16, 20–21, 32, 42, 46, 287

"Brahma" (Emerson), 95, 108

Brahman, 182, 209

British poetic tradition, ix, xxv, xxvi, 7–10, 17–18, 31, 62

Brontë, Emily, 245

Brooks, Cleanth, 132

Brown, Norman O., xii, 173–174, 183, 190n, 192–193

Browning, Robert, 274

Bryant, William Cullen, 1–4, 63–67, 71; Poe on, 130, 132

Buddha, 182n

Buddhism, 109

Bulkeley, John, 16–17

Burroughs, John, 162

"But—should the play" (Dickinson), 235

Byles, Mather, 18–19, 22

Byron, George Gordon, 116, 117, 119, 120

"Byron and Mary Chaworth" (Poe), 120

Calamus (Whitman), 211, 220

Calvary, 244

Calvinism: and Bradstreet, 20; and Taylor, 34, 36, 37, 41; and Bryant, 63, 65, 66–67; and Emerson, 68; and Tate, 122; and Poe, 122, 145; and Dickinson, 223, 225, 228–230, 235, 245. *See also* Puritan literary theory

Cambridge University, 16

Canticles, 36. See also *Song of Solomon, The*

Cantos (Pound), 32, 80, 102, 110–111, 164

Capps, Jack, 224

Carlisle, E. Fred, 164n

Carlyle, Thomas, 58, 67, 130, 156, 160

Catholicism, 22

Channing, W. H., 61

"Chanting the Square Deific" (Whitman), 188–189, 279

Chase, Richard, 164n, 192, 205

Chaworth, Mary, 120

childhood traumas, 200

Children of Adam (Whitman), 161, 207, 210, 220

Chirico, di, Giorgio, 145

"Choice, The" (Yeats), 223

Christ: as Bread of Life, 29–30; and Taylor, 29–30, 33–36, 39–40; types of, 45; and Emerson, 68, 108; and Whitman, 188–190; and Dickinson, 241

Christianity, 45, 108, 190n; Incarnation, 33–37, 41–46, 51, 68, 70, 108, 122; communion, 34, 36, 43–44, 68; Emerson on, 68; Trinity, 188–189. *See also* Calvinism; God

Christographia (Taylor), 34, 49

"Church Porch, The" (Herbert), 23

circle image: Emerson's, 106, 269, 273; Dickinson's, 269–270, 271

"Circles" (Emerson), 269, 273

Circumference metaphor: Dickinson's, 268–279, 282, 296

Index

Index

Index

Index

Index

Index

Index